Steps of the Seekers " Madaarij Al-Salikin"

1

Ibn Qayyim al-Jawziyya

Alreshah.net

Canada

Steps of the Seekers " Madaarij Al-Salikin" 1 / Ibn Qayyim al-Jawziyya . -- 1st ed.
ISBN 978-1-9991711-5-5

Contents

Introduction

In the name of God, The Entirely Merciful, the Especially Merciful

All praise is due to God, The Creator of the universe, blessed be the pious and no aggression but inflicted on the transgressors. I testify that there is no deity but God, Alone, with no associates or partners; the Lord of the world; the Lord of the messengers, the Lofty in Heaven and Earth. I testify that Muhammad is His servant and messenger commissioned with the Clear Book; the separator between guidance and aberrance; right and wrong; doubt and certainty. The Quran has been revealed to us to read through it in-depth, insightfully pondered over; to be grasped with its utmost subtle meanings and connotations; to believe in and follow its commands and eschew its interdictions. We have to reap the harvest of its beneficial sciences leading to the trees of the Almighty, and fragrant wisdom scented among His orchards and flowers. This Book is a revelation of God, the Almighty, to whomever wants to reach Him; the through-way seekers. It is God's clear light which dispelled darkness; His mercy sent for the good of all the creatures, the line bonding Him with His servants when they are cut off worldly relations. It is His great passable door; never slammed when all entrances are blocked. It is the Straight Path that is not tilted by personal discretions and the wise remembrance freed from passions and fixations. It is the noble revelation, of which the thirst of the scholar is not slated. It is the endless miracle with enumerable signs and unchanged significances. The more insightful seekers delve deeply in with contemplation and thinking, the more guided and mindful they become. Whenever its springs run off the surface, they overflow of rivers of wisdom. It is the light to the eyes and the remedy to the heart diseases and passions; the life of the heart; the pleasure to the souls; the gardens to the heart and the soul's shepherd to the land of joy. It is calling night and day: come people of success! Come to success. The caller to faith calls people to the Straight Path.

God, the Almighty, says:

"O our people, respond to the Messenger of God and believe in him; God will forgive for you your sins and protect you from a painful punishment."" يَاقَوْمَنَا أَجِيبُوا دَاعِيَ اللَّهِ وَآمِنُوا بِهِ يَغْفِرْ لَكُم مِّن ذُنُوبِكُمْ

(35:31): "وَيُجِرْكُم مِّنْ عَذَابٍ أَلِيمٍ"

I can hear its summoning, I swear. It would be heard if received by heedful ears and insightfully permeated through transparent hearts void of corruption. However, the wind of passions and fixations struck these hearts and extinguished their spiritual flames. Besides, the personal predilections took over and shut their doors and wasted away their keys. Hearts were so blocked that they could not receive the facts of the Quran and the ailments of ignorance became so chronicle that hearts could not benefit from the good deeds.

I wonder how hearts thrived on these lean and meager views and refrained to be nurtured by the wordings of the Lord of the universe and the content of His Messenger's message. I wonder how these hearts could be guided through the obscurity of these unjust thoughts to distinguish between the right and wrong, albeit, being too blind to see through the light radiant from the Quran and Sunnah!

I wonder how they could differentiate between the sound and awkward views; the accepted and the refuted; the most right and the least right! How they acknowledged their inability to perceive the guidance and knowledge from the wording of that Whose Words are protected and sanctified against the least imperfections. The One Who vouchguards clarifying the truth in the utmost articulate and subtler eloquence and the best collective and informative verbatim. The One whose speech is the absolute eloquence.

This is unbelievable! It is a sedition that blinded the hearts and swerved them from the Straight Path, misdirected minds from the well-determined and through ways; a sedition where the mediocre is signaled out while the well-learned is outcast.

The gang of the corrupters thought that they are the milestone where all race to reach, and the end where all compete and throng over to achieve. This is impossible! They are just a speck of sand compared to the huge planets! Their outlandish and small talk is groundless compared to the well authenticated wording of the infallible one, Muhammad, (PBUH). How can we hold a comparison between the views whose highest standards could be graded as "acceptable to be followed" and the obligatory provisions that every Muslim must follow and recourse to incase of disputes? Or the views whose holder prohibited imitating them and alerted against and the binding provisions that every Muslim servant has to follow and abide by? Where are the ideologies perishing by the death of their originators compared to the never-ending divine texts which are eternal even after the removal of heaven and earth?

Exalted is God! How lost those who are averse to the revealed divine text as they failed to gain knowledge from its bountiful source! How much they missed out from enjoying the life of heart and enlightenment! They sufficed themselves with the petty ideas inferred by worldly thinkers and fought tooth and nail for their prominence. They were satisfied with the worldly pleasures and deserted the Quran.

They disregarded the features of the Quran and became ignorant of and failed to cultivate its tenets. They even could not raise high standards of the Quran that fell off their hands. Its bright stars were set in their hearts and consequently they loathed them. They no longer see its sun because their astray and unjust views eclipsed its rays

The divine revelation of truth was dethroned, and relentless tirades of false interpretation were launched against it. Their raids are endless; they are so determined with their malicious intent as if it (the revelation) sought the accommodation of some misers who maltreated it and failed to offer the proper duties of hospitality and respect to it. They turned their back to it as if they raised a No- entry sign to avoid its authorized access, and if they are to remove it for certain urgency, they allow it to just sneak peek. They made the divine provisions as powerless as the honorary caliph of these days. The one committed to the Quran and

Sunnah is labeled as presumptuous and is outcast, and the one embracing the conflicting and contradicting ideas is the accepted model. The people of Quran and Sunnah who prioritize these texts over any other texts are labeled as ignorant and defective. In this realm, the verse reads: "And when it is said to them, "Believe as the people have believed," they say, "Should we believe as the foolish have believed?" Unquestionably, it is they who are the foolish, but they know [it] not"." وَإِذَا قِيلَ لَهُمْ آمِنُوا كَمَا آمَنَ النَّاسُ قَالُوا

(2:13) "ِأَنُؤْمِنُ كَمَا آمَنَ السُّفَهَاءُ أَلَا إِنَّهُمْ هُمُ السُّفَهَاءُ وَلَكِن لَّا يَعْلَمُون

How deprived they are, I swear, from reaching the truth by deviating from the revelation way and tampering with the original sources and fundamentals. They adhered to frameless pursuits and ideals which let go of them easier than they expected. Their relations to these vacuumed ideals were severed at the time they were mostly in need of at the time when they were resurrected from their tombs after death to be accountable for their deeds and every nation is to go under reckoning for the good and evil. Then, the truth of the disbeliefs is unearthed and their deeds are on the scale: "And there will appear to them from God that which they had not taken into account." وَبَدَا لَهُم مِّنَ

اللَّهِ مَا لَمْ يَكُونُوا يَحْتَسِبُون"""(39: 47)

The wrongdoers will grieve when they see the consequences of their void and malicious intents are of no avail. What a loss the defaulter encounters when he finds that his pursuits were in vain! How disastrous for the wrongdoer to find out his expectations are dashed and his hopes are false and prejudiced! What are the expectations of those who accommodate themselves to innovations, passions and personal intents and desires at the time when it is due to meet their Lord on the Day when all intents are revealed? What excuse can those who overlooked the revelations provide on a Day when the excuses of the wrongdoers are unbeneficial!

Does the one who is averse to the Book of his God and the Sunnah of his Messenger think that he would be salvaged by the polemics of the worldly thinkers? Or he will ward off God's power and might by the multiplicity of his search, arguments, analogies, diversities, allusions or the philosophical vagaries and illusions?

It's unbearable! They believed in the most unbelievable! Their egos promised them of the most impossible! The salvaged are those who give predominance to the guidance of God, the Almighty, over others, provided themselves with proof-based piety, groped the straight Path and clung to the inseparable bond of God, He is All Hearing, Omniscient.

Man's perfection is realized only by useful knowledge and good deed i.e. the divine guidance and the true religion- and by advising others to opt for them as God, Glorified is He, says: "By time. Indeed, mankind is in loss. Except for those who have believed and done righteous deeds and advised each other to truth and advised each other to patience" " وَالْعَصْرِ إِنَّ الْإِنسَانَ لَفِي خُسْرٍ لَّا الَّذِينَ آمَنُوا وَعَمِلُوا الصَّالِحَاتِ وَتَوَاصَوْا بِالْحَقِّ وَتَوَاصَوْا بِالصَّبْرِ" (103:1-3)

God, the Almighty, takes the oath that mankind is in loss except those who have crowned their scientific power with faith and righteous deeds and concluded them with advising others to truth patiently. The right is inclusive of faith and deed which are not fully established save by patience and advice. A Man has to spend his life time – till the last breath- in the pursuit of the holier perquisites to debar one's self from the clear loss or failure. This is unattainable save by heeding to the Quran by in-depth study, interpretation, extracting its treasures and hidden meanings, attending it wholeheartedly and enthusiastically adhering to it. It vouch guards the salves' interests in this world and the Hereafter; it is the trodden path for the way of guidance. Clear truth, methodology, tastes and perceptions are only extracted from its niche; they only fruit in its trees.

We- with God's assistance- will discuss and apply this on Surah of Alfatihah; Umm Alkittab (the most comprehensive Surah of). I will concern myself of these requirements included in this Surah as well as the refutations against the allegations of the innovators and corruptors. Also the ways of the seekers, statuses of the divinely well-versed will be addressed in order to distinguish between their means and ends, talents and gains to show that no Surah of can be lifted to its status or even replace it. It is a one of a kind with no resemblances neither in the Quran or the Gospels.

May God assist us, He is Ever Reliable and no power or might except by God, the Highest, and the Most Glorified.

Alfatihah is inclusive of the most comprehensive divine prerequisites

You have to know that Alfatihah is all inclusive and comprehensive of all the high divine prerequisites and perfectly opts for them.

It includes the identification of the Worshiped, God; Glorified is He, by three names of which all the good names and high attributes of God are related to and hinging on. They are "God (The Lord to be worshipped), (The One) and (the Merciful). The Surah is based on (lordship), (the Oneness of God) and Mercy; "It is You we worship" إِيَّاكَ نَعْبُدُ (1:5) addresses (Lordship); "and You we ask for help". وَإِيَّاكَ نَسْتَعِينِ (1:6) addresses (the Oneness of God) and asking guidance to the Straight Path is implored through God's Attribute of "Mercy". The praise is inclusive of the three; He, the Almighty, is the praised in His Lordship, Oneness and Mercy. Praise and Glorification are worthy of His Status.

It features verification of the Hereafter, retribution of the servants on their deeds- good or bad. God, Almighty, singled Himself out by judging mankind on that day; He is the utmost Justice. This all comes under "Sovereign of the Day of Recompense." "مَالِكِ يَوْمِ الدِّينِ" (1:4)

It further elaborates on verification of prophethoods from various perspectives:

First: Being the Lord of the universe, it is impossible for Him to leave His servants go astray without highlighting the useful and the harmful for them in this world and the Hereafter as this is disqualification of the role of Oneness of God, and a defective and improper attribution to the One, the Almighty. Such a faulty diminutive stature is away beyond sound judgment on the One.

Second: These names are taken from the name "God" and He is the One Worshiped; servants can't find their ways to worshipping Him except via His Messengers.

Third Position: His name Ar-Rahman "The Entirely Merciful" shows that His Mercy incorporates heedfulness of His salves and informing them of the ways of attaining the utmost perfection. True knowledge of the name Ar-Rahman makes one realize that it entails sending Messengers, revealing Books and best inclusions represented in sending down rains, growing plants and germinating seeds. Mercy reiterates attainment of eternal life of hearts and souls rather than that of bodies; yet, those who are astray and disposed of spirituality grasped nothing from that name. Accordingly, they are degraded to the level of the mindless animals. On contrary, the men of understanding realized what the implicit meaning lurking beyond.

Fourth Position: Mentioning "the Day of Recompense" يَوْم "الدِّين" " means that it is the day when servants are 'recompensed' for their deeds; either they are rewarded for their good deeds or punished for their sins and ill-deeds. God, Almighty, is not to torture anyone save after providing proof; the proof here is established by sending His Messenger and Books. Accordingly, reward and punishment are put into effect, and they are accountable; the pious are rewarded by eternal bliss; whereas the oppressors are dragged to Hell fire.

Fifth Position: In the verse that reads "It is You we worship" "إِيَّاكَ نَعْبُدُ" " God, Almighty, is only worshipped through the means He likes and favors. His worship – inclusive of praise, love and fear- is instinctively common to sound minds. However, the way and means of worship are only acknowledged through His Messengers and their messages. This indicates that sending Messengers is a well-settled matter in minds; it can neither be relinquished by the enlightened or the Creator. Therefore, the one who denies the Messenger is meant to deny the Sender as well and that he disbelieves in Him. God, Almighty, prescribed that disbelieving in His Messengers reiterates disbelieving in Him.

Sixth position: in the verse that reads "Guide us to the straight path". "اهْدِنَا الصِّرَاطَ الْمُسْتَقِيم" . Guidance is statement and signification, then followed by attunement and inspiration. Statement and signification are only realizable through Messengers; they are attained together with definition and the guidance of attunement and inspiration follows suit, planting faith, endearing, beautifying and making it influential in one's heart so that man becomes satisfied and content with it.

They are two independent ways of guidance; success cannot do without. They are comprehensive of what we are unaware about the truth jointly and severally, inspiring us to it and promoting us to follow it outwardly and inwardly. Furthermore, they hone our potential to act in accordance with guidance in utterances, deeds and determination and permanently accommodating it for us to abide by till death.

Therefore, a servant is required to ask for guidance in the time of need. This nullifies the allegations of those who say; if we are already guided; why do we seek guidance? The truth unknown to us is double fold what is known. What we are reluctant to do out of carelessness and laziness is like what we want or even more or less. And what we are unable to do – from what we need – is likewise. The matters we acknowledge in their entirety and unaware of their niceties are enumerable. We need total guidance. Whoever attained all these matters, his pursuit of guidance will be for eternal maintenance and persistence.

The last category of guidance is that guidance on the Day of Judgment to the way to Heaven; the path leading to it. The one who is guided in this life to God's Straight Path to which He sent His messengers, and to which He revealed His Books, will be guided in the Afterlife to the Straight Path leading to Heaven, the eternal abode of reward. As much as one's feet is firmly maintained and fixed on the Path that God, Almighty, has erected for His servants in this life, his feet will be maintained on the path erected to Hell fire; the distance he covers on this path is as long as that he crossed on that path. Servants are transported across the path in speeds according to their deeds; some will cross like a flash, some will hurry, some will walk and others will crawl. Some will be salvaged after receiving some scratches and others will be flung into eternal Hell fire. A servant is to be vigilant and heedful of his march on this path and the other one. Everyone will receive his right recompense "and it will be said, "Are you recompensed except for what you used to do?" " هَلْ تُجْزَوْنَ إِلَّا مَا كُنتُمْ تَعْمَلُونَ" (27:90)

A servant has to examine the lusts and fixations that hold him back from the Straight Path; they are the clamps on the two sides of the path that hinder him and block his transportation, once increased and strengthened, they will be the same in the Hereafter. "And your Lord is not ever unjust to [His] servants". " وَمَا رَبُّكَ بِظَلَّامٍ لِّلْعَبِيد" (41:46)

Seeking guidance entails attainment of all the good and salvage from every evil.

Seventh Position: To know the characteristics of the element responsible, namely the Straight Path. A path is not straight unless it included five aspects: straightness, direction to the goal, nearness, expansion to the passersby and specifying it as a way to the goal. Certainly, the Straight Path is inclusive of these five aspects.

Straightness entails nearness as well, because the straight line is the nearest line separating two points; the bumpier the farther. Its straightness means its direction to the goal and render it accommodating for the passersby which require its expansion. Attributing it to the Bestower and describing it as a way not trodden by those who have evoked anger or astray necessitates specifying it as a path.

The path is sometimes attached to God, the Almighty, as He is the One who created and specified it as He, the Almighty, says: "And, [moreover], this is My path, which is straight"," وَأَنَّ هَٰذَا صِرَاطِي مُسْتَقِيمًا (6:153). And He, the Almighty, says: "And indeed, [O Muhammad], you guide to a straight path - The path of God"" وَإِنَّكَ لَتَهْدِي إِلَىٰ صِرَاطٍ مُسْتَقِيمٍ

"صِرَاطِ اللَّهِ" (42:52-53)

And at others, it is attached to the servants as in Alfatihah, being the passersby and it is ascribed to them

Eighth Position: Mentioning the Bestower of grace on them and distinguishing them from those who have evoked anger or those who have gone astray.

Those who know the truth and act upon it are divided into three categories; a servant can be heedful or unheedful of the truth. The one heedful of the truth may act upon or contrary to it; those are the exclusive categories of those who are accountable. The one heedful of the truth and act upon it is the one bestowed with favors; he is the one who purified himself with beneficial knowledge and good deed. The successful is the one who "has succeeded who purifies it" "قَدْ أَفْلَحَ مَن زَكَّاهَا". (91:9)

The one who is heedful of truth and follows his passions is the one who evoked God' anger and the ignorant of the truth is the one who has gone astray. The one who has evoked God's anger is one who has deviated from the guidance of act and the one who has gone astray evoked God's anger for his ignorance of the knowledge that obligates action. Both have gone astray and thus evoked God's anger. Yet, the one who altogether abandoned acting upon the dictates of the truth knowledge – after being acquainted with - is the one most deserved and worthy to be categorized as "those who have evoked God's anger". Therefore, the Jews are most deserved to evoke God's anger; they are even more dramatically subject to aggravated penalties. God, the Almighty, says: "How wretched is that for which they sold themselves - that they would disbelieve in what God has revealed through [their] outrage that God would send down His favor upon whom He wills from among His servants. So they returned having [earned] wrath upon wrath. And for the disbelievers is a humiliating punishment"" بِئْسَمَا اشْتَرَوْا بِهِ أَنفُسَهُمْ أَن

يَكْفُرُوا بِمَا أَنزَلَ اللَّهُ بَغْيًا أَن يُنَزِّلَ اللَّهُ مِن فَضْلِهِ عَلَىٰ مَن يَشَاءُ مِنْ عِبَادِهِ ۖ فَبَاءُوا بِغَضَبٍ عَلَىٰ غَضَبٍ ۚ وَلِلْكَافِرِينَ عَذَابٌ مُّهِين (2:90)

God, Almighty, also says: "Say, "Shall I inform you of [what is] worse than that as penalty from God? [It is that of] those whom God has cursed and with whom He became angry and made of them apes and pigs and servants of Taghut. Those are worse in position and further astray from the sound way"." قل هَلْ أُنَبِّئُكُم بِشَرٍّ مِّن ذَٰلِكَ مَثُوبَةً عِندَ اللَّهِ ۚ مَن لَّعَنَهُ اللَّهُ وَغَضِبَ عَلَيْهِ وَجَعَلَ مِنْهُمُ الْقِرَدَةَ وَالْخَنَازِيرَ وَعَبَدَ الطَّاغُوتَ ۚ أُولَٰئِكَ شَرٌّ مَّكَانًا وَأَضَلُّ عَن سَوَاءِ السَّبِيل (5:60)

The one ignorant of truth is most deserved of misguidance; the Christians have been described in God' words: "Say, "O People of the Scripture, do not exceed limits in your religion beyond the truth and do not follow the inclinations of a people who had gone astray before and misled many and have strayed from the soundness of the way"" قُلْ يَا أَهْلَ الْكِتَابِ لَا تَغْلُوا فِي دِينِكُمْ غَيْرَ الْحَقِّ وَلَا تَتَّبِعُوا أَهْوَاءَ قَوْمٍ قَدْ ضَلُّوا مِن قَبْلُ وَأَضَلُّوا كَثِيرًا وَضَلُّوا عَن سَوَاءِ السَّبِيل (5:77)

The former verses came in the context of addressing the Jews, while the latter came with the Christians. In Alturmuzy and Sahih ibn Heban from a narration quoted by Aidday ibn Hatem that the Prophet, (PBUH), said: "Jews are those who have evoked God's anger, while the Christians are those who have gone astray."

In stating the categories of those who are bestowed with favors – those who are heedful of the truth and act accordingly, those who have evoked God's anger – those who are heedful of the truth and followed their passions and desires , and those who are ignorant of the truth, it is required to verify the message and the prophethood. This categorization of people is the matter of fact reality and it is obligated by the verification of the message.

God, Almighty, ascribed the favor to Himself and omitted the subject (doer) of the anger for many aspects:

Favor is the good and grace; while anger stems from vindication and justice; as mercy is predominant over wrath, God, Almighty, attached the more perfect, the more deserved and the mightier of the two. This is the methodology employed all through the Quran in ascribing good and grace to Him and omitting the subject (the Doer) otherwise. Such is manifested in the wording of the believing Jinn: "And we do not know [therefore] whether evil is intended for those on earth or whether their Lord intends for them a right course."

(72:10)   "وَأَنَّا لَا نَدْرِي أَشَرٌّ أُرِيدَ بِمَن فِي الْأَرْضِ أَمْ أَرَادَ بِهِمْ رَبُّهُمْ رَشَدًا"

Moreover, in Alkhider's utterances concerning the wall and the two orphan boys: "So your Lord intended that they reach maturity and extract their treasure, as a mercy from your Lord."

(18:83) "فَأَرَادَ رَبُّكَ أَن يَبْلُغَا أَشُدَّهُمَا وَيَسْتَخْرِجَا كَنزَهُمَا رَحْمَةً مِّن رَّبِّكَ" .

As for causing a defect the ship, Alkhider said "So I intended to cause defect in it.:" "فَأَرَدتُ أَنْ أَعِيبَهَا" Then he said: "And I did it not of my own accord." "وَمَا فَعَلْتُهُ عَنْ أَمْرِي" (18:82)

Ponder over God's words: "It has been made permissible for you the night preceding fasting to go to your wives, for sexual relations" "أُحِلَّ لَكُمْ لَيْلَةَ الصِّيَامِ الرَّفَثُ إِلَىٰ نِسَائِكُمْ" (2:187)

He, Almighty, says: "Prohibited to you are dead animals, blood, the flesh of swine" "عَلَيْكُمُ الْمَيْتَةُ وَالدَّمُ وَلَحْمُ الْخِنزِيرِ" (5:3). He also says: "Prohibited to you [for marriage] are your mother" " حرمت عَلَيْكُمْ أُمَّهَاتُكُمْ" (4:23), "And lawful to you are [all others] beyond these" "وَأُحِلَّ لَكُم مَّا وَرَاءَ ذَٰلِكُمْ" (4:24)

Gratifying the people who tread the Straight Path with grace and favor indicates that the absolute grace is the perpetual and everlasting success. Yet, the believer and the disbeliever are bestowed with grace and favor in general, not that of the absolute perception. All mankind enjoy God's grace and favor; this is to resolve the question of: Does God, Almighty, bestow grace on the disbeliever?

The absolute grace and favor is exclusively gratified for the people who attained to faith; the grace and favor in the general realm is for the believer and the disbeliever. God, Almighty, says:

"And if you should count the favor of God, you could not enumerate them. Indeed, mankind is [generally] most unjust and ungrateful." (14:34) "وَإِن تَعُدُّوا نِعْمَتَ اللَّهِ لَا تُحْصُوهَا إِنَّ الْإِنسَانَ لَظَلُومٌ كَفَّارٌ"

Favor is a type of Ihsan (all the qualities of goodness); it is the goodness in itself; God, Glorified is He, bestows His goodness on the grateful and ungrateful, the believer and the disbeliever.

The absolute charity and goodness are for those who are truly God-fearing and they are righteous

The second aspect is that: God, Glorified is He, is the sole Bestower of favors. God says:

"And whatever you have of favor - it is from God" "وَمَا بِكُم مِّن نِّعْمَةٍ فَمِنَ الله" (16:53)

What is exclusively His is attributed to Him; has it been attributed to others, it is because others are the vehicle to His grace and gratification. The anger against His enemies is not attributed to God, Almighty, but to His angels, Messengers and the truly God-Fearing servants; they are outrageous because of God's wrath. The wording "those who have evoked God's anger" came in the realm of the consent of those who are His Awliyaa (the God-conscious). The absolute favor is only from God, He is the sole Bestower thereof.

The third aspect: the omission of the (doer) -the One Who is angry-is instrumental in the disgrace, diminution and degradation of "those who have evoked God's anger". It can be a way of glorification and elevation of the Bestower's status, a means unrealizable save by such an omission. In other words, identifying the active subject is more influential in demonstration of praise and glory than using the passive form. This can be illustrated in these two sentences: "This is the man whom the Sultan honored and gifted" is stronger and more influential than: "This is the one who was honored and gifted by the king."

Ponder over the magnificence and splendor in mentioning the cause and recompense of the three categories in the briefest expression. Bestowing them with favors is inclusive of His gratification of guidance, i.e.: the beneficial knowledge and good deed. It is the true guidance and the true religion. It also incorporates the absolutism of gratification by good reward and recompense. It is the perfection of favors. The words "upon whom You bestowed favor" is inclusive of the two matters.

Stating His anger on those who evoked God's anger incorporates two matters; firstly, their retribution is the anger, the apex of which is torture and humiliation and secondly, the reason for God's anger; He, the Almighty, is more Merciful and Compassionate to be Angry unless they have transgressed severely and the inflicting anger on them requires their being misguided. Mentioning those who have gone astray evokes His anger and punishment. Misguidance obligates punishment which is enacted upon being misguided and God's anger accordingly.

Brevity and eloquence are clearly accentuated by mentioning the doer with the happy people, omitting it from the category of those who deserve God's anger and attributing the action to the reason in the case of those who have gone astray.

Reflect on the juxtaposition between guidance and favor on the one hand, and anger and misguidance on the other; "those who have evoked God's anger" and "those who have gone astray" were mentioned in contrast to the guided and favored. This pattern is prevalent in the Quran; God, the Almighty, combines between misguidance and sufferings on one hand, and guidance and success on the other. The latter example is traced in verse: "Those are upon [right] guidance from their Lord, and it is those who are the successful""أُولَٰئِكَ عَلَىٰ هُدًى مِّن رَّبِّهِمْ وَأُولَٰئِكَ هُمُ الْمُفْلِحُونَ" (2:5) and in the verse: "Those will have security, and they are [rightly] guided""أُولَٰئِكَ لَهُمُ الْأَمْنُ وَهُم مُّهْتَدُونَ" (6:82).

And the meaning of the former can be traced in the verse: "Indeed, the criminals are in error and madness"" إِنَّ الْمُجْرِمِينَ فِي ضَلَالٍ وَسُعُرٍ" (45:47).

It is also evident in God's words: "God has set a seal upon their hearts and upon their hearing, and over their vision is a veil.

And for them is a great punishment". " خَتَمَ اللَّهُ عَلَىٰ قُلُوبِهِمْ وَعَلَىٰ سَمْعِهِمْ

وَعَلَىٰ أَبْصَارِهِمْ غِشَاوَةٌ وَلَهُمْ عَذَابٌ عَظِيمٌ" (2:7)

God, Glorified is He, combined the four matters in the verse: "And if there should come to you guidance from Me - then whoever follows My guidance will neither go astray [in the world] nor suffer [in the Hereafter]". " فَإِمَّا يَأْتِيَنَّكُم مِّنِّي هُدًى فَمَنِ اتَّبَعَ هُدَايَ فَلَا يَضِلُّ وَلَا يَشْقَىٰ"(20:123).

This is the true guidance and happiness. Then God, Almighty, says: "And whoever turns away from My remembrance - indeed, he will have a depressed life, and We will gather him on the Day of Resurrection blind." He will say, "My Lord, why have you raised me blind while I was [once] seeing?" [God] will say, "Thus did Our signs come to you, and you forgot them; and thus will you this Day be forgotten"" وَمَنْ أَعْرَضَ عَن ذِكْرِي فَإِنَّ لَهُ مَعِيشَةً ضَنكًا وَنَحْشُرُهُ يَوْمَ الْقِيَامَةِ أَعْمَىٰ، قَالَ رَبِّ لِمَ حَشَرْتَنِي أَعْمَىٰ وَقَدْ كُنتُ بَصِيرًا، قَالَ كَذَٰلِكَ أَتَتْكَ آيَاتُنَا فَنَسِيتَهَا وَكَذَٰلِكَ الْيَوْمَ تُنسَىٰ" (20:124-126)

Hence, He, the Almighty, mentioned misguidance and sufferings collateral.

God, the Almighty, mentioned "the Straight Path" "Al-Sirat Al-Mostaqeem" in the singular form and used the Arabic definite article "al", i.e.: "the", for the purpose of specifying and distinguishing it as only one way. Yet, God, Glorified is He, pluralize the ways of the people who evoked God's anger and those who have gone astray in sometimes and singularize the same in others. God, the Almighty, says: "And, [moreover], this is My path, which is straight, so follow it; and do not follow [other] ways, for you will be separated from His way. This has He instructed you that you may become righteous." " وَأَنَّ هَٰذَا صِرَاطِي مُسْتَقِيمًا فَاتَّبِعُوهُ وَلَا تَتَّبِعُوا

"السُّبُلَ فَتَفَرَّقَ بِكُم عَن سَبِيلِهِ ذَٰلِكُمْ وَصَّاكُم بِهِ لَعَلَّكُمْ تَتَّقُونَ (6:153)

The "Path" and "His Way" are singularized, whereas the ways other than His Way, are pluralized.

Ibn Masoud said "the Messenger of God drew a line with his hand (in the sand) and said, "This is God's path. He then drew some lines to the right and on the left of that line and said, these are the other paths; on each path there is a devil calling to it and then he recited:

"And, [moreover], this is My path, which is straight, so follow it; and do not follow [other] ways, for you will be separated from His way. This has He instructed you that you may become righteous. "" وَأَنَّ هَٰذَا صِرَاطِي مُسْتَقِيمًا فَاتَّبِعُوهُ وَلَا تَتَّبِعُوا السُّبُلَ فَتَفَرَّقَ بِكُمْ عَن سَبِيلِهِ

"ذَٰلِكُمْ وَصَّاكُم بِهِ لَعَلَّكُمْ تَتَّقُونَ (6:153)

This is to say there is only one way leading to God, the Almighty, and it is that for which He sent His Messengers and revealed His Books. Nobody reaches this destination but through this path. If people are to tread different paths and knock all their doors, all paths will be blocked and their doors will all be shut except for this Path. It is linked and leading straight to God, the Almighty. In this fashion, God, the Almighty, says: "This is a path [of return] to Me [that is] straight"". "قَالَ هٰذَا صِرَاطٌ عَلَيَّ مُسْتَقِيمٍ". (15:41)

Mujahid said: the verse means that truth is attributed to God, the Almighty; the path of God. the Almighty, is the path of the truth. This is similar to Alhassan's interpretation or even clearer and the rightest view in the interpretation of this verse. "To Me" indicates obligation i.e.: God, the Almighty, obligated Himself to show and clearly define the Straight Path. The two views can be applied on the Verse in Surah of Alnahl "And upon God is the direction of the [right] way" "عَلَى اللَّهِ قَصْدُ السَّبِيلِ" (16:9). Identically, the right path is the straight path, this of God, that leads to Him

Accordingly, the tradable path – is the Straight path – and it returns and leads to God, the Almighty.

In the Arabic language the preposition "ala", i.e.: "on" is used instead of "إلى", i.e.: "to", in order to point to reaching a destination. While it would be linguistically wise to use the latter – as it indicates reaching a destination – than the former because "ala" indicates obligation. It is noteworthy that in the English translation the preposition "to" is used when the two Arabic preposition "ala" and "ela" are employed. There are many examples of using the preposition "ela" in many verses, indicating reaching a destination or a goal, such as: "Indeed, to Us is their return. Then indeed, upon Us is their account"" إِنَّ إِلَيْنَا إِيَابَهُمْ، "ثُمَّ إِنَّ عَلَيْنَا حِسَابَهُم (88:25-26)

He, Almighty, says: "To Us is their return" "إِلَيْنَا مَرْجِعُهُم" (31:23) When God, the Almighty, wanted to indicate obligation, He used the preposition 'ala'. "Indeed, upon Us is its collection [in your heart] and [to make possible] its recitation""إِنَّ عَلَيْنَا جَمْعَهُ وَقُرْآنَه" (75:17)

And He also says: "And there is no creature on earth but that upon God is its provision, and He knows its place of dwelling and place of storage. All is in a clear register"" وَمَا مِن دَابَّةٍ فِي الْأَرْضِ إِلَّا عَلَى اللَّهِ رِزْقُهَا وَيَعْلَمُ مُسْتَقَرَّهَا وَمُسْتَوْدَعَهَا كُلٌّ فِي كِتَابٍ مُّبِينٍ" (11:6)

And many examples are set. It is said that the preposition "ala" has a subtle meaning; it makes you feel that the one who treads this Path is guided and it is the right path. As God, the Almighty, says about the people attained to faith. "Those are upon [right] guidance from their Lord, and it is those who are the successful"."أُولَئِكَ عَلَى هُدًى مِّن رَّبِّهِمْ وَأُولَئِكَ هُمُ الْمُفْلِحُونَ" ـ (2:5)

And in the same realm, He, the Almighty, says to His Messenger, (PBUH), "So rely upon God; indeed, you are upon the clear truth". "فَتَوَكَّلْ عَلَى اللَّهِ إِنَّكَ عَلَى الْحَقِّ الْمُبِينِ"" (27:79)

God, Glorified is He, is the truth and His path is true and His religion is true. Therefore, the preposition ala was a subtler vehicle for conveying the meaning than 'ela'.

Why 'ala' is used here too? How can a believer be 'ala Alhaq' (on truth and guidance), as it gives the sense of being above or superior to truth?

"The one who is on the truth and guidance path" means that a believer is scaled up to the status of truth and guidance for holding on this path firmly and straightforwardly. "Ala" here is not used pejoratively; it is not connotative of "pride". Conversely to the meaning of misguidance and doubt; the preposition "في", i.e.: "in" is employed to reflect being immersed and soaked in misguidance. This is reflected in the verse: "And they, in their doubt, are hesitating"." "فَهُمْ فِي رَيْبِهِمْ يَتَرَدَّدُونَ" (9:45). And the verse: "But those who deny Our verses are deaf and dumb within darknesses. Whomever God wills - He leaves astray; and whomever He wills - He puts him on a straight path". " وَالَّذِينَ كَذَّبُوا بِآيَاتِنَا صُمٌّ وَبُكْمٌ فِي الظُّلُمَاتِ مَن يَشَإِ اللَّهُ يُضْلِلْهُ وَمَن يَشَأْ يَجْعَلْهُ عَلَىٰ صِرَاطٍ مُّسْتَقِيم" (6:39). And the verse: "So, leave them in their confusion for a time." " فَذَرْهُمْ فِي غَمْرَتِهِمْ حَتَّىٰ حِين" (23:54). And to the same effect came the verse: "And indeed, they are, concerning the Qur'an, in disquieting doubt". "وَإِنَّهُمْ لَفِي شَكٍّ مِّنْهُ مُرِيب"" (11:110)

Reflecting on this verse, "We or you are either upon guidance or in clear error." "وَإِنَّا أَوْ إِيَّاكُمْ لَعَلَىٰ هُدًى أَوْ فِي ضَلَالٍ مُبِينٍ" (34:24), one realizes that the truth path uplifts to the Highest, whereas the misguidance path abase the misguided to be the lowest of the low.

In a third interpretation for the verse: "God said, "This is a path [of return] to Me [that is] straight" "قال هَٰذَا صِرَاطٌ عَلَيَّ مُسْتَقِيمٌ" (15:41), Alkisaiy viewed that it is intended for menace and intim-idation just like the case with the verse: "Indeed, your Lord is in observation. "إِنَّ رَبَّكَ لَبِالْمِرْصَادِ" (89 :14). Yet, this interpretation conflicts with the context herein. As the verse came as a reply for Satan's machination to mislead mankind."[Satan] said, "My Lord, because You have put me in error, I will surely make [diso-bedience] attractive to them on earth, and I will mislead them all. Except, among them, Your chosen servants"" قَالَ رَبِّ بِمَا أَغْوَيْتَنِي "لَأُزَيِّنَنَّ لَهُمْ فِي الْأَرْضِ وَلَأُغْوِيَنَّهُمْ أَجْمَعِينَ إِلَّا عِبَادَكَ مِنْهُمُ الْمُخْلَصِينَ" (15:39-40). Satan has no way to cross through to tempt the guided servants of God.

God, the Almighty, made a clear and decisive statement that "the chosen servants", the sincere, are on the Straight Path of God. God, the Almighty, states that Satan has no power or might hover around God's chosen servants who are on this Straight Path. It is well-fortified with God's protection. The enemy of God cannot reach His chosen God-fearing servants. This is the most proper interpretation of the verse accepted by Salaf.

Alkisay's interpretation is unactable as the verse that reads: "[God] said, "This is a path [of return] to Me [that is] straight" as the connotation of the meaning has no relevance to the position of menace and intimidation. The path of the one menaced, by no means, can be straight; menace cannot come in the realm of straightness. The path of the misguided cannot lead him straight to God. Accordingly, this view is totally irrelevant and unactable.

Those who interpreted it in the fashion of obligation in the sense that God, the Almighty, obligated Himself of showing its straightness and guiding to it. However, I am not convinced of it as a sound interpretation of the verse at hand for some linguistic considerations. I more likely believe in the view embraced by Salaf.

I heard Taqayy Aldin Ahmed ibn Taymeyah, may God be pleased with him, said: They are equal to God's saying: "Indeed, [incumbent] upon Us is guidance. And indeed, to Us belongs the Hereafter and the first [life]" "إِنَّ عَلَيْنَا لَلْهُدَىٰ. وَإِنَّ لَنَا لَلْآخِرَةَ والأُولَىٰ" (92:12-13)

These are three positions bearing this meaning in the Quran.

I said that most scholars rested to the meaning of obligation in the interpretation of Surah of Alayel (the Night) i.e.: God, the Almighty, made it incumbent upon Himself to clarify for us the paths of guidance and falsehood. Others, like Albaghaway, accepted only this meaning in the interpretation of Surat Alnahal (the Bees). The three meanings were adopted in Surat AlHijir.

The straight path is God's path; He, the Almighty, states that He is on the path, as previously mentioned, and He Himself, the Almighty, is the Straight Path. This was mentioned in two positions in the Quran in Surah of Hud and Surah of Alnahl. God, the Almighty, says in Hud: "There is no creature but that He holds its forelock. Indeed, my Lord is on a path [that is] straight". " مَّا مِن دَابَّةٍ إِلَّا هُوَ آخِذٌ بِنَاصِيَتِهَا إِنَّ رَبِّي عَلَىٰ صِرَاطٍ مُّسْتَقِيمٍ" (11:56)

God, Almighty, says in Surah of Alnahl: "And God presents an example of two men, one of them dumb and unable to do a thing, while he is a burden to his guardian. Wherever he directs him, he brings no good. Is he equal to one who commands justice, while he is on a straight path?" " وَضَرَبَ اللَّهُ مَثَلًا رَّجُلَيْنِ أَحَدُهُمَا أَبْكَمُ لَا يَقْدِرُ عَلَىٰ شَيْءٍ وَهُوَ كَلٌّ عَلَىٰ مَوْلَاهُ أَيْنَمَا يُوَجِّههُّ لَا يَأْتِ بِخَيْرٍ هَلْ يَسْتَوِي هُوَ وَمَن يَأْمُرُ بِالْعَدْلِ وَهُوَ عَلَىٰ صِرَاطٍ مُّسْتَقِيمٍ" (16: 76)

God, the Almighty, sets an example of the deaf mute and dumb idols and those whoever worship them. Idols need to be carried, deposited and serviced by the worshipper, so how is it likely they equate them with God, the Almighty, Who commands justice and monotheism? He is the Able, the Speaker, the Rich and He, the Almighty, is on the Straight Path in terms of utterances and deeds. His utterances are truth, preaching and guidance on the one hand, and His deeds are wisdom, justice, mercy and benefits on the other. It is the rightest view interpreting this verse and which has been most related by the exegetes than other views. Those who related otherwise – as Albaghawy - prioritized his view over others and then related others. He then mentioned Alkalbiy's view and said God, the Almighty, is the One who guides mankind to the Straight Path.

I believe that God's guidance to the Straight Path stems from His Being, Glorified is He, on it whether this guidance is via deeds or utterances and He, the Almighty, is on the Straight Path in His deeds and utterances and this does not contradicts with the views holding that: He, Glorified is He, is on the Straight Path.

It is also said the verse refers to the Messenger, peace and blessings of God be upon him, is the one who commands justice and he is on the Straight Path.

I believe that this view, likewise, does not conflict with the first interpretation as God, the Almighty, is on the Straight Path and His Messenger is on it too; he, (PBUH), neither commands nor does anything save according to God's pronouncements.

Hence, the example related is to the leader and the guide to the disbelievers, namely the mute Idol which is incapable of guidance or good on the hand, and to the leader of the pious, the Messenger of God, (PBUH), who commands justice and who is on the Straight Path.

According to the first view, the example in the verse is referring to the one worshiped by the disbelievers and the One worshipped by the pious. The two views are conjoined; some hold the first view and others mentioned the other and both incorporate the purpose of the verse.

Some viewed that the verse refers to both the believer and the disbeliever as narrated by Attaiyah ibn Abbas; Attaa said: the mute is Ubbay ibn Khalaf and those who command justice are Hamza, Uthman ibn Affan and Uthman ibn Madhhun.

I hold that this view can be plausible too and not conflicting with others. Since God, the Almighty is on the Straight Path and so are His Messenger, (PBUH), and His Messenger's followers. Juxtaposed is the guide and the one worshipped by the disbelievers; the disbeliever is follower, the one followed and the one worshipped. Some Salaf related the highest types, others mentioned the guide and some mentioned the responsive; the verse can be interpreted according to all the views jointly. The Quran abounds in the same pattern.

As for the Verse is in Surah of Hud, it is clear and holds only one meaning which is God, Glorified is He, is on the Straight Path, He is Most Worthy of Being on the Straight Path. All His words are filled with truth, sound judgement, guidance, justice and wisdom. God, the Almighty, says: "And the word of your Lord has been fulfilled in truth and in justice. None can alter His words, and He is the Hearing, the Knowing". "تَمَّتْ كَلِمَتُ رَبِّكَ صِدْقًا وَعَدْلًا لَّا مُبَدِّلَ" "لِكَلِمَاتِهِ وَهُوَ السَّمِيعُ الْعَلِيم" (11:115)

Besides, His entire acts are of benefit, wisdom, mercy, justice and good. Evil is irrelevant in the deeds and utterances of those who are on the Straight Path, on the contrary it is included in the deeds and utterances of those who swerve from the Straight Path.

In the Messenger's invocation "O God! Here I came to you humbly. The entire good is in Your hand and Evil is totally away from You." Those who interpreted this by assuming that we can't approach God through evil or that evil does not come up to you are erroneous. The implicit meaning is subtler and loftier; His entire Names are good, His entire Attributes are perfect; His acts are perfectly enumerable, His entire acts are abounding in truth and justice. It is impossible for evil to be among His Names, Attributes, Acts or Utterances. This meaning is quite identical with God's words "My Lord is on a path [that is] straight." "إِنَّ رَبِّي عَلَى

صِرَاطٍ مُسْتَقِيمٍ" (11:56) which came rightly after God's saying: "Indeed, I have relied upon God, my Lord and your Lord" " إِنِّي تَوَكَّلْتُ عَلَى اللَّهِ رَبِّي وَرَبِّكُم" (11:56)

It means that He is my Lord; He will never let me get lost or astray. He is your Lord too i.e. He is not to let you empower over or oppress me. He overpowers; you can't do anything except through His Will. He holds the forelock of creature (He is Sole Controller of creatures), He direct them the Way He desires, The Disposer of all affairs. Although He directs and disposes all affairs of all the creatures, His disposition comes perfectly compatible with the Straight Path. Neither does He dispose the affairs unless they are by the virtue of wisdom, justice and interest. Even if God allows you to overpower me, He assuredly Wise and well deserved of praise, because the dictates of this Who is on the straight Path are just and wise. This is the true consciousness of God, the Almighty, which is totally at odds with that of Al-Qadraiayyh AlMajosiyyah (the adherents of Mazdeism), or Al-Qariyyah Jabriyah (the adherents of Fatalism) who negate the sound judgment, interests and causation. God, Glorified is He, is the Assistant.

The seeker for the Straight Path is engaged in the most laborious mission; especially that many have swerved of this path and accordingly those who grope for it are a few or even rare.

Human beings are innately abhorrent of the anguish of loneliness and seeking good escorts, God, the Almighty, drew our attention to this and directed us to the nature of the companions on the Straight path and that they are: "Those will be with the ones upon whom God has bestowed favor of the prophets, the steadfast affirmers of truth, the martyrs and the righteous. And excellent are those as companions". " فَأُولَٰئِكَ مَعَ الَّذِينَ أَنْعَمَ اللَّهُ عَلَيْهِم مِّنَ النَّبِيِّينَ وَالصِّدِّيقِينَ وَالشُّهَدَاءِ وَالصَّالِحِينَ وَحَسُنَ أُولَٰئِكَ رَفِيقًا" (4:69)

Thus, He, the Almighty, attached the path to its companions from among those whom God, the Almighty, has bestowed favor upon. This was intended to assure the seekers of the path of guidance and relieve them of the pain and anguish of loneliness for being forsaken by their contemporaries and fellow citizens. Being acknowledged that the companions of the path are those whom God bestowed them with favors, this seeker should not be concerned by those who abandoned or swerved from it. They are least in status, even if, the largest in number. In this realm, some Salaf said:

"Go on the path of truth and don't feel no feel lonely because who take it are few, and beware of the path of falsehood, and do not be deceived by the multitude of the perishers" whenever you entertain the pain of loneliness, seek for the previous companion, be careful to catch up with them and abandon the dissidents/ any other. They will be of no avail to you before God, if even accompanied you on your way and you heeded them, they would distract you to lead you astray.

Let me set two examples:

First example: a man gets out of his house for the sole purpose which is praying. On his way he came across one of the human devil. The latter started to insult him. Accordingly, he answered back till they engaged into a fight. The human devil could be stronger and overpowers him and prevents him from going to the mosque till he missed the prayer. Reservedly, the man could be stronger than the human devil; yet, engaging in altercation delayed him from attending the first row in mosque. This made him imperfect the requirement of congregational prayer. If he heeded the human devil, he might discourage him. If of emboldened resolve and consciousness, he might hasten his pace to be as much as the lapse of time spent in such a distraction. Ignoring such distractions and focusing on his intent so as not to miss the prayer or time, foils his enemy's machinations.

The second example: An antelope is faster than a dog; however, fears and turning to the dog dampen the antelope's resolve and consequently the dog nails it.

The purpose of setting these examples is to show that the companion of the path can relieve the pain of loneliness and encourage catching up with them.

This is one of the benefits entertained in Invocation of Qunut "O God! Guide me to be among those whom You have bestowed guidance" i.e. make me an affiliate of this group to be one of their companions."

Second benefit: it is a way of imploring to God through His favors and grace he bestowed on others; namely, the grace of guidance. It was Your favor, so I implore before You to gift me with share of this favor and make me one of those upon whom You bestowed favors. it is beseeching through God's grace and favor.

Third benefit: as if someone is imploring before the Most Generous: I wish I could be as blessed with favors as the entirety upon whom You have showered them with favors, I wish You teach me as those whom You have taught and I wish I could be as gifted as those whom You have embraced with Your favor.

As long as asking guidance from God, the Almighty, for the Straight Path is one of the most significant requests, and the attainment of which is the best bliss, God, the Almighty, taught His servants the way of supplicating Him. He, the Almighty, commanded them first to praise, extol and glorify Him. Then, to confess their being servants to Him and attesting to His Oneness. There are two vehicles for granting their request: first imploring before Him through His Names and Attributes and second imploring Him by worshipping Him. Imploring God through these two means guarantee fulfillment of the invocation. They are supported by the two means mentioned in the two narrations relating the Great Name of God – narrated by Ibn Hiban, Imam Ahmad and Alturmuzy.

The first narration related by Abdullah ibn Buraida on the authority of his father that the Prophet, (PBUH), heard a man supplicating God and saying:

"O God, indeed, I ask you by my testifying that You are the Lord, there is none worthy of worship except You, the One, As-Samad (the Eternal), the one who does not beget, nor was begotten, and there is none who is like Him." He said: 'By the One in Whose Hand is my soul, he has asked God by His Greatest Name, the one which if He is called upon by it, He responds, and when He is asked by it, He gives.

He supplicated God by testifying to His oneness and the testimony of the one supplicating of His Oneness, and the authentication of His attributes by the significance of the name As-Samad which ibn Abbas said that it means "the Most Perfect in Knowledge and abilities." In another version, it is meant: the

Most Perfect Master who contained all the potential of mastery." And in a third version by Saeed ibn Gabir: "the Most perfect in all Attributes, acts and utterances. "He, the Almighty, has no resemblance or equivalence Nor is there to Him any equivalent." "لَمْ يَكُن لَّهُ كُفُوًا أَحَدٌ" (112:4)

This is the doctrine of Sunnis to supplicate God by abiding by this belief and through attesting to His Great Name.

The second is narration by Anas ibn Malik that:

The Prophet (PBUH) entered the mosque and there was a man who had performed prayer and was supplicating. He was saying in his supplication: "O God, none has the right to be worshipped but God, You are the One Who gives blessings, Originator of the heavens and the earth, Possessor of glory and generosity." So the Prophet (PBUH) said: "Do you know what he has supplicated God with? He has supplicated to God by His Greatest Name, the one which if He is called upon by it, He responds, and when He is asked by it, He gives."

This is a means of supplicating God by His Names and Attributes.

Surah of Alfatihah combined the two means, supplicating by praise, extolling and glorification and through worship and attesting to His Oneness. Then came the most important and significant request reflected in asking for guidance after statement of the two means. The one supplicating God by these means, his invocation will be granted.

Parallel is the Prophet's supplication which he used to say when he performs his evening prayers at night.

When the Prophet (PBUH) got up at night to offer the late-night prayer, he used to say:

O God! All the praises are for you. You are the Light of the Heavens and the Earth And all the praises are for You; You are the King of the Heavens and the Earth; And all the praises are for You; You are the Truth and Your Promise is the truth, And to meet You is true, Your Word is the truth And Paradise is true And Hell is true And all the Prophets (Peace be upon them) are true; And Muhammad is true, And the Day of Resurrection is true. O God! I surrender (my will) to You; I believe in You and depend on You. And repent to You, And with Your help I argue (with my opponents, the non-believers) And I take You as a judge (to judge between us). Please forgive me my previous And future sins; And whatever I concealed or revealed And You are the One who make (some people) forward And (some) backward. There is none to be worshipped but You.

Thus, he supplicated God by praise, extolling and worship and then he asked for forgiveness.

Alfatihah including all categories of Tawhid (Oneness of God)

This Surah of Alfatihah includes the three kinds of Oneness agreed upon by all the Prophets.

Oneness of God entails two categories: the first incorporates knowledge and belief, and the second incorporates will and intent. The former is called the Tawhid of statement and the latter is called the Tawhid of will and intent. The first is related to informing and knowledge and the second with intent and will. The second includes (Tawhid of Lordship) and (Tawhid of worship).

As for Tawhid of statement, it entails confirmation of all attributes of perfection to God and negation of any possibility of resemblance and equivalence to God and glorifying Him against all drawbacks and shortcomings. This meaning was elaborated on jointly and severally: jointly in term of assuring that praise is for Him, Glorified is He, severally by mentioning the relevance of (worship) and (Lordship); namely Mercy and Possession. God's Names and Attributes are to be added to these four categories.

Praise encompasses this as it features laudation of the One praised by the attributes of His perfection and faculties of Glory embraced by love and content and full submission to Him. The one who is ungrateful to the attributes of the praised and shunned offering love and full submission to Him can't be categorized as praiser. The more enumerable the attributes of Perfection of the praised , the more perfect his praise is. Likewise, the fewer are the attributes of perfection, the less perfect praise is. Accordingly, all the praise is due to God; none but Him is worthy by the virtue of perfection and multitude of His Attributes; and so are all the faculties of His Glory. Therefore, God, the Almighty, disgraced/ condemned/ dispraised all the gods of the polytheists and caused fault/ dishonored/ demeaned/ them by taking away/denying them all their merits of perfection. They were degraded as being deaf and blind, mute and that they provide neither guidance nor benefit nor harm; the god of Jahmiyyah could be one of them. They have attributed idols to

God; Glorified is He from all the allegations of the unjust and the ungrateful. God, the Almighty, relates in the Quran on the tongue of His Prophet and Companion, Ibrahim: "[Mention] when he said to his father, "O my father, why do you worship that which does not hear and does not see and will not benefit you at all?"" ("إِذْ قَالَ لِأَبِيهِ يَا أَبَتِ لِمَ تَعْبُدُ مَا لَا يَسْمَعُ وَلَا يُبْصِرُ وَلَا يُغْنِي عَنكَ شَيْئًا") 19:42)

Should Ibrahim's God have these characteristics and status, Azar would have said" Your God has the same stature, why do you condemn me?" Albeit being a disbeliever, he was more aware of God than Jahmiyyah. The disbelievers of Quraish, though disbelievers, they admitted the attributes of the Creator and His Being the Highest over His creatures. "And the people of Moses made, after [his departure], from their ornaments a calf - an image having a lowing sound. Did they not see that it could neither speak to them nor guide them to a way? They took it [for worship], and they were wrongdoers."" اتَّخَذَ قَوْمُ مُوسَىٰ مِن بَعْدِهِ مِنْ حُلِيِّهِمْ عِجْلًا جَسَدًا لَّهُ خُوَارٌ أَلَمْ يَرَوْا أَنَّهُ لَا يُكَلِّمُهُمْ وَلَا يَهْدِيهِمْ سَبِيلًا اتَّخَذُوهُ وَكَانُوا ظَالِمِين " (7:148)

Had God of the creations been like this, He, the Almighty, would not have denied or condemned them or even relying on this for the invalidity of their godhood.

Haphazardly, they claimed, "God, the Almighty, does not speak to his servants."

Their allegation is refutable; He, the Almighty, spoke to some through veil, He spoke to others directly without any veil, like Prophet Moses and He sends messengers to reveal by His permission what he wills. God talked to all mankind on the tongues of His messengers. He revealed His words to them and they informed people with. The messengers said: "This is God's speech which He spoke and revealed it to us to transmit/ inform you with. Accordingly, Salaf stated that whoever denies the fact of God Being a Speaker, he denies, thereupon, the message of the entire messengers. God, the Almighty, when talking about Alsamariy says: "And he extracted for them [the statue of] a calf which had a lowing sound, and they said, This is your god and the god of Moses, but he forgot. Did they not see that it could not return to them any speech and that it did not possess for them any harm or benefit?" فَأَخْرَجَ لَهُمْ عِجْلًا جَسَدًا لَهُ خُوَارٌ فَقَالُوا هَٰذَا إِلَٰهُكُمْ "وَإِلَٰهُ مُوسَىٰ فَنَسِيَ، أَفَلَا يَرَوْنَ أَلَّا يَرْجِعُ إِلَيْهِمْ قَوْلًا وَلَا يَمْلِكُ لَهُمْ ضَرًّا وَلَا نَفْعًا (20:88-89)

God also says: "And God presents an example of two men, one of them dumb and unable to do a thing, while he is a burden to his guardian. Wherever he directs him, he brings no good. Is he equal to one who commands justice, while he is on a straight path?" "وَضَرَبَ اللّٰهُ مَثَلًا رَّجُلَيْنِ أَحَدُهُمَا أَبْكَمُ لَا يَقْدِرُ عَلَىٰ شَيْءٍ وَهُوَ كَلٌّ عَلَىٰ مَوْلَاهُ"

"أَيْنَمَا يُوَجِّههُّ لَا يَأْتِ بِخَيْرٍ هَلْ يَسْتَوِي هُوَ وَمَن يَأْمُرُ بِالْعَدْلِ وَهُوَ عَلَىٰ صِرَاطٍ مُّسْتَقِيم

(16:76)

Negating the attribute of God's talking features the disbelief in Lordship. It is well-known to the common sense, sound minds and in according with the dictates of the divine books that the one who is short of the attributes of perfection is not a Lord nor a Disposer of affairs nor a Rabb (Divinity); he is detested, defective not worthy of praise whether in the Herein or the Hereafter. Praise in the Herein and Hereafter is due to the One Who possess all the attributes of perfection, faculties of glory for which He is well- Deserved of praise. The Salaf called their compilations "taxonomies of Tawhid" as it elaborates on Sunnah and confirmation of the Attributes of God and His being of elevated status over His creation and His speech and talking to others ". Negating or denying or disbelieving in all of this is a denial and ingratitude to The Creator. Attesting to His Oneness is via confirmation of His attributes, extolling Him over any resemblance or defects. The sect of MuatGod considered denying the attributes of God, the Creator a kind of Tawid. They claimed that these attributes are ascribed to people and cannot be ascribed to God. They called the truth falsehood and vice versa. Most people believe in the outward rather than the inward without scrutinizing the real truth. God says: "He whom God guides is the [rightly] guided, but he whom He leaves astray - never will you find for him a protecting guide." "مَن يَهْدِ اللَّهُ فَهُوَ الْمُهْتَدِ وَمَن يُضْلِلْ فَلَن تَجِدَ لَهُ وَلِيًّا مُّرْشِدًا" (18:17)

The one praised is not praised for nothingness and muteness, unless negating the shortcomings and imperfections, the thing that implicitly implies affirmation of opposite attributes which are indictive of evidenced perfections. the groundless negation is heavily frowned upon.

God, the Almighty, praised Himself by negating the likelihood of having partners or associates. He, the Almighty, singled Himself out by Oneness, Lordship and all the unique attributes of perfections, none can be equivalent to deserve being a partner or associate. Negation of these attributes discredits His Existence and, accordingly, every existent being will be more perfect than Him; existence has predominance over nothingness. God, the Almighty, is not to praise Himself by negating a certain attribute unless this negation is the very core of verification of perfection. For example, God, the Almighty, negated His demise to prove the very perfection of His Ever-living. Furthermore, He, the Almighty, praised Himself by not be overtaken by neither drowsiness nor sleep to indicate that He is the most perfect Sustainer of all existence. Likewise, He extoled Himself that "nothing is absent from Him even if it is an atom's weight within the heavens or within the earth or [what is] smaller than that or greater, except that He is well-aware of by the virtue of the perfection of His knowledge and well-Encompassing." The attribute of injustice, also, was negated to prove the utmost perfection of justice and goodness. He, the Almighty, is not perceived by visions to underpin the utmost perfection of His Glory; He is seen albeit Unperceived. He is the Most Knowledgeable but none can encompass the boundaries of His knowledge; the negation of vision and perception is not a perfection in itself as nothingness is unseen, i.e.: the very being of unseen is not, by any means related to perfection, whilst the very essence of perfection resides in the fact of the impossibility of encompassing His boundaries whether through vision or perception. He is Most Glorified by Himself, He is way above the perception of His creations. He, the Almighty, negated the imperfections of heedlessness and forgetfulness for His perfect insightfulness.

God, the Almighty, enunciated the pattern of negation all through the Quran to praise Himself to verify its opposite, affirmation and to include the perfection of verifying its opposite.

To conclude, the essence of praise is related to affirmation of the attributes of perfection, and their negation entails denial of the praise which obligates proving the affirmation of its opposite.

This is the proof of the Oneness of Names and Attributes of God, the Almighty.

The five Names of God, the Almighty; God (Lord), Rabb (the One), Ar-Rahman, (the Especially Merciful), Ar-Rahim, (the Entirely Merciful) and the King prove the Oneness of Names and Attributes. This is built on two facts:

First: all the Names of God, Glorified is He, are indicative of the descriptions of His utmost perfection; they stem from His Attributes. They are names as well as descriptions. Hence, they are the best names, if they were just meaningless utterances, they would have been neither beautiful nor indicative of any praise nor perfection. If such, it would have been sensible to replace the names denoting God's vengeance and wrath with that of mercy and goodness and vice versa. We can supplicate God, the Almighty, by "O' God! I have wronged myself, so forgive me! You are the Avenger. O' God! Gift me With Your Favors. You are the Afflicter, the Preventer", and the like.

Negation of the meanings of God's best Names is the gravest degree of deviation concerning His Names. God, the Almighty, says:

"And leave [the company of] those who practice deviation concerning His names. They will be recompensed for what they

7) وَذَرُوا الَّذِينَ يُلْحِدُونَ فِي أَسْمَائِهِ سَيُجْزَوْنَ مَا كَانُوا يَعْمَلُونَ" "." have been doing
180:)

Had they been incomprehensive of meanings and descriptions, He, the Almighty, would neither have referred to them by their masdar (close to its English equivalent 'verbal noun') nor employed them as adjectives. However, God, the Almighty, referred to Himself using their masdar, established them for Himself and were established for Him through His Messenger, Prophet Muhammad (PBUH) as in the verse:

"Indeed, it is God who is the [continual] Provider, the firm possessor of strength". "إِنَّ اللَّهَ هُوَ الرَّزَّاقُ ذُو الْقُوَّةِ الْمَتِينُ" (51: 58). One of God's Name is the Strong and the described meaning of which is Strength' ['Strength' is the masdar (verbal noun) of the verb 'strengthen'. And this masdar exemplified in strength الْقُوَّةِ is used to describe God, the Almighty, by His being possessor of this strength (the masdar). Masdar, here, is the grammatical vessel to add vitality to names to transcend their significance from just mere names into vitalized meanings attributed to God's names.]

Likewise, in the following verse; the Honorable is the One who possesses honor; had not strength and honor been well-established and evidenced, He, the Almighty, would have been called neither the Strong nor the Honorable. "Then to God belongs all honor." "الْعِزَّةَ فَلِلَّهِ الْعِزَّةُ جَمِيعًا" (35:10)

This is applicable on the following verses too; "to that which He has revealed to you". "أَنزَلَهُ بِعِلْمِهِ" (4:166), and the verse, "then know that the Qur'an was revealed with the knowledge of God" "أَنَّمَا أُنزِلَ بِعِلْمِ اللَّهِ" (11:14), "and they encompass not a thing of His knowledge except for what He wills". "وَلَا يُحِيطُونَ بِشَيْءٍ مِّنْ عِلْمِهِ" (2:255)

It has been reported in Sahih Albukhari that the Messenger of God (PBUH) said, "Verily the Exalted and Mighty God does not sleep, and it does not befit Him to sleep. He lowers the scale and lifts it. The deeds in the night are taken up to Him before the deeds of the day, and the deeds of the day before the deeds of the night. His veil is the light. If He withdraws it (the veil), the splendor of His countenance would consume His creation so far as His sight reaches." The masdar 'sight' from which His name, All-Seer, is derived.

Lady 'Aisha, may God be pleased with her, was quoted saying: "Praise be to God Whose Hearing is expanded to comprehend/include all sounds (redress all grievances)"

In the narration of asking God's consultation, the Prophet (PBUH) advised us to say "O God! I consult You, for You have all knowledge, and appeal to You to support me with Your Power and ask for Your Bounty, for You are able to do things while I am not;" God, the Almighty, is All-Capable and He, the Almighty, possesses the Power.

God, the Almighty, says to (Moses):

[God] said, "O Moses, I have chosen you over the people with My messages and My words [to you]"." قَالَ يَا مُوسَىٰ إِنِّي اصْطَفَيْتُكَ عَلَى النَّاسِ بِرِسَالَاتِي وَبِكَلَامِي" (7:144). God, the Almighty, is a Speaker of speech.

He is the Glorified to Him belong the glorification, as the Messenger (PBUH) was quoted as saying:

God, the Exalted and Glorious, said: Glory is His lower garment and Majesty is His cloak" He, the Almighty, is the just to Whom belongs judgment. "So the judgement is with God, the Highest, the Grand."" "فَالْحُكْمُ لِلَّهِ الْعَلِيِّ الْكَبِيرِ" (40:12)

The Muslim scholars unanimously agreed that if a person is to take an oath by God, the Almighty, by imploring His Eternity, Hearing, Sight, Power, Honor or Glory, his oath is to be granted and it is expiatory for his sins. Given to the fact that they are the attributes of God's perfection and they are derived from His names.

Furthermore, should not His names be inclusive of meanings and attributes, it would not be fitting to refer to God, the Almighty, by using their verbs i.e.: it would be insensible to say" God, the Almighty," hears. Sees, knows, can, and wants."

Establishing the rules of adjectives is secondary to their establishment; once the root of the adjective is negated, it is impossible to establish its rule.

Besides, had not His names entail significances and descriptions, they would have been lifeless exactly like mere proper names whose denotation bears no relevance to their nomination, thus they would be of flat sameness and their connotations would not expand to diversity. This is a real contention and apparent falsehood! How can one assume that the meaning of the name the All-Capable is equal to that All-Hearer or All-Seer, and the All-Repenting to that of the Vindicating or the Bestower with the Preventer? This assumption is horrendously at odds with the sound mind, language and common sense. Accordingly, the negation of the connotations of His names (denominations) is the gravest deviation for them. This deviation incorporates many kinds and this is one of them.

The Second deviation: they attributed His Names to their idols which they called deities. Ibn Abbas and Mijahid said, "they deviated the names of God from their connotations and called their idols after these names. They went so far by adding or decreasing some letters to the original names; they derived Latt from God, Uzza from Aziz (Honored) and Manat from God's name Manan (the Sustainer). It was narrated that this is ibn Abbas's interpretation of the verse," those who deviate from His names."

and that they lie to God, the Almighty. This is the literal meaning.

The deviation here features deviating from the true meaning, and inclusion of weird meanings that have no shades of any relevance to them. It also parades devoicing them of their true meanings. This is the essence of deviation in this realm. Those who are engaged in this act are lying to God, the Almighty. Ibn Abbas interpreted Ilhad 'deviation' by lying to God, or this is the very evil intent of the deviant concerning God's Names. If he is to include weird meanings that have no relevance to their meanings, devoiced them of all or some of their true meanings, he, hence, deviates them from the right and truth. This is the meaning of deviation.

Ilhad "Deviation" can be their rejection or negation, rejection or deference of their significances, distortion of their true meanings, vacating them from their contextual true significance by some false assumptions. Erratically, they ascribe His names to the fabricated creations; like that the deviation of the adherents of doctrine of Ahl Al-Ithad (Oneness of being), so faulty is their deviation that they lent His names to all the beings, the benign and the malignant. Their mentor said: "He is named after each and every praised name intellectually. Legally and customarily.

May God, the Almighty, be highly raised above the assumptions of the deviant.

The second origin: the name is from among God's names and it is indicative of Being and the Attribute of which was derived by conformity. It also incorporates two significances by inclusion and necessity. It refers to the adjective alone by the virtue of inclusion, the being devoid of attribute and refers to the other attribute by virtue of necessity. His name "the All-Hearer" denotes the Being of God (the One) and His Hearing by conformity, and the Being alone and the Hearing alone by inclusion. It is also indicative of All-Eternal and the attribute of Eternity by the virtue of attachment. This rule is applicable to the totality of God's Names and Attributes. The acknowledgement or the negation of the attachment varies from someone to another, and here lies their disagreement as per many names, attributes and judgments. The one who grasps that volitional act is a prerequisite for Eternity, and that the Hearing and Sight are the prerequisite of perfect Eternity and that all the perfection is needed for the perfect Eternity, is proving his argument that the names, attributes and acts of God against all those who denied them for their unheedfulness to their necessity. They are really unconscious of the truth and the prerequisites of Eternity or that of all God's attributes.

God's name AlAzim "the Great" has its prerequisites, denied only by those who don't know the greatness of God and its pre-requisites.

This can be applied on God's name AlAli "Highest", AlHakim "the All-Wise" and all of the names. The prerequisite of the name "the Highest" is the Absolute Highness in any fashion. To Him belongs the Absolute Highness in all aspects; Highness of Status, Subjugation and Highness of Being. Rejection of the Highness of Being prompts for rejection of the prerequisites of His name "the Highest"

God's name "the Manifest", also, has its requirements; there is nothing above Him as mentioned in the authentic Hadith of the Prophet (PBUH) who was quoted as saying about God: You are the Manifest, nothing is above You," He, the Almighty, is above everything; the rejection of His 'Aboveness' (Elevation) to everything implies a similar rejection to the prerequisites of His name "the Manifest". It is unbefitting that the Manifest has Ele-vation over fate only in the like of "gold is above silver (in terms of value or so), jewelry is transcending glass. This Aboveness is related to manifestation, or even the above can be more mani-fest than what is underneath it. It is insensible for God, to ascribe to Him the manifestation of subjugation and victory only albeit God, the Almighty is manifested through the hallmarks of subjugation and victory. This is parallel to His name the Most Hidden, denoting to the fact that He is the One that nothing is above Him and nothing is beneath Him. By the same token, God's name AlAwal "the First", the One Whose Existence is without a beginning, is juxtaposed to God's name, AlAkhir "The Infinite Last", the One Whose Existence is without an end.

God's name, AlHakim "The All-Wise", constitutes establishment of the praised goals intended for Him via His acts, His sagacious disposition of affairs in the best fashions. Denial of this prompts for a total denial of the name and its prerequisites. This can be drawn on all God's best Names.

By this the two tenets have been established. God's name God (the Lord) is comprehensive of all His best names and the supreme attributes of the three significances i.e. It is indicative of His Divinity embracing all the verification of His divine attributes and negation of any other opposites attributed to Him.

The Divine attributes draw on His perfection which is distant from and devoid of any resemblance, equivalence, defects and shortcomings. Given that, God, the Almighty, attaches all His best names to this great name as exemplified in the verse "And to God belong the best names"" "وَلِلَّهِ الْأَسْمَاءُ الْحُسْنَىٰ فَادْعُوهُ بِهَا" (7:180). We can attach God's names to the name God; Ar-Rahman (the Merciful), Ar-Rahim (the Extremely Merciful), Al-Kudoos (the

Extolled), As-Salam (the Peaceful), Al-Aziz (the Almighty). However, His name "God" can't be related to be one of the names of Ar-Rahman or Al-Aziz or the like.

So we are to acknowledge His name "God" to be embracing of the meanings of His best names, indicative to them in their entirety. God's best names detail for and clarify the divine attributes from which the name 'God' is stemmed. His name 'God' constitutes His being a Lord to be worshipped. All creatures worship Him as Lord by the virtue of their love, extolment and subjugation to Him. Therefore, they seek His refuge when afflicted by mishaps and calamities. This necessitates the utmost perfection of His Oneness and Mercy that are, in turn, encompassing the perfection of Sovereignty and Praise. His Uluhiyyiah (Lordship), Rububiyyah (Oneness of God), Mercy and Sovereignty require the availability of all His attributes of perfection. Impossible is to establish this for that who is inanimate, deaf, unheedful, disable, mute or unable to act upon his own accord or acting irrationally.

The attributes of glory and beauty are exclusive to the name 'God', whilst, the attributes of acting, ability, the uniqueness of inflicting harm or benefit, bestowing and preventing, enforcement of Will, perfection of strength and disposition of all affairs of creation are exclusive to the name Rabb (the One)

Whereas the attributes of Ihsaan (goodness), generosity, benevolence, Kindness, bestowing, giving, mercy and softness are mostly deserved to His name Ar-Rahman. They have been repeated to proclaim the establishment of description, attainment of its effect and relevance to its attachments.

Ar-Rahman (the Entirely Merciful) is the One Whom been described by Mercy. Ar-Rahim is the One who extends his mercy to his slaves. In this realm, God, the Almighty, says: "And ever is He, to the believers, Merciful." "وَكَانَ بِالْمُؤْمِنِينَ رَحِيمًا" (33:43) and in the verse, "Indeed, He was to them Kind and Merciful." "إِنَّهُ بِهِمْ رَءُوفٌ رَّحِيم" (9: 117). God does not describe Himself as Rahman of His slaves or the believers though this "wazan", Arabic verb form, Falaan, is spacious enough to add more nouns and establish of the meanings of which it has been described. They usually say in Arabic ghadban to show that he is extremely angry and nadman (remorseful) and the like this formula is used for comprehension and adding more intensity to the adjective in question. The verb form ('f'allan' is used to show extension and comprehensiveness. Building on this, God's establishment above the Throne is mostly conjoined with this name. God, the Almighty, says, "The Most Merciful [who is] above the Throne established"."" الرَّحْمَنُ عَلَى الْعَرْشِ اسْتَوَىٰ (20:5)

He, the Almighty, established Himself on His Throne by using the name Ar-Rahman; the Throne is well-encompassing all the creations and it was extended to embrace all of them and so is the Mercy which is all encompassing and extended to all the creations. God, the Almighty, says: "but My mercy encompasses all things" ". "وَرَحْمَتِي وَسِعَتْ كُلَّ شَيْءٍ (7:156)

Accordingly, He, the Almighty, was well established above the entirety of creations by His most encompassing attributes. This is the interpretation of that His mercy encompasses all things. It was narrated by Abu Hurayrah, may God be pleased with him, that the Messenger of God (PBUH) said: "When God created the creation as He was upon the Throne, He ordained for Himself in His Book: "Verily, My mercy predominates My wrath."

Reflect on the specification of this Book by mentioning Mercy therein, putting it down with Him above the Throne together with the God's verses: "The Most Merciful [who is] above the Throne established. الرَّحْمَٰنُ عَلَى الْعَرْشِ اسْتَوَى" "" (20:5)and "then established Himself above the Throne" "ثُمَّ اسْتَوَىٰ عَلَى الْعَرْشِ الرَّحْمَٰنُ" (25:59). These reflections will warrant you a great gateway for the true knowledge of God, Glorified is He, if not blocked and marred by the deviation of the Jahamites and Mu'atilah.

The attributes of justice, restraining and extending, demeaning and elevating, giving and withholding, honoring and dishonoring, dominance, judgment and the like are unique to His name The Sovereign and associated with the Day of Retribution i.e. the just retribution for He, the Almighty, singled Himself Alone with Judgment. It is the Day of Truth and what is prior to it is only like an hour-time according to the Divine reckonings. It is the utmost goal and all the worldly life is just a step to it.

Mull over the association between the creation and disposing affairs on the one hand and God's three names, God, Rabb and Ar-Rahman on the other. How do creation, disposing the affairs, rewards and punishment evolve from these names? How do these names unite and disunite creations? What potential do they have to do the unity and disunity jointly?

The name Rabb (the One) is collective of all creations; He is Only God of everything and the Creator of all things, the One attributed with Power, nothing goes beyond His Rububyiyyah (Oneness of God). All those who are in heavens and on earth are His slaves in His grip and force. All believed in His Rububuyyah, yet, disagreed in terms of His Uluhiyyah (the Lord to be worshipped). Those who won the pleasure of God declared their submission to His worship, they, on their own accord, acknowledged that He is God (The Lord) Alone, Who has no other partners or deities, Who is exclusively most deserved of worship, trust, hope, fear, love, deputation, submission, awe, imploring and subjugation.

Here people were dissected into two groups: the first are the disbeliever whose abode is Hellfire and the second who testify His Oneness and lordship and Paradise is their eternal abode.

Religion and Divine law, Command and prohibition are attributes of Lordship formally and subjectively. Whilst creation, existence, disposition and action are the attributes of Rububiyyah; reward, punishment, paradise and Hell are attributes of His Sovereignty. He is the Sovereign of the Day of Retribution. Therefore, He commanded them to worship Him by the virtue of His Lordship and supported, directed, guided and made them astray within the dictates of His Rububiyyah (Oneness). In the realm of His Sovereignty and Justice, He, the Almighty, rewarded and punished them. All these matters are coherently interwoven.

Mercy is the linking cord between God, the Almighty, and His slaves; it is reciprocity - based relation; they worship Him, and He is Heedful of them in the context of His Rububyyiah. Mercy is a linking yoke between Him and His slaves by concordance to its prerequisites, He, the Almighty, sent down His messengers and books to them, the potency of God's Mercy vouchguarded for them guidance, attainment of the abode of reward, sustenance, the health, favors and blessing. They are linked to God by the cause of their worship and He, the Almighty is linked to them by the cause of this mercy.

The identification between His Rububiyyah and His Mercy is mirrored in the conjoining between His establishment on the Throne and His Mercy. God's Saying: "The Most Merciful [who is] above the Throne established."""" (20:5) الرَّحْمَنُ عَلَى الْعَرْشِ اسْتَوَى is commensurate with Lord of the worlds -. The Entirely Merciful, the Especially Merciful, رَبِّ الْعَالَمِينَ. الرَّحْمَنِ الرَّحِيمِ (1:2-3).

The well –tight extending and comprehending nature of Rububuyyiah meets with that of Mercy. He, the Almighty, is en-compassing everything through His mercy and Rububuyyiah, His being the Lord of the worlds, nonetheless, is the evidential of His Elevation above His creations as well as everything as it will be detailed later.

Mentioning these names after God's praise and laying praise in their context and requirements manifests that He, the Al-mighty, is praised in His Uluhiyyah, Rububiyyah, Mercifulness and Sovereignty; He, the Almighty, is a praised as Lord, Rabb, Rahman and Sovereign. All the categories of perfections belong to Him; perfection respective of one name Alone and the other name alongside with that is realizable through their association together. "Then indeed, God is Free of need and Praiseworthy." وَاللَّهُ "(35:15) "وَاللَّهُ هُوَ الْغَنِيُّ الْحَمِيدُ" "And God is Knowing and Wise"" ."

عَلِيمٌ حَكِيمٌ (4:26) And "God is competent, and God is Forgiving and Merciful"." "وَاللَّهُ قَدِيرٌ وَاللَّهُ غَفُورٌ رَّحِيمٌ" (60:7). "Being free of need" is an attribute of God's perfection, and being "Praiseworthy" is another attribute of perfection; the combination between both of them implies perfection as well. God's knowledge is perfection and so is His Wisdom; the conjoining between knowledge and wisdom is perfection too. The same is applicable on His Competence and forgiveness. In the same realm, "Indeed, God is ever Pardoning and Forgiving." ""إِنَّ اللَّهَ كَانَ عَفُوًّا غَفُورًا"" (4:43) Pardoning after Competence and conjoining Knowledge with forbearance as in the verse: " and God is Knowing and Forbearing". وَاللَّهُ عَلِيمٌ "حَلِيم"ٌ (4:12).

The Bearers of God's Throne are four angels: Two of them supplicate God "O God! Glory and Praise be to You. Praise be to You for Your Forbearance following Your Knowledge." And the Other two supplicate God "O God! Glory and Praise be to You. Praise be to You for Your Pardon following Your Competence." This is God's Uniqueness; not everyone pardons after being competent nor do all those who pardon have the competency. Likewise, not all those who know are tolerant and forbearing nor every forbearing one has knowledge. Nothing has been correlated to something else better than the conjuncture of Forbearance with Knowledge, pardon with competency, sovereignty with praise, and honor with mercy. To this effect, God, the Almighty, says: "And indeed, your Lord - He is the Exalted in Might, the Merciful". "وَإِنَّ رَبَّكَ لَهُوَ الْعَزِيزُ الرَّحِيمِ"(26:9) That's why Prophet 'Aissa (Messiah) said to God, as revealed in the Quran: "If You should punish them - indeed they are Your servants; but if You forgive them - indeed it is You who is the Exalted in Might, the Wise." "إِن تُعَذِّبْهُمْ فَإِنَّهُمْ عِبَادُكَ وَإِن تَغْفِرْ لَهُمْ فَإِنَّكَ أَنتَ الْعَزِيزُ الْحَكِيمِ" (5:118) That is much better than saying but if You forgive them, You are the Forgiving and the Merciful. As this indicates that If He, the Almighty, is to pardon them, His pardoning is based upon Your Competence and Power which is the utmost of perfection, wisdom and knowledge. Those who pardon out of feebleness and ignorance of the default of the perpetuator is not entitled to win the status of being capable, wise and knowledgably. One pardons only if he possesses total power, knowledge and wisdom to manage the affairs properly. That is to say it is more aptly place than the Forgiving and the Merciful. As the meaning underlying the latter alludes that Prophet 'Aissa is asking for God's Pardoning and Forgiveness would be out of place. It foreshadows the implication of undeserved empathy and allusion of requesting for pardon for those who are unworthy of- the status of Messiah is avowed of this certainly, particularly that is a situation of glory and exaltedness and vengeance on those who associated a son to God, the Almighty, and offered worship unto him in the lieu of God, the Almighty. Therefore, he mentioned the power and wisdom which are more properly poised than mention the mercy and pardon. Conversely, Prophet Ibrahim, the Companion, may God be pleased with him, said: "My Lord, make this city [Makkah] secure and keep me and my sons away from worshipping idols. My Lord, indeed they have led astray many among the people. So whoever follows me - then he is of me; and whoever disobeys me - indeed, You are [yet] Forgiving and Merciful"." وَاجْنُبْنِي وَبَنِيَّ أَن نَّعْبُدَ الْأَصْنَامَ رَبِّ إِنَّهُنَّ أَضْلَلْنَ كَثِيرًا مِّنَ النَّاسِ فَمَن "تَبِعَنِي فَإِنَّهُ مِنِّي وَمَنْ عَصَانِي فَإِنَّكَ غَفُورٌ رَّحِيم" (14:35-36)

He didn't say You are the Exalted in Might as this is a situation of begging for empathy and allusion of invocation i.e. to pardon them and grant them with Mercy by the means of Your Guidance to relinquish shirk polytheism to Monotheism, from disobedience to submission. This is parallel to Prophet Muhammad's invocation "O God, forgive my people for they do not know."

Certainly, this more clearly stresses the fact that the names of God stem from attributes and significances are well established in Him, and that each name is commensurate with what is mentioned and correlated with respective of His Act and Command.

May God guide us to say the right.

CHAPTER 4

Special and general guidance; they fall into ten categories

First category: the category of God's speaking to His slave directly without any intercessor. This is the highest degree, and can be traced in God's speech to Moses ibn Imran, may God be pleased with them and our Prophet (PBUH). God says: "And God spoke to Moses with [direct] speech". "وَكَلَّمَ اللَّهُ مُوسَىٰ تَكْلِيمًا" (4:164). In the beginning of the verse, God, the Almighty, mentioned His revelation to Noah and the Prophets after him and then he singled Moses out among them by stating that He, the Almighty, spoke to him. Clearly is that the speech to him is more specific than the revelation to other Prophet at the very beginning of the verse. To the same of effect of confirmation, God, the Almighty, used the true masdar (verbal noun) Takleem (speaking) from the verb Kalama (spoke to) to negate any doubts raised by deviant sects such as Mu'atGod , Jahmites and Mu'tazila and others that it might be an inspiration or signal or psychological identification but without speaking. Thus, the masdar was employed for assertion and removing any illusion of the metaphorical speaking. The Grammarian Abu Alfara said: the Arabs state that whatever is transmitted to a person by any means is called speech and it was not affirmed by the usage of masdar, otherwise, it is called a true speech ascertained by the use of masdar. For example in expressing one's need, they used to say arada erada (meaning he needed that need). This rules out the possibility of figurative usage. God, the Almighty, says: "And when Moses arrived at Our appointed time and his Lord spoke to him, he said, "My Lord, show me [Yourself] that I may look at You." " وَلَمَّا جَاءَ مُوسَىٰ لِمِيقَاتِنَا وَكَلَّمَهُ رَبُّهُ قَالَ رَبِّ أَرِنِي أَنظُرْ إِلَيْكَ"(7:143)

This speaking is different from the first time when God, the Almighty, sent Moses to Pharaoh. This time, Moses besought God's Sight not in the first time. In this time also Moses was give the tablets .after God, the Almighty, arranged an appointment, while the first speaking the meeting was unarranged and God, the Almighty, said to him [God] said, "O Moses, I have chosen you over the people with My messages and My words [to you]. So take what I have given you and be among the grateful." "قَالَ يَا مُوسَىٰ إِنِّي اصْطَفَيْتُكَ عَلَى النَّاسِ بِرِسَالَاتِي وَبِكَلَامِي فَخُذْ مَا آتَيْتُكَ وَكُن مِّنَ الشَّاكِرِينَ" (7:144) Scholars unanimously agreed that "my words" here refers to God's speaking.

God, the Almighty, states in His Book that He called Moses and confided to him. The act of calling necessities that the one called is a far from the caller, and confiding takes place when one is brought closer. Our father, Adam, while arguing with Moses is quoted as saying: "You are Moses whom God, the Almighty, has chosen over the people with His words and wrote the Torah for with His own Hands. And the same is repeated by people on the Day of Judgment when they seek his intercession before God, the Almighty. A similar conversation is mentioned in the event of Israa (Ascension) at Musa's visit to the sixth and seventh Heavens with different versions in the realm of God's selection for him over people and favoring him with His speech. Had this speech been the same as any other conversations taking place between God, the Almighty, and His other Prophets, this specification in these hadith would have been worthless and Musa wouldn't have been called Kaleem Ar-Rahman (the interlocutor of God). God says:" And it is not for any human being that God should speak to him except by revelation or from behind a partition or that He sends a messenger to reveal, by His permission, what He wills. Indeed, He is Highest and Wise. " وَمَا كَانَ لِبَشَرٍ أَن يُكَلِّمَهُ اللَّهُ إِلَّا وَحْيًا أَوْ مِن وَرَاءِ حِجَابٍ أَوْ يُرْسِلَ رَسُولًا فَيُوحِيَ بِإِذْنِهِ مَا يَشَاءُ إِنَّهُ عَلِيٌّ حَكِيمٌ"(42: 51). God, the Almighty, made a distinction amid speaking through revelation or sending messengers or from behind a partition.

Second category: station of Wahi (revelation) specially sent-for sent Prophets

God, the Almighty, says,"Indeed, We have revealed to you, [O Muhammad], as We revealed to Noah and the prophets after him.)إِنَّا أَوْحَيْنَا إِلَيْكَ كَمَا أَوْحَيْنَا إِلَىٰ نُوحٍ وَالنَّبِيِّينَ مِن بَعْدِهِ"4:163".)

And He, the Almighty, says," ," And it is not for any human being that God should speak to him except by revelation or from behind a partition or that He sends a messenger to reveal, by His permission, what He wills. Indeed, He is Highest and Wise."" وَمَا كَانَ لِبَشَرٍ أَن يُكَلِّمَهُ اللَّهُ إِلَّا وَحْيًا أَوْ مِن وَرَاءِ حِجَابٍ أَوْ يُرْسِلَ رَسُولًا فَيُوحِيَ بِإِذْنِهِ مَا يَشَاءُ إِنَّهُ عَلِيٌّ حَكِيمٌ" (42:51). God, the. He, the Almighty, made revelation in this verse one division of speaking and made it in the chapter of An-Nisaa a subdivision of speech for two reasons: it is the subdivision of private speech which is without intercession, and a division of general speech which is conveying the meaning through different methods.

Linguistically, Wahi (revelation) is the hidden quick informing.

Third Category: sending the Heavenly Messenger to the human Messenger

The Heavenly Messenger reveals to the human Messenger what God, the Almighty, commanded him to reveal.

These three categories are only for the prophets.

This Heavenly Messenger comes to the human Messenger in the form of a man whom the human messenger can see with his own eyes and speak to. He can also see him in the form which God, the Almighty, has molded him in. or he integrates with his body, breathes revelation and then disembodies him. Prophet Muhammad (PBUH) experienced the three methods of conveyance of revelation.

Fourth Category: Tahdith (the recipients of Divine inspiration)

There had been among the people before you inspired persons and if there were any such among my Umma Umar ibn. Khattab would be one of them. Ibn Wahb explained the word Muhaddathun as those who receive hint from the High (Mulhamun)

I heard sheikh –ul-Islam ibn Taimiyyah, say: the prophet (PBUH) asserted that those inspired people 'Muhaddathun' were present in the nations existed before us, yet, their presence in this nation was conditional though we are the best of nations.

The nations before the Muhammad's nation were in a dire need of this kind of inspired people, whilst our nation was dispensable of for the perfection of our Prophet (PBUH) and his message. God, the Almighty, made this nation dispense with any inspired or people of intuition, soothsayer or interpreters of visions and dreams. The conditional case is functional to highlight the perfection rather than the imperfection of this nation and its dispensability of this category.

Muhdathith is the one inspired or have predomination.

Our sheikh said: As-Sadiqq (the truthful) is more perfect than Muhdith (the inspired), the perfection of his truthfulness and guidance made Tahdith (inspiration), Ilham (inspiration) and Kashf (enlightenment) dysfunctional. He wholeheartedly internalized his surrender in heart and mind, inwardly and outwardly to the Prophet and this made him dispense with other matters.

He also said: this inspired person used to compare what is inspired to him with the prophet's preaching, if they are in conformity, the inspired person accepts his inspiration, otherwise he rejects it. As a result, he acknowledges that the status of truthfulness is more elevated than that of inspiration.

He also said: As for those who acquiesce to imaginations and ignorance by claiming that" his heart inspired him about God", Assumingly, his heart inspired him, but about what? Or about whom? About his devil or his God? If he claimed that his heart inspired him about God, he would be ascribing the speech to the one who doesn't know that he was inspired with and this is lying. The true inspired person of the nation (Umar ibn Alkhattab) never speaks of that inspiration or even never utter a bit of it one day because God, the Almighty, protected him against disclosing this inspiration, one day his scribe wrote" This is what has been inspired to the commander of the believers, Umar ibn Alkhattab." He commanded his scribe to wipe this and re-write," this is what Umar ibn Alkhattab views, if it is right, it is by God's inspiration, if it is wrong, it is Umar's and God and His messenger disavow of," it was reported in Kalala" This is what I believe as true, if it is true, it is from God and if is wrong it is my fault and the shaytan's" This is what is quoted from the exemplary true inspired person in accordance with the Prophet's testimony.

Unfortunately, we see many heretical from the adherents of Hulul (Unity with the divine oneness).and the mongers of obscenity Shatah and Alsama'iyy who flagrantly proclaims his fabrication in public by saying that "my heart was inspired by God".

The comparison between the imposters and truly inspired persons, their situations and attitudes helps us to separate the wheat from the chaff.

Fifth category: Granting understanding

God, the Almighty, says: "And [mention] David and Solomon, when they judged concerning the field - when the sheep of a people overran it [at night], and We were witness to their judgement " "وَدَاوُودَ وَسُلَيْمَانَ إِذْ يَحْكُمَانِ فِي الْحَرْثِ إِذْ نَفَشَتْ فِيهِ غَنَمُ الْقَوْمِ وَكُنَّا لِحُكْمِهِمْ شَاهِدِينَ" (21:78-79) "And We gave understanding of the case to Solomon, and to each [of them] We gave judgement and knowledge". "فَفَهَّمْنَاهَا سُلَيْمَانَ وَكُلًّا آتَيْنَا حُكْمًا وَعِلْمًا" (21:78-79)

God, the Almighty, has mentioned those two honorable Prophets and praised them for their knowledge and wisdom and distinguished Solomon with his being granted the faculty of perception and understanding in this incident.

I heard Abu Juhaifa saying, "I asked `Ali 'Have you got any Divine literature apart from the Qur'an?' (Once he said...apart from what the people have?) `Ali replied, 'By Him Who made the grain split (germinate) and created the soul, we have nothing except what is in the Qur'an and the ability (gift) of understanding God's Book which He may endow a man with and we have what is written in this paper.' I asked, 'What is written in this paper?' He replied, 'Al-`Aql (the regulation of Diya), about the ransom of captives, and the Judgment that a Muslim should not be killed in Qisas (equality in punishment) for killing a disbeliever." In a letter sent to Abu Musa by Umar ibn AlKhattab, may God be pleased with them, he said; "Understanding, and repeated twice to what has been sent to you."

Understanding is a bliss granted by God to his slaves and a light poured into a slave's heart by which he is recognized and perceives what others don't and understands what others don't though being equal in cherishing and getting the very basic meanings.

Perception of what is preached by God, the Almighty, and His messenger is intrinsic to righteousness, the very essence of prophetic guardianship. The scholars' stations of elevation differ in proportion to their understanding; one scholar can be equal to a thousand in respect of their delving into the bottom of matters.

Let's consider the understanding of ibn Abbas when he was asked by Umar and some of those who witness the battle of Badr about the meaning of the chapter of Fatah "When the victory of God has come and the conquest" "إِذَا جَاءَ نَصْرُ اللَّهِ وَالْفَتْحُ"(110-1). He was given the special gift of understanding and interpreted that this chapter is a death notice from God, the Almighty, to the His messenger (PBUH) and informing him with the nearness of his death. Umar agreed with him too. He was given the gift of special understanding from among all the Companions, albeit he was the youngest. There is no clear noticing in this chapter but for his implicit understanding of the hidden meanings. Some matter might need extra and more focused understanding, many can't get the core of it and consequently they need other sources to help him understand it and these extra-curricular teats are indispensable for them. However, men of understanding have no recourse to other sources but the text given.

Sixth category: general statement

Clarifying the truth and distinguishing it from the falsehood while providing evidence, signs and cases till it becomes as known to the heart as visible things are seen to the eyes. This stage is God's authoritative evidence against creations; no man is tormented or led astray till reaching stage. "And God would not let a people stray after He has guided them until He makes clear to them what they should avoid. Indeed, God is Knowing of all things. " وَمَا كَانَ اللَّهُ لِيُضِلَّ قَوْمًا بَعْدَ إِذْ هَدَاهُمْ حَتَّىٰ يُبَيِّنَ لَهُم مَّا يَتَّقُونَ إِنَّ اللَّهَ بِكُلِّ شَيْءٍ عَلِيم" (115: 9)

Leading them astray was God's punishment for them after He, the Almighty, made the truth clear for them and they unheeded it and turned and acted otherwise. Therefore, they have been punished by being distanced from the guidance. Never Did God, the Almighty, lead anyone astray unless being notified by this statement.

Seventh category: elite statement

If this point is well-perceived, man truly knows the secret behind the destiny, many doubts are dispelled and suspicions lifted in this concern. We are to get God's wisdom from misguidance. Actually, the Quran clearly proclaims that in more than one position as when He, the Almighty, says,"[Even] if you should strive for their guidance, [O Muhammad], indeed, God does not guide those He sends astray, and they will have no helpers." إِن تَحْرِصْ عَلَىٰ هُدَاهُمْ فَإِنَّ اللَّهَ لَا يَهْدِي مَن يُضِلُّ وَمَا لَهُم مِّن نَّاصِرِينَ (16: 37) God, the Almighty, says: "Indeed, [O Muhammad], you do not guide whom you like, but God guides whom He wills. And He is most knowing of the [rightly] guided." إِنَّكَ لَا تَهْدِي مَنْ أَحْبَبْتَ وَلَٰكِنَّ اللَّهَ يَهْدِي مَن يَشَاءُ وَهُوَ أَعْلَمُ بِالْمُهْتَدِينَ And He, the Almighty, says:" (28: 56)

The first statement is an essential prerequisite and it's binding.

Eighth category: Causing to hear

God, the Almighty, says: "Had God known any good in them, He would have made them hear. And if He had made them hear, they would [still] have turned away, while they were refusing."" وَلَوْ عَلِمَ اللَّهُ فِيهِمْ خَيْرًا لَّأَسْمَعَهُمْ وَلَوْ أَسْمَعَهُمْ لَتَوَلَّوا وَّهُم مُّعْرِضُونَ (23: 8)

God, the Almighty, says "Not equal are the blind and the seeing, Nor are the darknesses and the light, Nor are the shade and the heat, And not equal are the living and the dead. Indeed, God causes to hear whom He wills, but you cannot make hear those in the graves." " وَمَا يَسْتَوِي الْأَعْمَىٰ وَالْبَصِيرُ، وَلَا الظُّلُمَاتُ وَلَا النُّورُ، وَلَا الظِّلُّ وَلَا الْحَرُورُ،وَمَا يَسْتَوِي الْأَحْيَاءُ وَلَا الْأَمْوَاتُ ۚ إِنَّ اللَّهَ يُسْمِعُ مَن يَشَاءُ ۖوَمَا أَنتَ بِمُسْمِعٍ مَّن فِي الْقُبُورِ" (35:19-23) This causing to hear is more specific than authoritative evidence and statement; it is a combination of the two. By which God, the Almighty, gave them well-grounded argument. The former stage was special to conveying the truth through corporeal hearing and the latter is concerned with spiritual clairvoyance of hearts and souls. Any speech entails an utterance and a meaning; the former is processed through the ears while the latter through the heart; causing to hear utterance is functional to ears, whereas causing to hear its true significance and meaning is functional to heart. God, the Almighty, negated the possibility of the polytheists' hearing of significance which belongs to the hearts and confirmed their hearing of its utterance. "No mention comes to them anew from their Lord except that they listen to it while they are at play. With their hearts distracted"" مَا يَأْتِيهِم مِّن ذِكْرٍ مِّن رَّبِّهِم مُّحْدَثٍ إِلَّا اسْتَمَعُوهُ وَهُمْ يَلْعَبُونَ، لَاهِيَةً قُلُوبُهُمْ ۗ وَأَسَرُّوا النَّجْوَى الَّذِينَ ظَلَمُوا هَلْ هَٰذَا إِلَّا بَشَرٌ مِّثْلُكُمْ ۖأَفَتَأْتُونَ السِّحْرَ وَأَنتُمْ تُبْصِرُونَ" (21:2-3)

This kind of hearing is of no value to the hearer save that it establishes the ground against him that he was fully informed, however, the real intent behind hearing and its fruits is unrealizable when hearts are distracted and caught in the snares of unheedfulness and rejection. Lamentably, this hears comes out of any discussion asking other attendees" they say to those who were given knowledge, "What has he said just now? Those are the ones of whom God has sealed over their hearts and who have followed their [own] desires"." مَاذَا قَالَ آنِفًا أُولَٰئِكَ الَّذِينَ طَبَعَ اللَّهُ عَلَىٰ قُلُوبِهِمْ وَاتَّبَعُوا أَهْوَاءَهُم" (47:16) This stage is different from that of granting understanding in the sense that this stage occurs through the ears and the stage of granting understanding is more comprehensive, it is special in this respect and the stage of understanding is special from another in the sense that it has to do with the significance, signs and relevances. The stage of causing to hear encompasses channeling the significance of speech to the heart and subsequently this hearing reaches the stage of acceptance.

Accordingly, causing to hear has three stages: hearing through ears, through heart and finally the hearing of acceptance and response.

Ninth Stage: Ilham (inspiration)

God, the Almighty, says," And [by] the soul and He who proportioned it. And inspired it [with discernment of] its wickedness and its righteousness" "وَنَفْسٍ وَمَا سَوَّاهَا.فَأَلْهَمَهَا فُجُورَهَا وَتَقْوَاهَا"" (91:7-8). The Prophet (PBUH) said to Husain ibn Mundhir when he embraced Islam" say: O God! Inspire me to Guidance and protect me against the evils of myself."

The author of Manazil Al-Saereen (Stations of Wayfarers) made no distinction between ilham and Tahdith (a superior form of inspiration). He assumed that Ilham is a status higher than foresight (Farasah) because foresight may be unattainable, difficult or eluding. Ilham is attainable only in transcendental statuses.

I said that Tahdith is more specific than Ilham. Ilham is more general for the totality of believers according to the ranks of their faith; each believer is given special inspiration to receive guidance by which he attained to faith, whereas Tahdith, the prophet said "if there was no muhdith in this nation it is Umar. Tahdith is a special Ilham which is the Wahi (revelation) to non-prophets or among whom God has assigned with a special mission: "And We inspired to the mother of Moses, "Suckle him" وَأَوْحَيْنَا إِلَىٰ أُمِّ مُوسَىٰ أَنْ أَرْضِعِيهِ""(28:7) And [remember] when I inspired to the disciples, "Believe in Me and in My messenger Jesus." They said, "We have believed, so bear witness that indeed we are Muslims [in submission to God]." " وَإِذْ أَوْحَيْتُ إِلَى الْحَوَارِيِّينَ أَنْ آمِنُوا بِي وَبِرَسُولِي قَالُوا آمَنَّا وَاشْهَدْ بِأَنَّنَا مُسْلِمُونَ (111: 5) or it is granted for the unassigned like the case of bees: "And your Lord inspired to the bee, "Take for yourself among the mountains, houses, and among the trees and [in] that which they construct." " وَأَوْحَىٰ رَبُّكَ

(16: 68) "إِلَى النَّحْلِ أَنِ اتَّخِذِي مِنَ الْجِبَالِ بُيُوتًا وَمِنَ الشَّجَرِ وَمِمَّا يَعْرِشُون

As for his assumption that Ilham is in a status higher than Farasah (foresight), he argues foresight can be rarely attainable as above- mentioned, and no binding judgment on rarity. Further, it may be difficult or elusive especially that Ilham is only attainable in transcendental statuses i.e. the sublime status of nearness and mindfulness to God, the Almighty.

To conclude both Farasah and ilham are divided into general and specific; the specificity of each of them is above the general of the other; the general of each occur mostly, and their specificities occur rarely. The most right distinction between the two is that Farasah (foresight) is related to gaining and attainment whilst ilham (inspiration) is purely a gift, never acquired through gaining.

Degrees of Ilham (inspiration)

He said: Ilham has three degrees

First degree: it is a certain piece of news communicated through revelation associated with hearing: news means a statement of worth, not every piece of news is a statement. It is news mostly stating the unseen.

Wahi (revelation) and Ilham (inspiration): it is a kind of imparting information which gives no clue about the way it was communicated. It can be done either through hearing sounds or it is informing without intermediaries.

As for its occurrence by the means of hearing sounds: it is not ilham (inspiration); it is a kind of speech, there is no scantiest chance for it to occur to non-prophets. This is the type which God, the Almighty, distinguished Prophet Musa with; the Speaker is God, Glorified is He.

What is communicated to some of the self-disciplined elite through hearing sounds is done via only three methods. The highest in rank is that of the angels talking to people, this is common with people other than prophet. Angels used to greet Omran ibn Hasin by Salam. When he got sick and was treated by moxibustion (heat therapy by moxa plant), they stopped greeting. When he stopped this kind of therapy, the angels returned to speak to him anew. The angels' speech is of two kinds:

The first one is a speech heard by ears, which is rare to the laymen among the believers.

The second is a speech breathed into one's heart as the angel talks to this person's soul. This is evident in the famous hadith," that the Messenger of God (PBUH) said: "Indeed the Shaytan has an effect on the son of Adam, and the angel also has an effect. As for the Shaytan, it is by threatening evil repercussions and rejecting the truth. As for the effect of the angel, it is by his promise of a good end and believing in the truth. Whoever finds that let him know that it is from God, and let him praise God for it. Whoever finds the other then let him seek refuge with God from the Shaytan (the outcast) then recite: "Satan threatens you with poverty and orders you to immorality, while God promises you forgiveness from Him and bounty. And God is all-Encompassing and Knowing."" الشَّيْطَانُ يَعِدُكُمُ الْفَقْرَ وَيَأْمُرُكُم بِالْفَحْشَاءِ وَاللَّهُ يَعِدُكُم مَّغْفِرَةً مِّنْهُ وَفَضْلًا "وَاللَّهُ وَاسِعٌ عَلِيم (2:268) God, the Almighty, says: "[Remember] when your Lord inspired to the angels, "I am with you, so strengthen those who have believed.." " إِذْ يُوحِي رَبُّكَ إِلَى الْمَلَائِكَةِ أَنِّي مَعَكُمْ فَثَبِّتُوا الَّذِينَ "آمَنُوا (8:12). It was interpreted as follows: God, the Almighty, inspired to the angels to strengthen the hearts of the believer and to convey the good tidings of victory to them. Another version views that God, the Almighty, ordered the angels to engage in fight with them. Both are quite correct as they engaged in fight and empowered them. "

Another mode of this speech is God's inspiration to the hearts of his believing slaves. As it was reported in Altirmizzy and Musnad Ahmad on the authority of Abu AlNawas ibn Saman that the Messenger of God (PBUH) said: "Indeed God has made a parable of the straight path: At the sides of the path there are walls with open doors, each door having a curtain. There is a caller at the head of the path calling, and a caller above it calling. And God invites to the abode of peace and guides whomever He wills to the straight path. The doors which are on the sides of the path are the Hudud (legal limitations) of God; no one breaches the Hudud."

This Caller to the hearts of the believers is the Divine Inspiration through the angels.

As for the Ilham without intermediaries: it is not clear yet. It is difficult to give conclusive evidence since it is based on proof. Only God knows.

The second mode of the heard speech; the speech of the inspired jinn; the addresser can be a righteous believing jinn or a shaytan (devil). This also can fall into two kinds:

First: A jinn communicates with a human through sounds that can be heard by ears.

Secondly: to breathe into the human's heart when he possesses him and promises him to arouses desires in them. Then, he takes hold of him and starts giving commands and prohibitions. As God, the Almighty says: "Satan promises them and arouses desire in them. But Satan does not promise them except delusion"."يَعِدُهُمْ وَيُمَنِّيهِمْ وَمَا يَعِدُهُمُ الشَّيْطَانُ إِلَّا غُرُورًا" (4:120)

Both heart and ears have their share of this speech. All people err; infallibility was only granted to the Messengers of God.

How can addressee perceive that this speech is inspired by God or through the angels? What is the proof? Which evidence can one recline to? Shaytan breathes his inspiration to one's self and communicates his speech through one's ears. The deluded self-conceited brags about his being inspired and raves by saying; " I was inspired and being spoken to". So good to be true, however, it is significantly enough to consider the situation of the addresser and the addressee. In this realm, Umar ibn AlKhattab, may God be pleased with him, said to Hailan ibn Salamah, who is one of the Prophet's Companions, when he divorced his women and divided his wealth among his children,: I think that Shaytan- while overhearing from the world of the Unseen- knew about your death and inspired this to your heart."

The third mode is: self-talk; it begins in one's psyche and returns to it while one imagines that it was an external inspiration while it is purely psychological internal monologue.

Too often is the seeker confronted by this type and mistakes it to be God's speech inspired to him. The reason for his erratic understanding is that had the subtle part of one's heedful perception been disciplined and cut off its intense worldly inclinations, it would overtake by the virtue of prevalence of soul and heart over the body. They, in turn, prevail and then one's self and heart engage in the abstraction of the affixed significances, soul transcends to replace these inclinations and preoccupations till it fills the heart. Then, these abstract meanings usually find their headways to logic and spiritual speech of heart and thus soul abstraction endures and then meanings are formed to the hearing ability in the form of the audio/ heard sounds as well as the sight ability in the form of the visible figures, so that one can see the picture and hear the speech. The whole process take place inwardly rather than outwardly. So he takes an oath that he already saw a figure and heard a sound. He believes himself but he is not certain if the hearing and sight were processed outwardly or inwardly?

The weakness of the ability of distinction, the diminutiveness of knowledge, the hegemony of these meanings over the soul and its relinquishment of inclination collaborate together to reach this conclusion

These are the three modes of speech; externalizing one's internal speech is self-conceitedness and deception as well as illusions. This is the point in case and it bids well for those who verify and perceive it.

He added" the second degree": it is a direct Ilham. Its correctness is evidenced by the fact that it doesn't unearth a veil nor transgress a limitation nor ever errs"

The distinction between this kind and Ilham in the first degree is that it is nearly necessary knowledge which can't be vacated from the heart. It is a revelation and unveiling. It is higher in rank than the first type, and more apparent. It is as clear to the heart as the visible items to the eyes. It has three signs:

First: it doesn't unearth a veil; if the one experiencing this case was inspired to reveal hidden matter, he never unveil it to others, good or bad, or that he never unveils what God, the Almighty, has covered up from people or even he shields himself and the one whose affairs have been revealed.

Second; he never transgresses limitations; it may have two interpretations:

First is that he never manipulates this gift to engage in wrongdoings nor violates the legal limitations ordained by God, the Almighty, just like the soothsayers and oracles and those with diabolic unveilings.

The second is that he never acts against the pronouncements of the legal limitations Hudud by spying on others to expose their secrets, an act forbidden by God, the Almighty. Whoever peeped into one's secrets through this unveiling, his inspirational motivation is considered diabolic rather than divine.

The third is that he never errs unlike the diabolic one, he always errs. When the Prophet (PBUH) said to Ibn Sa'ed : what do you see? He said: I see two truthful and a liar or two liars and one truthful. Thereupon God's Messenger (PBUH) said: Leave him He has been confounded. A diabolic unveiling has to be untrue, its truthfulness never persists.

He said; "the third degree: Ilham that unveil the truth to reach enlightenment. Ilham is an end that should not be disclosed."

The scrutiny of the core of True enlightenment: means annihilation in pursuing the truth where everything beyond it fades away in the pursuit. Where egos are reduced to nothing. Ilham in this degree totally clears one's vision where it is not mixed with any of the percepts of minds or senses, if they are the least traces of sensual or mindful percepts, the core truth would not be in clairvoyance. The one who speaks of this enlightenment, for them, is understood by none but those whom he is among and participates with him. The supporters of Kashf believe that all creations are under veil. They also believe that knowledge, mind and being are veil upon him and the speech of the creatures is at the tongue of this veil. Further, they don't get the language beyond the veil from the covered meaning. Therefore, they should neither disclose nor express it. Signals and expressions are media of the sensual and the sensible and this is transcendental over senses and minds.

To conclude, this ilham witnesses the elevation, reduction and annihilation of the media but for the pursuit of truth rather than the existence. But Alitahadiah adherent believe in the unity of being; they made this quest for truth a reduction and annihilation through the unity with the divine being.

CHAPTER 5

Tenth category of guidance: true dreams

It is part of prophethood as evidenced by the prophetic tradition the dream of a believer can hardly be false; and the dream of a believer represents one part from forty-six parts of Prophethood."

It is said that the reason behind the mentioned specification is that the beginning of the Wahi revelation was the true dreams as it lasted for half a year. Then it was transformed into the wakefulness revelation for twenty three years starting from the Prophet's mission till his demise. The percentage of Wahi duration in sleepiness one to sixty four parts and that is a sound percentage. In another authentic version it was mentioned that" it is a part of seventy parts."

As for coupling them together: it is according to the state of the dreamer, the dreams of the truthful believers can be reckoned with the 46 percentage while the true dreams of the believing laymen belong to 70 percentages.

Dreams; they are the first form of Wahi and its correctness depends on the dreamer's truthfulness. "The most truthful of you in their speech are those who see the truest visions." he Prophet (PBUH) said, "When the time draws near (i.e., near the end of the world), the dream of a believer can hardly be false for being distant from the time of prophethood and its impact. So that the believers are compensated with the true visions. Whereas during the epoch of the prophethood, they were worthless compared to the dawning of prophethood and its illumination.

They are an alternative for the Karamat (supernatural powers by Muslim saints) which emerged after the epoch of the Prophet's companions; the strength of their faith spurred for its dispensability. Those who came after them needed them for their waning of faith. Imam Ahmad referred to this meaning. Ebadah ibn Assamat said: "A believer's dream is the speech of Lord to His slave during his sleep."

The Prophet (PBUH) said: "O people, nothing of the glad tidings of prophecy is left except a good dream that a Muslim sees or is seen about him." A dream is true as long as it is concurrently agreed upon among more than a considerable number of Muslims.

Some of the Companions of the Prophet (PBUH) saw Lailat-ul-Qadr (Night of Decree) in their dreams in the last seven nights of Ramadan, whereupon the Messenger of God (PBUH) said, "I see that your dreams all agree upon the last seven nights. Whosoever seeks it, let him seek it in the last seven nights."

Dreams have something in common with Kashf (enlightenment); they can be divine unveiling, psychic or diabolic. The Prophet (PBUH) said: "Good visions are glad tidings from God, a terrifying vision caused by the devil, and the ideas which come from within a man in his wakefulness and sees during his sleep."

Particularly the vision from God, the Almighty, is one of the reasons of guidance.

The visions of the prophets are Wahi (revelation); infallible, and the scholars unanimously agreed upon that. As such, Prophet Abraham, the Companion of God, proceeded to slaughter his son, Ishmael, may God be pleased with them, after seeing the vision.

As for the dreams of the non-prophets, they are to be compared to the true revelation, the Quran and Sunnah; they are to be endorsed upon if not at variance with them.

What is the ruling if such dreams are true or concurrently agreed upon by a number of Muslims?

If true, they are unlikely to contradict the true revelation but rather to be compatible, emphatic or affirmative of it concerning a special case in its realm which the dreamer is unaware of, and here the dream draws his attention to its relevance. If one wants to be gifted with true vision, he is to ascertain truthfulness, Halal (lawful) gains and attending to God's commands and interjections. Furthermore, one has to ascertain being on Tahara (fully purified through ablution) following the direction of Qiblah and engage himself in God's remembrance till he falls asleep, he will never miss a true vision.

The truest dreams are those happening before dawn time; it is the time of Divine descending, attainable mercy and forgiveness and the lull of devils. Conversely is the night dreams; it is the time of the spread of devil and evil spirits.

There is an angel entrusted with visions; he shows it to a man in examples befitting to him and his state, they vary according to every condition. Imam Malik says: "A dream from Wahi is a revelation in itself." And he admonishes on interpreting it without having sufficient knowledge.

Dreams are of different rulings and methods of interpretations, and detailing on them would be out of place here.

Inclusion of Alfatihah of two remedies:

[cure for the hearts and cure for the bodies]

As for being a cure for the heart, it is fully inclusive of it. The very essence of the ailments of heart is: the ignorance and ill intent.

They bring about two lethal diseases: misguidance and anger. The former is caused by ignorance whereas the latter is caused by the ill intent. They are the very distinct diseases of the heart. The guidance to the Straight Path constitutes remedy of misguidance ailment. Hence, asking for it is the most incumbent request on every slave. It requires endurance: day and night and in every prayer for its urgency and significance to move ahead to the required guidance.

Working within the framework of "It is You we worship and You we ask for help." through recognition, knowledge, deeds and state guarantees healing of corruption of heart and ill intent. The ill intent relates to ends and means; whoever seeks fractured temporary end and tries every gimmick crocked way to get it is of ill intent. This holds to be true to those whose utmost ends alienate them from God and His worship such as the polytheists, followers of vain desires, and those who pursuit extending their hegemony and commandership by any means, true or false. Truth is to be ground and trodden once it impedes their malicious advances. If they are incapable of removing it altogether, they swerve into other crocked ways while intending to push it forcefully to the edge or they cause it to be impotent powerless framework. If truth is supportive of their intents, they hail it as crowned king to whom they are faithful henchmen, not for its effectiveness but for its conformity with their wicked desires and ill intents; it won them a victory. God, the Almighty, says: "And when they are called to [the words of] God and His Messenger to judge between them, at once a party of them turns aside [in refusal]. When they are called to [t But if the right is theirs, they come to him in prompt obedience. Is there disease in their hearts? Or have they doubted? Or do they fear that God will be unjust to them, or His Messenger? Rather, it is they who are the wrongdoers". وَ"إِذَا دُعُوا إِلَى اللهِ وَرَسُولِهِ لِيَحْكُمَ بَيْنَهُمْ إِذَا فَرِيقٌ مِّنْهُم مُّعْرِضُونَ وَإِن يَكُن لَّهُمُ الْحَقُّ يَأْتُوا إِلَيْهِ مُذْعِنِينَ أَفِي قُلُوبِهِم مَّرَضٌ أَمِ ارْتَابُوا أَمْ يَخَافُونَ أَن يَحِيفَ اللَّهُ عَلَيْهِمْ وَرَسُولُهُ بَلْ أُولَئِكَ هُمُ الظَّالِمُونَ" (24:48-50)

Essentially, both their ends and means are corrupt. They are struck by the greatest loss and regret when the truth rise over untruth and their worldly relations are cut off. Their situation is mimicked in this world, and is more apparent at their death, intensifies at Barzakh (In Islam, it is generally viewed as the barrier between the physical and spiritual worlds) till they become blatantly exposed on the Day of Judgment. The truthful are the winners of heavenly bliss, whereas the spoilers are the losers.

The same holds to be true in the case of those who seek the highest end and the most elevated requirement and yet they mistook the course thinking that it is their headway means for their end. They are, likewise, of ill intent. No remedy is for this disease except for clinging to," It is You we worship and You we ask for help."

This cure is based on six components: (1) the worship of God alone, (2) associating no deities with Him, (3) in accordance with His Divine laws (4) not personal affixations nor the discretions of human beings, their positions, statuses and idiosyncrasies (5) through asking God's assistance for abidance by His worship (6) not relying on the slave's self but through the Might and Power of God.

This is the formula of "It is You we worship and You we ask for help." Prepared by the Greatest Physician, the Well-Aware of the disease and used by the patient, the full recovery will ensue. Its ineffectiveness is caused by skipping a component or more.

A heart may be afflicted with two great diseases, namely, hypocrisy and haughtiness, if not cured, they doom the slave to misguidance. The vice of hypocrisy is to be remedied by "it is You we worship.", and haughtiness is by "and You we ask for help." This is the view held by Ibn Tayimayyah too.

If a slave is cured from hypocrisy by declaring the worship of God, and from haughtiness by asking God's help and from misguidance and ignorance by asking guidance to the Straight path, he would be healed of all his diseases and ailments, thrive in health and grace. He will be one of the bestowed with favors not of those who evoked God's wrath of the people of ill intent.

Surah like Alfatihah which contains these two remedies is well deserved to be sought for healing.

Chapter

As for being a cure for the ailments of bodies as well, we will detail for it with evidence from Sunnah, science of medicine and experimentation.

It has been reported from the narration of Abu Almutawakel on the authority of Abu Saed Alkhadriy that he reported that: "some persons amongst the Companions of God's Messenger (PBUH) set out on a journey and they happened to pass by a tribe from the tribes of Arabia. They demanded hospitality from the members of that tribe, but they did not extend any hospitality to them. They said to them:

Is there any incantatory (any who can recite Ruqiah) amongst you, at the chief of the tribe has been stung by a scorpion? A person amongst us said: 'Yes. So, he came to him and he practiced incantation (Ruqiah) with the help of Surah of Alfatihah and the person became all right. He was given a flock of sheep (as recompense), but he refused to accept that, saying: I shall make a mention of it to God's Messenger (PBUH), and if he approves it, then I shall accept it. So, we came to God's Messenger (PBUH) and made a mention of that to him and he (that person) said: God's Messenger, by God, I did not practice incantation but with the help of the Surah of Alfatihah of the Holy Book. He (the Holy Prophet) smiled and said: How did you come to know that it can be used (as incantation)? - and then said: Take out of that and allocate a share for me along with your share."

The hadith contained treatment of the bitten by recitation of Alfatihah, and it cured him instead of medication, or it may have better off effect than usual medication.

Miraculously, its treatment worked with people unworthy of help, whether they are non-Muslims or miser or wicked people, how would it work if people we really worthy of?!

As for the medical evidence, the sting can be caused by any of the Arachnida poisonous lass. They are malicious selves of angry nature that adapt through over protective lethal methods that produce venom inside them. They inject their venom inside their prey. They vary in the degree of their malice, power and adaptation. Their malicious nature evokes certain ecstasy in them when they inject their venom in their prey. Identically, A man of venomous nature finds pleasure in injecting his evil in others and harming them, as if he is harmed himself if not ridding with his malice and afflicting others with. Then, he rests assured. This is parallel to the people of excessive erotic desires; they get agitated, till they give vent to their eroticism. One can find an equivalent analogy in giving release to one's anger as well.

God, the Almighty, imposed some restraint on this kind of selves, if not; the earth would have been corrupted by their un-scrupulousness. God, the Almighty, says: "And if it were not for God checking [some] people by means of others, the earth would have been corrupted, but God is full of bounty to the worlds." " وَلَوْلَا دَفْعُ اللَّهِ النَّاسَ بَعْضَهُم بِبَعْضٍ لَّفَسَدَتِ الْأَرْضُ وَلَٰكِنَّ اللَّه ذُو فَضْلٍ عَلَى الْعَالَمِين" (251: 2)

God, the Compassionate, granted these selves with spouses and maid-slaves (made lawful for mating) to tame their wild desires.

This means that if these angry malicious selves contacted with the object of influence, they affect it even if not touching it, others are of more disastrous effects.

One manifestation of malicious selves is evil eye. A person may be envious of another for a certain bounty or grace he possesses. His evil eye creates venomous effect that afflicts the one envied. This envy depends on the aptitude of this envied person, or his being unguarded and strength of power of evil eyed. When a pure elevated self goes under the spell of the envy of a malicious self, it has to recourse to Alfatihah by adopting and mulling over its facts, secrets and significances, reasons of Tawhid and trusting in God lying therein, praising God, mentioning of His names and attributes, remembrance of His Name which is of the power to uproot any evil and proliferate good. As such, this self can ward off this malicious diabolic eye by such adjustments and then it is to be cured. Yet, this cure is dependent on the power of the acting self and the acceptance of the acted upon self; if the one bitten is unresponsive of acceptance of Ruqiah, and the one who performs the Ruqiah was uninfluential, the cure is un-attainable.

To summarize, cure rests on a three –step therapy: the suitability of the medication to the disease, the skill of the therapist and the patient's acceptance of the therapy; skipping any element of the tri-formula foils the cure, however, if well- preserved cure is realizable.

One has to reflect on the true underlying secrets of Ruqiah.

As for personal experimentation; they are enumerable. I have tried it myself and performed on others and it was of miraculous effects particularly in Mecca. I used to recite Alfatihah on the positions of pains in my sored body, and it makes wonders and relieves my ailments. But it all depends on the strength of faith and the soundness of confidence in God's disposition.

Chapter

As regards the inclusion of Alfatihah to all refutations against the deviant groups and sects and the innovators and misguided of this nation.

This was addressed in a comprehensive and detailed approaches:

As regards the comprehensive approach: it is epitomized in the inclusion of the Straight Path of recognition of truth, its preference and prioritizing it over others, its love, abidance by, calling for it and striving against its enemies as much as possible.

The truth is manifested in the practices of the Prophet (PBUH) and his companions, his preaching and practices in the realm of the attributes of God, the Almighty, His names and Oneness, His commands and prohibitions, promise and menace and facts of faith which are the statuses of the seekers of the Path to God, the Almighty. This has to be ascribed to the instructions of the Prophet (PBUH) rather than the reasoning of men and their doctrines and beliefs.

Any knowledge, act or truth, state or condition should be exuding from the Prophetic niche.

There are three ways: the path of the Messenger (PBUH) and his preaching, the path of those who provoked God's wrath; those who know the truth and stood against and the path of those who have gone astray and those are misguided by God.

Abdullah ibn Abbas and Gabir ibn Abdullah held the view that "the Straight Path is Islam." While Abdullah Ibn Massoud and Ali ibn Abu Taleb believe it is the Quran. Suhail ibn Abdullah believes that: it is the path of Sunnah and Gam'ah (consensus).

This is the comprehensive tackling of the path, whatever is at variance with is falsehood i.e. it the path of the malicious and deviant groups.

As regards the detailed approach: it is the recognition of the unorthodox doctrines and the inclusion of the words of Alfatihah of their refutations.

People are of two categories; the believers in God, the Truthful, and the disbelievers. Alfatihah prompts for affirmation of the

Creator and refuting the claims of the disbelievers by establishing the Oneness of God, the Almighty.

The entire universe, higher or lower parts, all its parts witness the existence of a Creator, Cleaver and Sovereign. The rejection of a creator and denial in mind and common sense equals a similar denial of knowledge, no difference. The creator is evidenced by the creations, the actor denotes an act and the maker denotes his manufacture.

Clear common sense grasps this.

The reference to the created is recurring; however it is of considerable importance when it comes to the Creator. The messengers proclaimed that to their nations as they said: "Can there be doubt about God", "أَفِي اللَّهِ شَكٌّ" (14:10) can you doubt the existence God. They doubt God till finding the evidence of His existence which is vehemently clear with the existence of His creations. They underpinned this evidence by the verse: "Creator of the heavens and earth?", "فَاطِرِ السَّمَاوَاتِ وَالْأَرْضِ"(14:10)

The existence of God is as clear as the daylight for those of sound mind and Fitra (natural disposition).

The falsehood of those who believe in "the Unity of being" is clearly established. They believe that the existence of being is the very existence of God. They embrace the conviction of removing the difference between the Creator and what He created; they are combined and united. The worshiped is the same as the worshipper, the one Helping is the one to be helped, and the one Guiding equates the one to be guided. The God and his slave became one. The difference is only ascribed to figurative manifestations and disclosures which appear once in the figure of the one to be worshiped just like the case of Pharaoh, or a slave or the guiding ones exemplified by prophets, messengers and scientists. Meaning that in essence all the existence is One; the worshiped and the Worshipper share the same essence of being.

Alfatihah from its beginning till its end nullifies all these assumptions and exposes the corruption and deviation of those astray sects.

Those who publicize for the unity of being negate God's variance from His creatures. They claim that God is not two things. He is not described by two different descriptions. He does not have a highest and a lowest nor directions or sides, neither a right nor left, and neither is He light nor heavy, and He does not have color or a body, and nor is He known or understood. And everything that you imagine in your heart which is considered a thing, and then He is different to it.

Alfatihah rebuts these flawed assumptions from two perspectives:

First: affirmation of Rububiyyah (Oneness of God) over the universe. The very prerequisite of Rububiyyah is that the Essence (being) of God is at variance with the created universe. Identically God, the Almighty, distinguished Himself with attributes and acts. If the deity is not distinct from the universe, then he is unworthy of godhood. Negation of God's distinctiveness and variance from the universe necessities removing the lines separating the two entities and uniting them. Consequently, this group adopted the doctrine of the unity of being. Mu'talah and Itahidia were the proponents of such a doctrine.

Others hold that He is not two different things, nor inside nor outside.

A third group held a view pivoting on juxtaposing of two contradictions; establishing a deity at variance with the universe and at the same time negating such variance. Likewise, affirmation of the existence of a creator that stands alone by himself, His essence neither dwells in the universe nor the universe dwells therein, neither above nor beneath it.

The entirety of these flawed and corrupt beliefs is frowned upon by the Salaf (Fundamentalists) and whoever enjoys a sound heart devoid of any desires, fixations or fanaticism.

Those who approve of the existence of a Creator are of two categories:

Believers in Tawhid (Oneness of God) and polytheists. The polytheists are of two kinds:

First: those who disbelieve in His Rububiyyah such as the adherents of Mazdeism and the Determinists (Qadriyyah). They hold that there is another creator with God: even if viewing that it is not scaled up to His Status or being His equal. Qadriyyah (Determinists), the Magi-Like adherents, on the other hand promulgate that there are other creators of acts along with God; to them, the actions are neither predetermined by God nor created for them. There are divorced from His Will and volition; they are far beyond His power. Neither does He make deities causing them to occur. Man is the agent of actions out of their own free will.

The true prerequisites of the absolute and comprehensive Rububiyyah of God over the whole universe nullify all these offshoots. They necessitate extending His hegemony over all the existents; the beings, the attributes, movements and actions.

Qadriyyah deny that God is the agent of all actions because they, as alleged, overstep boundaries of His power, will, creating. This contradicts the very requirement of praise as it entails extoling Him for the obedience of His creatures as He is the One Who helps and guide them to do these acts of obedience. The existence of God's will has been recurrently accentuated in the

Quran. God, the Almighty, says;" And you do not will except that God wills" " وَمَا تَشَاءُونَ إِلَّا أَن يَشَاءَ اللَّهُ"(76:30)

They made themselves equals to God and more deserved of praise for being the initiating agents of action. They went step further in alleging of their eligibility of the reward; it is a genuine right.

God's saying: "It is You who help us." is a conclusive rebuttal of their allegations. Their recourse to Him for assistance is emphatically establishes His Oneness and the creatures spin in the domain of His power and will.

Another rebuttal is God's saying: "Guide us for the Straight Path." It is the absolute guidance prompting for the attainment of guidance, Had it not been exclusively in His Hand, they would have never asked for it. It is not a mere statement as claimed by the Determinists. Destination alone is short of actualization of guidance.

The second type is the disbelievers in His Lordship. He is the Alone, the Owner, the Possessor, the Creator of their ancestors and the Sovereign of Heavens and the One over the Throne. In overt denial of all His lofty status, they worship other deities and even worse, they made them His equals. They failed to fulfill the requirement of "It is You whom we worship." They had their lot of worship but not directed to Him. Subjugating themselves to the worship of God is the only way to avert Shirk (idolatry).

The polytheists failed to meet the prerequisites of Rububiy-yah and asking for the Straight Path, consequently they are astray and well-deserved of God's wrath and misguidance.

Refutation of the Jahmites's denial of God's attributes

This includes many aspects:

First: God's saying: "Praise be to God." is establishing the entirety of praise which necessitates the availability of all what He is praised for by the account of utmost perfection of His attributes and faculties of Exaltation. The lack of attributes of perfections or even one of them totally disqualifies deservedness of praise; it is the sole property of the One who singles Himself out of possessing the totality of the attributes of perfection.

This is applicable on attributing mercy to God as it constitutes affirmation of relevant attributes such as eternity, will, power, hearing and sight. Identically Rububiyyah is inclusive of the attribute of His being the Agents of all acts while divinity encompasses all attributes of perfection in respect of Essence and Acting.

God's encompassing of all these attributes and their negation simultaneously, is, by and large, contradictory.

This includes establishment of stative attributes from two perspectives:

First: they are prerequisites of His absolute perfection; His Being over the Throne is indicative of His elevation, His descending every night to earth after midnight is indicative of His mercy and Rububiyyah and the like with other stative attributes.

The second aspect: God's possessing of hearing includes praising to God and a way through which He acknowledges Himself to His slaves.

Negation or distortion of these attributes is conflicting with their original revealed significance.

Refutation of the Jabriyyah (Fatalism)

This can be addressed from different perspectives:

Establishing God's deservedness of praise requires that He, the Almighty, never punishes His slaves for actions that go beyond the boundaries of their will nor anticipated by them. May God be Exalted from doing this injustice. Humans are only accountable for the acts they have committed themselves, they are theirs not His. Being of evil nature, their deeds are ascribed to them. The actions of God include Justice, all acts of goodness and bliss. The Fatalists assume that all events are predetermined by fate i.e. God is the Agent of all acts, good or bad. If humans had no freedom of will or choice, none would deserve praise or blame for any action

The second perspective is that establishing God's mercy and compassion nullifies their allegations as it is unbefitting for God to possess these attributes and punishes a powerless slave who does not act upon his own free will. Neither does God appoint His slaves with what he is intolerable of. This goes at odds with and negates the attribute altogether.

The third is establishment of God's worship and His help for them.

They claim that worship and assistance here are figuratively used; they are relative and that it is detracting to God to ascribe worship and help to him since these are the actions of His slaves.

However, the slave is basically the one who worships and asks for help from God and God is the One worshipped and to Whom we recourse for help.

Refutation of the statement maintaining that God is non-referential (self-evident); undifferentiated by an act of His will or intellect and

Establishing that God, the Exalted is He, is self-referential

First: establishing God's praise; a non-referential being that is non-existing before any existent thing; undifferentiated by his will or act or any prediction of predicates is undeserved of being praised. Whereas a self-referential Being; differentiated by His will and acts of goodness is instinctively worthy or praise to sound minds; otherwise will be at odds with Fitra (natural composition) and mind.

Those who maintain those corrupt premises are undeniably take haughtiness in being debarred from the context of the divine laws and Prophethood dictates.

Second: proving His Rububiyyah (Oneness): this necessitates acknowledging God's will, selection, pre-disposition and power; for it conflicts with common sense to hold that the sun is the author- creator- of its light; or coolness or the sprouting of plants are the derivative referential to water; these predicates are, naturally, attributed to a Subject, a Creator or else it would be flagrantly outward negation of Rububiyyah.

Third: Proving God's Sovereignty: ability to act or reason is flawed; so the begotten here who has free will and reason will be more complete and perfect than the Begetter and this is impossible. God, the Almighty says: "Then is He who creates like one who does not create? So will you not be reminded?" " أَفَمَن يَخْلُقُ كَمَن لَّا يَخْلُقُ أَفَلَا تَذَكَّرُون"ـ (17: 16)

Fourth: Proving God's help: we recourse to the One who act out of His will as the opposite is detectably illogical.

Five: proving God's responsibility for the Guidance of His slaves: It's unlikely to ask guidance from he who lacks the power to guide and likewise His being a bliss-Bestower.

Refutation of God's knowledge of all matters of substance

This is imbued in many perspectives:

First: the perfection of praise: how is he deserved of praise that he who knows nothing about the surrounding world, its details, planets, stars, the obedient and the disobedient, those who supplicate Him and those who don't?

Second: He can be neither a lord nor a god; the worshipped Lord and the Disposing God must know His slave and his state.

Third: proving His mercy; it can't be that He has mercy on whom He doesn't know.

Fourth: proving His sovereignty: It is not befitting for a Sovereign not knowing any of his slaves, the conditions of His kingdom.

Fifth: His being a Helper

Sixth: His being responsible for guidance and fulfillment of a seeker.

Seventh: His being the Guiding One.

Eighth: His being the Bestower

Ninth: His being Wrathful to the disobedient.

Tenth: His being a Judge, holds people accountable for their deeds

The negation of God's knowledge of all matters of substance is at odds with all foregoing.

The refutation of deniers of prophethood

This falls into some aspects:

First: proving His absolute praise: this necessitates the perfection of His wisdom that includes that He does not create anything without a purpose or leave them untended, nor being enjoined for the good and prohibited against the bad. Therefore, God, the Almighty, extolled Himself in more than one position in the Quran against all these shortcomings. He, the Almighty, informed that the deniers of revelation, Prophethood and messengers do not really know the truth of God nor abide themselves by extolling Him rightfully.

Those who truly appreciate praise- out of recognition, knowledge and insight- can easily deduce the testimony: "I bear witness that Muhammad is the Messenger of God." the same way they deduced that: "There is no deity but God."

The negation of Prophethood is at variance with praise just like the case with negation of the Attributes of God and associating other deities and partners with Him.

Second: His lordship: being a Lord requires His being worshipped and the medium accessible for the knowledge of His ordinance and preaching is His Messengers.

Third: Being a God: Godhood requires giving ordinances and interjections to slaves; rewarding the obedient and punishing the disobedient. This is the truth of Rububiyyah, unattainable except through divine messages and Prophethood.

Fourth: His being especially Merciful and Compassionate: the prerequisites of His perfect mercy incorporate His identification of Himself and His Attributes to His slaves; guiding them to what makes them near or what divorces them from Him, rewarding for their obedience and rewarding them in abundance. This is achievable only through divine messages and Prophethood.

Fifth: sovereignty; which requires disposition through act and verbatim. The sovereign is the Disposer of affairs; His ordinances and decrees are to be followed the way he desires.

God's disposition through verbatim is of two kinds: the verbatim of His divine "Be" words and His revealed words; the perfection of Sovereignty is realized through the integration between them

Sending Messengers: requires the perfection of His sovereignty and authority; this is the common norm for people; a king is not accountable if not sending his messengers all through his kingdom.

Through this medium His angels are known, faith in them is among the prerequisites of faith in His Sovereignty. They are the messengers of God for His slaves to fulfill His orders.

Sixth: proving the Day of Judgment; it is the day of Retribution when God's accountability of   people's deeds is rendered only after establishing the message and Prophethood and laying the grounds upon which the obedient and the disobedient are decided upon.

Seventh: His being a worshipped; He is not worshipped except through what pleases and satisfies Him and no access to know this but through messengers.

Eighth: His being a Guiding to the Straight Path which incorporates acknowledgement of the truth and working accordingly; it is the nearest ways leading to the desired destination which is known only through messengers.

Ninth: His being the Bestower of the Straight Path to the guided ones; this favor of grace is done to them by sending messengers, being open to accepting the message and responsive to it too.

Tenth: the categorization of people to those who have won God's favors and those who evoked God's wrath and those who have gone astray. This categorization is a must according to their hierarchy in truth knowledge and acting accordingly; some recognize it and act accordingly and those are the people of grace; some recognize it and then oppose it and those are who evoked God's wrath and the third who are unaware of and those are the astray. It is identified only after sending messengers; but for them all people would have been one undifferentiated ranks.

This includes refutation of the allegations of the deniers of the corporeal resurrection and established the necessity of reward, punishment, promotion of virtue and the prevention of vice. It is the truth based on which the creation of heavens and earth, the worldly life and the hereafter; the very essence of creation and ordinance and negation of whatever at variance with.

Establishing of Prophethood and message is evidence of the attribute of kalam (speech) and taklim (talking to others)

The essence of the message communicates the messenger's speech; should it not be there any speech what a messenger is to communicate? How can he be a messenger? Therefore, more than one of the Salaf hold that he who denies that God is a Speaker and that the Quran is His revealed wording, denies the Prophethood of Muhammad and all the Messengers as well who are basically communicating God's revealed speech. Those who deny the Prophethood of Muhammad (PBUH) said that the

Quran is: "This is not but magic imitated [from others]. This is not but the word of a human being." " فَقَالَ إِنْ هَٰذَا إِلَّا سِحْرٌ يُؤْثَرُ إِنْ هَٰذَا إِلَّا قَوْلُ الْبَشَرِ" (74: 24-25) (They meant the Quran communicated to them as a warning.

Those who view that God does not speak are like those doubters and detractors. May God be Exalted against what those unjust deniers claim.

CHAPTER 8

Statement of the Refutation of the infinity of the universe from many perspectives

First: proving His praise; it requires providing evidence for his acts; given that God's praise throughout the Quran is dedicated to acts. Here, God praised Himself for His Godhood which is inclusive of His willful acts; it is impossible to compare the act to the actor; for no intelligent mind is deluded about that. Rather, an action is basically far preceding the actor. Actions are linked to will, influence and power rather than infinity.

Second: proving His Rububiyyah for the whole universe. The universe is everything different from His being; and they are all

created and every creation is contingent after being non-exist-
ent. Consequently His Godhood for the whole universe requires
His being a head of it and the contingency of the created subject.
An infinite universe can't be created since it's self-referential by
the fullness of its eternity and dispensable with a creator or doer.
Certainly every subject is poor; the created is neither rich nor infinite.

Third: proving His Oneness. Its prerequisite precludes not
sharing any of His attributes of Oneness with any of the created;
willful power is exclusive to His oneness. Tawhid negates the existence of that power to others and establishing the
distinctiveness of His Rububiyyah and divinity rather than others.

.

CHAPTER 9

Statement of Rebuttal of the Rafidah by God's words "Guide us to the straight Path"

A rebuttal of their argument incorporates that God, the Almighty, has divided people into three categories: those who were bestowed with favors and they are on the Straight Path; those who evoked God's anger who are aware of the truth and rejected it and those who have gone astray of the ignorant of the truth.

Those who are most well-versant with and abiding by the truth are more deserved of the Straight Path.

Undoubtedly, the Companions of Prophet Muhammad (PBUH) are more worthy of this honor than the Rafidah; for it beggars belief that the companions are unaware or reject the truth whilst the Rafidah are aware of it.

The imprints of each group are manifest; the companions opened the unbelieving countries and turned them into Muslims and open up hearts by the Quran, knowledge and guidance. Their legacy is that of the people who tread the Straight Path. On the contrary, the Shia every time and place, collude with the opponents of Islam and they caused harm on Muslims by their malicious machinations. They collaborated with the Tatars, were the cause behind wreaking havoc with the mosques, burning the parchments of the Quran, killings of the Muslims, their scholars. Their backing up to the polytheists and the Christians is known for the elite and the laymen.

Some Salaf interpreted that the Straight path is meant to describe Abu baker, Umar and the companions of the prophet (PBUH). It is the path they tread following in the footstep of their prophet and they are who are bestowed with favors and their enemies are those who evoked God's anger and they are judged to be astray.

Chapter

If this became clear, then Know that: a slave cannot fulfill this statement (it is you we worship إِيَّاكَ نَعْبُدُ)(1:5) except by fulfilling two great principles:

The first is: to follow the prophet (PBUH).

The second is: to be sincere to the one who is worshipped. By these two principles, this statement (it is you we worship إِيَّاكَ نَعْبُدُ) is implemented.

People, according to these two principles can be divided into four categories:

The first Kind: the people of sincerity to God who follow the prophet. Those are the real implementer of (إِيَّاكَ نَعْبُدُ). So, all their deeds are for the sake of God and their sayings are for God. When they give, they give for the sake of God and when they prevent, they prevent for the sake of God. All their treatments outwardly and inwardly are only for the sake of God.

They do not do that in order to be rewarded or thanked by people. They do that neither wishing for position or gratitude nor fearing from being blamed by people. They consider people equals to the people of the grave; they grant not them any harm or benefit and possess not (power to cause) death or life or resurrection. Therefore, to act for the sake of people, wishing they may give you status or position and asking them for benefits or to ward off harm cannot be an act of one who knows people. Nay, it is an act of one who is very ignorant of people and also very ignorant of his Lord. Because whoever knows people, he should give them only what they deserve. And whoever knows God, he should make his deeds, sayings, giving, prevention, love and hate only devoted to God alone. And whoever directs himself to people in everything and not to God, he is truly ignorant of God and ignorant of people. For if he really knew God and knew people, he would surely give preference and priority to God's treatment over people's treatment.

Also, all their deeds and worships are according to God's command, and according to what He love and accept. In fact, God accepts no act except this kind of act. And for the sake of this act God tested man by life and death, God says:

"[He] who created death and life to test you [as to] which of you is best in deed" "ٱلَّذِي خَلَقَ ٱلْمَوْتَ وَٱلْحَيَوٰةَ لِيَبْلُوَكُمْ أَيُّكُمْ أَحْسَنُ عَمَلاًۚ" (67:2) And He has made that which on the earth adornment for it that He may test them (as to) which of them is best in deed. Alfuḍayl ibn ʿIyāḍ said: the best deed (mentioned in the verse) is the sincerest to God and the most correct. They (people) asked him: O' abu Ali, what do you mean by "the sincerest and the most correct"? He answered: if a deed is done for God's sake but it is not correct, it will not be accepted. And if it is correct but not for God's sake, it will not be accepted. So It must be done correctly and for the sake of God.

The "sincere" act means: that is aimed to be done for the sake of God. And the "correct" means: what is done according to the Sunnah (tradition) of the prophet (PBUH). And this is mentioned in God's saying – Exalted is He- : "So whoever would hope for the meeting with his Lord – let him do righteous work and not associate in the worship of his Lord anyone.", " فَمَن كَانَ يَرْجُواْ لِقَآءَ رَبِّهِۦ "فَلْيَعْمَلْ عَمَلاً صَلِحًا وَلَا يُشْرِكْ بِعِبَادَةِ رَبِّهِۦ أَحَدًا"... (18:110). And also in his saying: "And who is better in religion than one who submits himself to God while being a doer of good", " وَمَنْ أَحْسَنُ دِينًا مِّمَّنْ أَسْلَمَ وَجْهَهُۥ لِلَّهِ "وَهُوَ مُحْسِنٌ"...(4:125).

So, God does not accept any act (of worship) unless it is for His sake and according to His commands. Otherwise, it is rejected and it will be reimbursed to his doer as dust dispersed while he is in a dire need for its reward. It is narrated in Sahih by Aisha, as the prophet (PBUH) said: "If anybody introduces a practice which is not authenticated by me, it is to be rejected". Every act is done without following the prophet in doing it, it will add to his doer nothing but grab him away from God. Since God is being worshipped according to His commands, not by opinions and desires.

The second kind: The people who have no sincerity to God nor do they follow the prophet (PBUH). So, the deeds of (one of those) are not in agreement with the Islsamic law, and they are not done for the sake of God as well. This status is like those who show off for the sake of people. They show their deeds off, however these deeds are not legislated by God or His messenger. those people are the worst creatures at all and the most despicable in the sight of God, and they would have the best share of God's saying: "And never think that those who rejoice in what they have perpetrated and like to be praised for what they did not do – never think them [to be] in safety from the punishment, and for them is a painful punishment." " لَا تَحْسَبَنَّ ٱلَّذِينَ يَفْرَحُونَ بِمَآ أَتَوا "...ۖ"وَّيُحِبُّونَ أَن يُحْمَدُواْ بِمَا لَمْ يَفْعَلُواْ فَلَا تَحْسَبَنَّهُم بِمَفَازَةٍ مِّنَ ٱلْعَذَابِ وَلَهُمْ عَذَابٌ أَلِيمٌ (3:188). They are rejoicing in what they have perpetrated and invented from heretics, misguidance and disbelief, and they like to be praised for being sincere to God and for being following the sunnah (the prophet).

You can find this category most frequent among those - who are engaged in knowledge, asceticism and worshipping - who deviated from the straight path. So they commit heretics, misguidance, showing off and pursuing reputation and they like to be praised for what they did not do; as being sincere, followers (to the prophet) and knowledgeable. For this, they are the people who deserve anger and misguidance.

Chapter

The third kind: Those people who are sincere in their deeds, but their deeds are not done according to the command (of God and His messenger), like the ignorant of the worships, and those who affiliate themselves to poverty and asceticism. Generally, it includes all those who worship God without following God's command, believing that this worship will make them nearer to God. Examples for those people are: whoever thinks that listening to whistling and handclapping is a kind of worship, or whoever thinks that solitude, which of course make him lose juma'ah (Friday) prayer and congregational prayers, is a kind of worship. And whoever believes that fasting during day and night as well is a kind of worship or whoever thinks that if he fasts a day on which all the people are not fasting, is considered a kind of worship, and so on.

The forth kind: The people who are doing acts in accordance with the commands (of God and His messenger), however these acts are not purely for the sake of God. For example: the obedience (worship) of those who are showing their deeds off. It is like the one who fights enemies for pride and haughtiness. And like the one who goes to pilgrimage that it might be said [of him](he is a performer of pilgrimage) or the one who recited the Quran that it might be said [of him] (He is a reciter). All the deeds of those people are apparently good deeds which God legislated, but in fact these deeds are not sound. And they will not be accepted: "And they were not commanded except to worship Allah, [being] sincere to Him in religion," " وَمَآ أُمِرُوٓاْ إِلَّا لِيَعْبُدُواْ ٱللَّهَ مُخْلِصِينَ لَهُ ٱلدِّينَ"(98:5). Therefore, everybody is ordered only to worship God according to His commands and to be sincere to God in religion, and those are the true people and implementers of "It is You we worship and You we ask for help.", " إِيَّاكَ نَعْبُدُ وَإِيَّاكَ نَسْتَعِينُ"(1:5).

Chapter

Now we move to the people and implementers of (it is you we worship إِيَّاكَ نَعْبُدُ) (1:5). Those people can be divided into four divisions, in discussing which kind of worship is the best, most beneficial and most recommended. So there are four opinions are held:

The first opinion: the best and most beneficial worship is the hardest one and the toughest on souls. They argued: because this kind of worship is the most far from one's desires and this is the essence of worship.

They also said: they reward (of worship) is defined on the basis of how hard and tough it is. They narrated a hadeeth- which has no basis - that: "the best act (of worships) is the hardest." i.e.: the most difficult and the toughest. Those are the people who strive against to the degree that they wrong themselves. They say: this is the only way by which the souls can be straightened. Because the soul trends by nature to laziness and humiliation. Therefore, no way to be straightened except by taking risks and enduring hardships.

The second opinion: those who held this opinion said that: the best (kind) of worships is to take this worldly life off, to practice ascetics and to practice austerity in the pleasures of this life and not to care about it.

The holders of this opinion are of two types:

· The majority thought that this (mentioned opinion) is a goal and purpose. So they rolled up their sleeves, worked hardly on it and called people for their way. They said: this is better than seeking knowledge and worship. They saw that practicing asceticism and austerity in this life is the purpose of every worship and the most important kind of worship.

· Few thought that this (mentioned opinion) is required to be done but not for itself, it is required for another purpose; which is, to make one's heart get preoccupied and full of God, free from everything but God, constantly repent to and trust God and engaged with God's obedience and satisfaction. They saw that the best (kind) of worships is to be in a company with God, to be in constant remembrance of him by both tongue and heart, staying away from whatever diverts or distracts the heart.

These few are also of two types: first: the knowers of God who follow the prophet's steps. Whenever those people are ordered by God and his messenger to do something or prevented from doing something, they rash and obey. Even if this order or prevention will lead to dispersing their company and taking away their solitude with God. Second: the deviants among them who say: the purpose behind worships is to make your heart engaged and in company with God. So, if anything is going to take it away from God, it should be neglected.

Worships are required from those who are of inattentiveness to God.... So, what about those who are constantly in attention.

And those deviants are also of two types: First: those who abandon the obligations and duties in respect of this company with God. Second: those who do obligations and duties but they leave the Voluntary and recommended worships (sunnah) and they abandon seeking knowledge for the sake of their "company with God".

One of those deviants asked a scholar and knower (of God) saying: the caller for prayer calls, while I am in my company with God...if I went to prayer, then my solitude will be broken. And if I keep on, my company with God will go on. What is the better for me to do in that case? He answered: If the caller for prayer called while you are under God's throne (in your Meditation), go and answer the caller of God then return to your place. Because this solitude is the right of the soul and heart while answering the caller is the right of God. And whoever gives priority to his soul's right over his God's right, then he is not one of the people of (it is you we worship إِيَّاكَ نَعْبُدُ)(1:5)

The third opinion: Those who held this opinion said that: the best of worships and the most beneficial are: those worships which have benefits for other people. They thought that serving the poor and working on people's interests and needs are the best of worships. So, they rolled their sleeves and worked hardly on this...arguing that the prophet PBUH said: "All creatures are the dependents of God and the most beloved of them to God is he who is most beneficial to His dependents" "narrated by Abu Ya'ala"

They also argued that: the benefit of the worshipper is limited to himself, while the benefit of the one who serve others reach many…. so how can they be equal?! They said: For this reason, the Prophet made the superiority of the learned man over the devout worshipper is like that of the full moon to the rest of the stars (i.e., in brightness). They also said: the Prophet (PBUH) said to Ali ibn Abu Talib (may God be pleased with him) "By God, if a single person is guided by God through you, it will be better for you than a whole lot of red camels.". They commented: this superiority is for the multilateral beneficial working. They make basis on the prophet's (PBUH) narrations: "If anyone calls others to follow right guidance, his reward will be equivalent to those who follow him (in righteousness) without their reward being diminished in any respect" and the narration: "Indeed God and His Angels, - say peace upon the one who teaches the people to do good".

And the narration "Everyone in the universe, in the heavens and on earth, prays for forgiveness for the scholar, even the fish in the sea and the ant in its hole "

They argued that: when a devout worshipper dies, his righteous deeds cease. While the one who serves and benefits others, his righteous deeds go on as long as these benefits exist.

They also argued that: the prophets were sent to do favors for people, guide them and benefit them in this worldly life and in the afterlife. They were not sent with monasticism or solitude; isolation from the world. For this reason, the prophet (PBUH) prevented those people who intended to be in solitude from people and worship God. He (PBUH) prevented them from doing so. Therefore, the holders of this opinion saw that: dispersing while performing God's order, benefitting His servants and doing good for them is better than being in a company with God without performing these (righteous) acts.

The third opinion: Those who held this opinion said that: the best of worships is: to be keen to satisfy God all the time with the most appropriate worship for this time. For example: the best worship at the time of war is to make jihad...even if this will lead to leaving usual worships like; the voluntary night prayer, fasting the day or even completing the obligatory prayer (as God legislated the war prayer is different from the usual prayer).

And the best worship at a time of having a guest is: to honor your guest and to serve him...even if this leads to leaving your usual recommended worship (like reading Quran). The same applies to giving the wife's and family's rights.

And the best worship at the time before dawn is: to pray, to read Quran, to make (supplications and remembrance of God) and to ask for forgiveness.

And the best worship at a time when a seeker of knowledge or an ignorant person wants to know and learn is: to teach them and to seek knowledge.

And the best worship at a time when the caller for prayer is calling is to leave any recommended worship you are engaged with, and to answer the call of God, by repeating the call and going to prayer.

And the best worship at the time of the five obligatory prayers is: to intend to perform it in the best possible way, to rash to it in the beginning of its time and to perform it in the mosque and the more far the mosque is the more reward you will take.

And the best worship at a time when a disadvantaged needs help is to assist him, to help the oppressed who appeal for help and to give this priority to your solitude (with God) and your usual worships.

And the best worship at the time of reading Quran is to make your heart present while reading in order to contemplate and understand it, to the degree that you feel like God is talking to you. By this, your heart will be ready to understand it and you will be determined to apply its instructions more than your willingness.

And the best worship at the time of standing at the mountain of Arafat is to do your best in supplication, imploring and remembrance of God, but not fasting this day.

And the best worship on the first ten days of Zul-Hijjah is to do much worshipping, especially to be regular (in remembering God by saying): "God is the Greatest"; "there is no lord but God"; "all praise is due to God". This is more recommended than the non-mandatory Jihad.

And the best worship at the time of the last ten days of Ramadan is to stick to the mosque; to stay for worship in it, far from mixing with people and getting busy with them. This is even better than teaching them or making them read the Quran, according to the majority of the scholars.

And the best worship at the time of sickness or death of your Muslim brother is to visit him, to attend his funeral and to accompany him until the burial is completed. It is preferable to give priority to this over your solitude and company with God.

And the best worship at the time of calamities and being abused and hurt by people is to be patient while mixing with them, but not to flee from them. Because the believer who mixes with people and endures their injury is better than the person who does not mix with people nor endure their injury. And the best is to mix with them while participating in doing good, this is better than keeping yourself away from them. And the best is to keep yourself away from them when they do evil, this is better than mixing with them. But if you know that, by mixing with them while they are doing evil, this will remove evil or reduce it, then your mixing with them is better than keeping away from them.

Hence, we know that, the best worship in a certain time is to engage with the most beloved worship to God in this specific time.

Those holders of the fourth opinion are the people of the absolute worship. And those before them (the holders of the first three opinions) are the people of the limited worship. So whenever one of them leaves the kind of worship he used to, he feels like he left worshipping. This man is worshipping God by only one way. Unlike the man of absolute worship who has not a specific preferable worship. His aim is to search for God's satisfaction. Where it be, he orbits with. So you find him all the time moving from a degree of worshipping to another. Whenever he finds a higher degree of worship than his current degree, he moves to it. This is the way of his life until it ends. So when you see the scholars, you will see him (learn) with them. When you see the worshippers, you will find him, worshipping there. When you see the mujahedeen (fighters in the sake of God), you will see him, fights with them. When you see those who remember God much, you will find him with them. When you see the givers of charity, you will find him with them. And when you see the people whose hearts are engaged with God's company, you also will see him there. Hence, this man is the absolute worshipper. He is not limited by restrictions. His worships are not chosen according his soul's desire and what he loves and wishes. His worships are chosen according to what His Lord loves, even if he loves other worships. Truly this man is the real implementer of "It is You we worship and You we ask for help.", " إِيَّاكَ نَعْبُدُ وَإِيَّاكَ نَسْتَعِينُ " (1:5). He wears what is available and eats what he finds and wherever he goes to a place, he sits where he found a place (i.e.: not arrogant). All the time he is engaged with God's orders, each in its preferable and suitable time. He is free from desires and whims, so nothing can capture him. Whatever God's orders him, he obeys. He is very loved by the people of the truth, and he is very disliked by the people of falsehood. He is like rain; wherever he falls, he will be beneficial for everything. And he is like a palm tree; its leaves do not fall, and every part of it is beneficial, even its thorns are beneficial. He is very forceful against those transgressors of God's orders and becomes very angry if one transgresses a matter prohibited by God. All the time, he is for God, with God and trust God. When he is in a company with God, he does not think of people. And when he is with people, his soul is away from them (his soul is with God); when he is with God he abandons people, and when he is with people, he (leaves his body with them and) takes his soul away to God. What a strange he is among people! What loneliness he feels when he is with them! And what tranquility, joy, peace and relief he feels when he is with God! God is the one from Whom help is sought and He is the one upon Whom is the reliance.

Chapter

People have four visions as to the benefit of worship, its wisdom and its goal. So they are four kinds:

The first vision: the denials of wisdoms and reason, those people deny the existence of wisdom and reason behind the divine order and prevention. They say: it is just the mere will and sheer volition of God (they mean: no reason, benefit or wisdom behind the worships). Those think that: they do worships because they were ordered by God and they must obey, without rendering these worships reason for happiness in this life or in the afterlife or reason for survival (in the afterlife). They do it just because they were ordered. As they said that: (God) has not created mankind for a reason. There is no purpose or wisdom behind this. And the creatures are not results for reasons (i.e.: there were no reasons that led to the creation of these creatures). Nor do they have powers or (different) natures. For example: Fire is not the reason for burning. And water is not the reason for irrigation, refrigeration and germination. Water has no power or nature to do so. Burning and irrigation do not happen because of fire and water, but because of the conjugate habits. (i.e.: God offered a conjugate habit which is when fire touches a combustible material, it will be burnt, and when water get absorbed by a soil which have a seed, the seed will be implanted. However fire cannot burn, nor water can implant). There is no difference in the essence between the commands and prohibitions. It is just the will of God which made this lawful and that prohibited. There is no characteristic that makes the order good, and there is no characteristic that makes the prohibition bad.

This opinion has many attachments and related issues which all are null. We (ibn Alqayem) mentioned them in detail in our book; named "the key of home of happiness, and goal of people of knowledge and will". In this book we have explained the invalidity of this opinion with about sixty reasons. This book is really unique in its field. We also discussed this opinion in our book;

named "the travel of the two migrations, and way of happiness in two lives".

Those (the holder of the pre-mentioned opinion) do not feel the sweetness or delight of worship. They do not enjoy it. Prayer is not their joy and comfort (as it is for others). The divine orders are not the protection for their hearts, nor do they the sustenance for their souls and lives. So they call them (the orders) the obligations. However, if somebody claims to love a king, while he is calling the king's orders as obligations; saying I am doing these obligations with hardship, he is no longer loves the king. For this reason many of those denied the servant's love for his God. They said: the servant only loves the God's reward and what He creates of pleasure for him. He does not love God Himself. By this, they denied the reality of servitude and its essence.

The reality of divinity: Being a most beloved God (to the servant). This love is associated with (the servant's) humiliation, submission, glorification and honor. So they denied His being beloved, which is a denial for His divinity. The master of those people is: Algaad ibn Derham who was killed by Khalid ibn Abdullah Alqasri in an Adha day (Adha Eid). He (Algaad) claimed that: "God did not talk to Moses, nor does he take Abraham as an intimate friend. He denied being God beloved. He did not deny Abraham's need for God. In fact, this is very known for

Jahmis (a deviated Muslim group) and named as "Khullah; friendship" which is common to all creatures. According to them: all creatures are intimate friends for God.

We have explained the invalidity of their opinion; their denial of God's love by people, with more than eighty ways in our book; named "the joy of lovers' eyes and the garden of knowers' hearts". We mentioned in this book that: love must be connected with the first beloved one (God). We asserted this with the textual, mental, physical and innate proofs. Also we asserted that: man has no perfection without this love (for his Creator). As it is the case: there is no perfection for his body except with the soul and life nor for his eye except with light nor for his ear except with hearing; (the same) he has no perfection except with this love. It is even beyond and greater than that.

Chapter

The second kind: The Qadriyyah; the deniers (a deviated Muslim group) those people saw that: there is some kind of wisdom (behind worships), but this wisdom is not connected with God, rather it is related to the benefit and interest of human.

So, according to their opinion, worships were legislated as prices for what servants are going to take of reward and pleasure (in the hereafter). So, it is just like the fare or wage obtained by the worker.

They said: that is why God made worship as recompense as His saying: "And they will be called, "This is Paradise, which you have been made to inherit for what you used to do.", وَنُودُوٓاْ أَن تِلْكُمُ ٱلْجَنَّةُ أُورِثْتُمُوهَا بِمَا كُنتُمْ تَعْمَلُونَ " (7:43), and (like) His saying: "Enter Paradise for what you used to do.", "ٱدْخُلُواْ ٱلْجَنَّةَ بِمَا كُنتُمْ تَعْمَلُونَ" (16:32), and (like) His saying: "Are you recompensed except for what you used to do?", "هَلْ تُجْزَوْنَ إِلَّا مَا كُنتُمْ تَعْمَلُونَ" (27:90), and (like) his saying (peace be upon him) in a narration sent by God: "O My slaves, it is but your deeds that I reckon for you and then recompense you for…", and (like) God's saying : "Indeed, the patient will be given their reward without account [i.e., limit].", " إِنَّمَا يُوَفَّى ٱلصَّـٰبِرُونَ أَجْرَهُم بِغَيْرِ حِسَابٍ"…(39:10).

They said: God named it as "recompense", "reward" because it returns (from the work) to its worker.

They also said: if it was not connected with (one's) work, it would be meaningless to call it recompense or reward.

They said: this is proved by the scales (in the hereafter). If reward and punishment were not the result of (one's) deeds, then the scales would be of no meaning or benefit. God says: "And the weighing [of deeds] that Day will be the truth. So those whose scales are heavy — it is they who will be the successful. And those whose scales are light — they are the ones who will lose themselves for what injustice they were doing toward Our

وَٱلْوَزْنُ يَوْمَئِذٍ ٱلْحَقُّ فَمَن ثَقُلَتْ مَوَٰزِينُهُ فَأُوْلَٰئِكَ هُمُ ٱلْمُفْلِحُونَ وَمَنْ خَفَّتْ مَوَٰزِينُهُ " ,".verses (7:8-9). "فَأُوْلَٰئِكَ ٱلَّذِينَ خَسِرُوٓاْ أَنفُسَهُم بِمَا كَانُواْ بِـَٔايَٰتِنَا يَظْلِمُونَ

And these two sects are very different from each other and very opposite to each other.

As for Jabriyyah, they think that: the deeds have no relation with the recompense at all. They said that: God can punish this one who spent all his life in God's obedience, and He can favor and reward this one who spent all his life in God's disobedience. Those two men are the same in the sight of God. They made it permissible for God to raise a person of little work over another who has more deeds and more degrees. According to them, eve-ryone's (recompense) is due to the mere will of God, without explanation or reason. There is no wisdom behind making the reward for this person and the punishment for that person.

As for Qadriyyah, they made it obligatory upon God to choose the best (for His servants). They made everything (reward and punishment) given only in return for (our) deeds. Deeds are the price of this (reward and punishment). They saw that: if a person is going to gain reward without his righteous deeds, then it would be unpleasant for him. Because he might think that, this reward was given to him as charity in return for nothing.

May God curse them! What arrogant they are! They made God's bounty and kindness given to His servant like one's charity given to another. They even said: "the reward that God gives for His servants in return for his deeds is much better, liked and pleasant for him than giving him reward as bounty; for no return or deeds.

Jabriyyah thought is the very opposite of this, they saw that deeds has no relation to or impact on the recompense at all.

The two sects are unjust and deviant from the straight path upon which God has created His servants, with which the messengers were sent and according to which the books were revealed. It (the straight path) proclaims that: deeds are reasons for reward and punishment, and lead to it, as God made every reason leads to its result. Righteous deeds are of God's bounty, blessings and charity to His servant. He gave His servant the help and guidance to do these righteous deeds, granted them the will and power to do them, made them loveable and made hateful to him their opposites. However, they are not the price of God's recompense and reward, nor do they up to the God's position. The ultimate success of these deeds – if the servant did his best and made it on the best way- is thanking for God for some of His blessings (upon His servant). So, if the servant asked God his right, he would still unthankful to Him, for many other blessings and also for the blessing of being thankful. Therefore, if God punished the dwellers of the heavens and the dwellers of the earth, He would not be unjust for them. And if He showed them mercy, His mercy would be good for them more than their deeds, as it is narrated by the Prophet (PBUH). For this, the Prophet (PBUH) denied being anyone would enter paradise by his deeds.

He (PBUH) said: "There is none whose deeds alone would entitle him to get into Paradise – in another narration: None amongst you can get into Paradise by virtue of his deeds alone . – in another narration: None of you can achieve salvation through his (good) actions.- They said: Allah's Messenger, not even you? Thereupon he said: Not even I, but that Allah should wrap me in His Grace and Mercy."

However, God proved that: getting into paradise would be according to the deeds, as His saying: "Enter Paradise for what you used to do." "ٱدۡخُلُواْ ٱلۡجَنَّةَ بِمَا كُنتُمۡ تَعۡمَلُونَ)(16:32)

(In fact), there is no contradiction between them (the hadeeth and the verse) because the meaning of negation is different from the meaning of affirmation. The negated matter is deserving reward by the mere deeds. This negation is response to and refutation of the thought of Majusi Qadriyyah, who claimed that giving reward for no return is a kind of giving charity (which abuses the servant).

This sect is the most ignorant of God among people and the most far from Him. They deserve for this to be the magi's of this nation. Very enough of being ignorant of God that: they do not know that the inhabitants of heavens and the inhabitants of earth are overwhelmed by His blessing, and that the perfection of this blessing, joy, pleasure, and delight is their joy of their Lord and Master's reward. In fact, their life is happy only by this blessing (i.e.: God's bounty and reward). The one who will have the best status in the sight of God and will be nearest to Him is most knowledgeable one of this blessing, who always satisfies with it, remembers it, and expresses its full thanksgiving, loves God for it. Is there anyone who not overwhelmed by His blessing?!! "They consider it a favor to you that they have accepted Islam. Say, "Do not consider your Islam a favor to me. Rather, Allah has conferred favor upon you that He has guided you to the faith, if you should be truthful." " يَمُنُّونَ عَلَيْكَ أَنْ أَسْلَمُواْ قُل لَّا تَمُنُّواْ عَلَيَّ إِسْلَمَكُمْ بَلِ اللَّهُ يَمُنُّ عَلَيْكُمْ أَنْ هَدَلكُمْ لِلْإِيمَٰنِ إِن كُنتُمْ صَٰدِقِينَ" (49:17)

A person's favor to another is considered embarrassing because the two persons are equal. So if someone conferred favor upon another, he might behave arrogantly towards him. And the one who received the favor might see himself in a lower degree than the giver (of favor, and this might hurt him). However, this is not the case with everyone. For example: the prophet (PBUH) has the favor upon this nation. For this, his companions used to say to him: "God and His messenger have the favor upon us". Also, there is no defect regarding one's favor to his child, and it is not embarrassing for his child to accept it. The same, with the master and his servant. Now, how about the Lord of the universe, the one in whose river of blessings and favors people are enjoying, without any return for this. And if their deeds are reasons for what they gained of His favor and bounty, then it is Him who is Most Bountiful to guide them for these deeds, help them and accept these deeds with all their defects from them. "for what you used to do." "بِمَا كُنْتُمْ تَعْمَلُونَ" (16:32)

This is response to the Qadriyyah and Jabriyyah; (the Jabriyyah) who say: there is no connection between the deeds and the recompense. Deeds are not reasons for recompense (reward). The best case is to be just signs (for the reward).

They (Jabriyyah) also said: deeds are not consistent; i.e.: it is not always reward for good deeds and punishment for bad deeds (it can be the opposite). Therefore, the matter relies only on the heavenly will and volition.

The texts nullify the sayings of those people (Jabriyyah), as they also nullify the sayings of the others (Qadriyyah). The proofs of reason (mind) and innate also invalidate the opinions of the two parties. The proofs show clearly for everyone who has a heart and a mind: the validity of the opinion of "Sunnah followers" who are the moderate sect. They confirm the generality of God's will and ability and His creation of people and their deeds. They also affirm His perfect wisdom which involves connecting the reasons with their results, making these reasons connected to their results by both the divine destiny and one's acquisition, and arranging them (reason and results) in the immediate and long-term time.

And each one of these two deviant has left one kind of truth and committed one kind of falsehood, rather many kinds. But God has guided the people of Sunnah to the truth concerning that over which the others had differed, by His permission "And Allah guides whom He wills to a straight path". " وَٱللَّهُ يَهْدِي مَن يَشَآءُ "إِلَىٰ صِرَٰطٍ مُّسْتَقِيمٍ" (2:213). And "That is the bounty of God, which He gives to whom He wills, and Allah is the possessor of great bounty." "ذَٰلِكَ فَضْلُ ٱللَّهِ يُؤْتِيهِ مَن يَشَآءُ وَٱللَّهُ ذُو ٱلْفَضْلِ ٱلْعَظِيمِ"(62:4)

Chapter

The Third Kind are people claiming that: the benefit of worship is to tame the self, to make it ready to acquire (receive) the knowledge thrown to it and to make it leave its powers which likened the powers of monsters and beasts. Because when the self gives up worships, it becomes a kind of the spirits of monsters and beasts. The worships change the habits and usual behaviors of these spirits, and make them mindful, knowledgeable and open to acquire knowledge and sciences. This opinion is held by two groups: the first: those philosophers who are accepting some way prophethood and messages, who believe that: this universe has no beginning, the celestial bodies have not splatted and there is no a free-will maker. The second: those who practiced philosophy from among the Muslim Sufis and approached the philosophers. They claim that worships are only for taming the soul and making it leave this (material) physical world and receive the inspiration and knowledge thrown to it.

There is a group among those people believe that worships are obligatory only for this mentioned reason. So, if the worshipper got this (heavenly inspiration and knowledge), then it is up to him to continue in his obligatory worship or to leave it, and to engage with these inspirations and Knowledge. And there is another group which believes that: it is obligatory for the worshipper to do his usual obligatory worships in a complete way. This group also has two parties. The first: they make worship obligatory in the sake of preserving God's laws and taming the souls. The second: they make it obligatory in the sake of preserving the inspiration and Knowledge and fearing that the soul may return, by giving up worship, to its first status of beast.

This is as far as the people of speech, they have gotten in this regard and the end of their knowledge about the wisdom behind worship and the reasons for which it was legislated. And you rarely find in their books (opinions) other than these three approaches, either collectively or separately.

Chapter

As for The Fourth Kind: they are the Abrahamic-Muhammad sect; the followers of the two (God)'s intimates (Ibrahim and Muhammad), the knowers of God and His wisdom behind His order, His law and His creatures. They are the people of sight regarding God's worship and His Wisdom behind it.

So, the first three sects are concealed from truth because of the void misconceptions and the null bases which they have. In fact, they have nothing beyond these (misconceptions and bases). They rejoiced in what they had of fake knowledge. And they are satisfied with what they invent of imagination. Even if they know that there exists beyond what they have invent that which is more authentic and greater, then they would not satisfy except with what they have of imagination. But even their mind did not reach such true knowledge. They were not guided by the light of prophethood. They did not even feel it to search for and pursuit it. They saw that what they have of this knowledge is better than ignorance and they saw the contradiction and invalidity of what the others have.

These mentioned reasons led them to prefer what they have to anything else. And, in fact, this is the calamity of the sects. The protected only the one to whom God gives protection.

Chapter

Therefore, know that: No one can reach the secret of servitude, its aim and its wisdom except the one who knows the attributes of God, Exalted is He, and he does not disrupt them. The one who knows the meaning of divinity and its essence. The one who knows that the reality of divinity cannot be except for Him. And that worship is the right obligation, impact and result of His Divinity. This worship is connected to divinity as it is the connection between the source of a specific attribute and the attribute itself; as it is the connection between what is known and knowledge, what is afforded and ability, the voices and hearing, kind treatment; and mercy and giving in charity and generosity.

So, how can it be for one who denies and does not know the reality of divinity to know the wisdom behind worships, their goals and aims and the purpose for which they were legislated? How can he know that this worship is the purpose behind their creation, for it they were created, for it the messengers were sent, for it the divine books were revealed and for it the Heaven and Hell were created? The supposition of worship cancelled or disrupted is considered an abuse to God by describing Him with that which is inappropriate for Him. Exalted is He (above all this); The One who has created the heavens and earth with truth. He has not created them heavens and earth in vain. He has neither created man uselessly nor did He leave him neglected .God says: "Then did you think that We created you uselessly and that to Us you would not be returned?"."أَفَحَسِبْتُمْ أَنَّمَا خَلَقْنَاكُمْ عَبَثًا وَأَنَّكُمْ إِلَيْنَا لَا تُرْجَعُونَ" (23:115), i.e.: for nothing and for no wisdom, not for worshipping God and getting recompensation. God stated this in His saying: "And I did not create the jinn and mankind except to worship Me."." "وَمَا خَلَقْتُ ٱلْجِنَّ وَٱلْإِنسَ إِلَّا لِيَعْبُدُونِ" (61:56).

So, the worship is very purpose for which jinn, humans, and the whole creatures were created. God says: "Does man think that he will be left neglected?".(i.e. to no end, without responsibility, or without being returned to the Creator for judgment.)." "أَيَحْسَبُ ٱلْإِنسَٰنُ أَن يُتْرَكَ سُدًى" (75:36). i.e.: neglected. Al-

Shafi'I said: "without being ordered or prevented". Others said: "without being rewarded or punished". The right interpretation is both of the two explanations. Because, reward and punishment are the impact of the order and prevention. The order and prevention are God's request and will to be worshipped. And the reality of worship is to obey and comply with the instructions. God says: "and they give thought to the creation of the heavens and the earth, [saying], "Our Lord, You did not create this aimlessly; exalted are You [above such a thing]; then protect us from the punishment of the Fire"" وَيَتَفَكَّرُونَ فِي خَلْقِ ٱلسَّمَٰوَٰتِ وَٱلْأَرْضِ رَبَّنَا مَا خَلَقْتَ هَٰذَا بَٰطِلًا سُبْحَٰنَكَ فَقِنَا عَذَابَ ٱلنَّارِ" (3:191).

And He also says: "And We have not created the heavens and earth and that between them except in truth". "وَمَا خَلَقْنَا ٱلسَّمَٰوَٰتِ وَٱلْأَرْضَ وَمَا بَيْنَهُمَآ إِلَّا بِٱلْحَقِّ" . (15: 85). In addition, "And Allah created the heavens and earth in truth and so that every soul may be recompensed for what it has earned". . "وَخَلَقَ ٱللَّهُ ٱلسَّمَٰوَٰتِ وَٱلْأَرْضَ بِٱلْحَقِّ وَلِتُجْزَىٰ كُلُّ نَفْسٍ بِمَا كَسَبَتْ" (45:22). So, He tells us that He has created the heavens and earth by truth which includes His order and prevention and His reward and punishment.

Hence, if the heavens and earth and what is in-between were created for this; which is the aim of creation, then how can be said that: there is no reason behind this creation or an intended wisdom for it?! Or how can be said it is worship only for hiring people in order that they do not be embarrassed or ashamed when taking their reward for no return?! Or it is just for making the souls ready for the mental knowledge and taming them to contravene the habits of beasts?

So, let the one of mind ponder over (and differentiate between) these sayings and what is proven by the clear texts of revelation. He will find out that the people of these opinions have not appraised God with true appraisal, nor do they know him truly.

God, Exalted is He, have created the creatures to worship Him. The worship includes the finer perfection of love, with submission to Him and compliance with His order.

The origin of worship is to love God. For God is not beloved because of someone else, rather others are beloved for Him and because of Him, as we like His prophets, His messengers, His angels and His allies. Our love for them is of the perfection of our love for Him, as it is the case with the one who takes others than God as equal to Him. They love them as they (should) love God.

And if love for God is the reality of worship and its secret, as mentioned, then it cannot be reached, or exist except by following His order and refraining from His prohibitions. For this reason, God made following the messenger as a sign for it, and a proof for the one who claims God's love. God says: "Say, [O

Muhammad], "If you should love God, then follow me, [so] God will love you"..﴿قُلْ إِن كُنتُمْ تُحِبُّونَ ٱللَّهَ فَٱتَّبِعُونِي يُحْبِبْكُمُ ٱللَّهُ﴾"(3:31). So, He made following the messenger is a condition for their love for God and a condition for them to be loved by God. The conditioned cannot be existed without the existence and achieving of the condition. Hence, we know that God's love cannot be existed in the case that following the Messenger does not exist. So, their love for God is negated because their following the messenger is negated. If they do not follow the Prophet, they will lose God's love. Therefore, their love for God and God's love for them are impossible to be proven or exist without following His Messenger.

This indicated that "following the Messenger" is: to love God and His Messenger and to obey his orders. Rather, this is not enough to be a true worshipper except by loving God and His Messenger more than anyone else. So, one must have nothing which is more loved than God and His messenger. God, Exalted is He, says: "Say, [O Muhammad], "If your fathers, your sons, your brothers, your wives, your relatives, wealth which you have obtained, commerce wherein you fear decline, and dwellings with which you are pleased are more beloved to you than God and His Messenger and jihad [i.e., striving] in His cause, then wait until God executes His command. And God does not guide the defiantly disobedient people." " قُلْ إِن كَانَ ءَابَآؤُكُمْ وَأَبْنَآؤُكُمْ وَإِخْوَٰنُكُمْ وَأَزْوَٰجُكُمْ وَعَشِيرَتُكُمْ وَأَمْوَٰلٌ ٱقْتَرَفْتُمُوهَا وَتِجَٰرَةٌ تَخْشَوْنَ كَسَادَهَا وَمَسَٰكِنُ تَرْضَوْنَهَآ أَحَبَّ إِلَيْكُم مِّنَ ٱللَّهِ وَرَسُولِهِۦ وَجِهَادٍ فِي سَبِيلِهِۦ فَتَرَبَّصُوا۟ حَتَّىٰ يَأْتِيَ ٱللَّهُ بِأَمْرِهِۦ وَٱللَّهُ لَا يَهْدِي ٱلْقَوْمَ ٱلْفَٰسِقِينَ " (9:24)

So, whoever gives precedence for obedience of one of those over God's and His Messenger's obedience, the saying of one of them over the saying of God and His messenger, then he is not one of those who ardently love God and His messenger. And (even) if he said this by his tongue, then it would be a lie and telling something against the truth and reality. The same case is the one who gave priority to someone's judgment over God's and His messenger judgment. But this may become a little dicey for someone who gives priority for a person's saying, judgment, obedience or satisfaction (over God's and His messenger's), thinking that this person say not, order not and judge not but according to the saying of the Prophet (PBUH). So, he obeys him, refers legislation to him and accepts (also all) his sayings. Then, this person is excused if he has no ability (to have knowledge) except this. But if he had the ability to reach the prophet's sayings, and know that someone else is more deserving to be followed in every matter or just in specific matters than the first one, but he did not care about the Messenger or the one who is more deserving to be followed, then this person is lost. And if he went to punish and humiliate the one who has disagreed with him and refused to follow his master, then he is among the unjust transgressors. And Indeed, God has already set for everything a decreed extent.

Chapter

And He God has built (It is You we worship إِيَّاكَ نَعْبُدُ) upon four pillars (bases): implementing what God and His messenger love and satisfy which are: worships by tongue and heart, the deeds of the heart and organs.

Therefore, worship is: a name includes these four ranks. So, the people of (It is You we worship إِيَّاكَ نَعْبُدُ) are its real owners.

The worship of the heart is: believing in God, Exalted is He, and His 99 names and attributes, His angels and His meeting with us) on the tongue of His messengers.

The worship of the tongue is: to tell the best about Him, to call people to worship Him, to defend Him (His religion), to explain and refute the heresies against Him, to establish His remembrance and spread His orders.

The worship of the heart is: to love Him, to rely upon him, to repent to Him, to fear from Him, to surrender to Him, to make your religion sincere to Him, to be satisfied with and about Him, to love for His sake, to hate for His sake, ... and many other heart worships which are more obligatory than the organs worships. In fact, the worships of organs without the heart worships are of no benefit or no much benefit.

Additionally, the worships of organs are like: prayer, jihad (fighting for the sake of God), walking to attend Friday prayer and the congregational prayers, helping the disabled, presenting kindness to people and so on and so forth.

Therefore, (It is You we worship إِيَّاكَ نَعْبُدُ) means: to stick to the rulings of these four bases and to admit them. And (and You we ask for help (وَإِيَّاكَ نَسْتَعِينُ means: to ask God to give us power, help and success to accomplish them. And (Guide us to the straight path...

(ٱهْدِنَا ٱلصِّرَٰطَ ٱلْمُسْتَقِيمَ)includes the definitions of these two points in details as well as asking God to grant us the motivation to establish both of them and to make us follow the way of the true walkers to God.

Chapter

All of the messengers call for (It is You we worship and You we ask for help إِيَّاكَ نَعْبُدُ وَإِيَّاكَ نَسْتَعِينُ). All of them called for the oneness of God and devoting worship for Him, from the first to the last one of them. Noah (PBUH) said to his people: "worship God; you have no deity other than Him.""ٱعْبُدُوا۟ ٱللَّهَ مَا لَكُم مِّنْ إِلَٰهٍ غَيْرُهُ"..

(7: 59). The same (was said) by Hud, Salih and Shu'aib (PBUH) and (also) Abraham (PBUH). God says: " And We certainly sent into every nation a messenger, [saying], "Worship God and avoid Taghut.".." (16:36). "وَلَقَدْ بَعَثْنَا فِي كُلِّ أُمَّةٍ رَّسُولًا أَنِ ٱعْبُدُواْ ٱللَّهَ وَٱجْتَنِبُواْ ٱلطَّـٰغُوتَ" And He says: "And We sent not before you any messenger except We revealed to him that, "There is no deity except Me, so worship Me".." "وَمَآ أَرْسَلْنَا مِن قَبْلِكَ مِن رَّسُولٍ إِلَّا نُوحِيٓ إِلَيْهِ أَنَّهُ لَآ إِلَـٰهَ إِلَّآ أَنَا۠ فَٱعْبُدُونِ" (21:25). God, Exalted is He, also says: "O messengers: eat from the good foods and work righteousness. Indeed I, of what you do, am Knowing. And indeed this, your religion, is one religion, and I am your Lord, so fear Me." " يَـٰٓأَيُّهَا ٱلرُّسُلُ كُلُواْ مِنَ ٱلطَّيِّبَـٰتِ وَٱعْمَلُواْ صَـٰلِحًا إِنِّي بِمَا تَعْمَلُونَ عَلِيمٌ وَإِنَّ هَـٰذِهِۦٓ أُمَّتُكُمْ أُمَّةً وَٰحِدَةً وَأَنَا۠ رَبُّكُمْ فَٱتَّقُونِ" (23:51-52).

Chapter

God, Exalted is He, has made the attribute of servitude the attribute of those who are most perfect among His mankind and the nearest to Him. God says: "Never would the Messiah disdain to be a servant of God, nor would the angels near [to Him]. And whoever disdains His worship and is arrogant –then, He will gather them to Himself all together" " لَّن يَسْتَنكِفَ ٱلْمَسِيحُ أَن يَكُونَ عَبْدًا لِّلَّهِ وَلَا ٱلْمَلَـٰٓئِكَةُ ٱلْمُقَرَّبُونَ وَمَن يَسْتَنكِفْ عَنْ عِبَادَتِهِۦ وَيَسْتَكْبِرْ فَسَيَحْشُرُهُمْ إِلَيْهِ جَمِيعًا" (4:17). He also says: "Indeed, those who are near your Lord [i.e., the angels] are not prevented by arrogance from His worship, and they exalt Him, and to Him they prostrate." " إِنَّ ٱلَّذِينَ عِندَ رَبِّكَ لَا

"يَسْتَكْبِرُونَ عَنْ عِبَادَتِهِ وَيُسَبِّحُونَهُ وَلَهُ يَسْجُدُونَ" (7:206). And this indicates that the complete pause in Surah of Alanbiaa', is "To Him belongs whoever is in the heavens and the earth.". "وَلَهُ مَن فِي ٱلسَّمَٰوَٰتِ وَٱلْأَرْضِ". (21:19) (to pause) here, then to begin with "And those near Him [i.e., the angels] are not prevented by arrogance from His worship, nor do they tire. They exalt [Him] night and day [and] do not slacken.". " وَمَنْ عِندَهُ لَا يَسْتَكْبِرُونَ عَنْ عِبَادَتِهِ وَلَا يَسْتَحْسِرُونَ. يُسَبِّحُونَ. "ٱلَّيْلَ وَٱلنَّهَارَ لَا يَفْتُرُونَ".....(21:19-20). Because they are two complete dependent sentences.

This means: to Him belongs what is in the heavens and what is on the earth including servants and kingdoms. And God also says: "A spring of which the [righteous] servants of God will drink; they will make it gush forth in force [and abundance].". ("عَيْنًا يَشْرَبُ بِهَا عِبَادُ ٱللَّهِ يُفَجِّرُونَهَا تَفْجِيرًا" (76:6) and He also says: "and remember Our servant, David,". "وَٱذْكُرْ عَبْدَنَا دَاوُدَ" (38:17), moreover "and remember Our servant Job", " وَٱذْكُرْ عَبْدَنَا أَيُّوبَ"(38:41), and "and remember Our servants, Abraham, Isaac and Jacob" "وَٱذْكُرْ عِبَادَنَا إِبْرَٰهِيمَ وَإِسْحَٰقَ وَيَعْقُوبَ" (38:45), and He says about Solomon "indeed he was one repeatedly turning back [to God]". "نِعْمَ ٱلْعَبْدُ إِنَّهُ أَوَّابٌ" (38:30), and He says about the Christ: "He [i.e., Jesus] was not but a servant upon whom We bestowed favor", "إِنْ هُوَ إِلَّا عَبْدٌ أَنْعَمْنَا عَلَيْهِ" (43:59), so He made His purpose and aim (behind the creation of mankind) is servitude (to be worshipped) not divinity – as His enemies of Christians say, and He described the most honored one among His mankind who will be in the highest degree with the description of servitude)and this is the best attribute and status as for the man, so He says "and if you are in doubt about what We have sent down [i.e., the Quran] upon Our Servant [i.e., Prophet Muhammad" " وَإِن كُنتُمْ فِي رَيْبٍ مِّمَّا نَزَّلْنَا عَلَىٰ عَبْدِنَا" (2:23), and He, Most honored, says : "Blessed is He who sent down the Criterion upon His Servant" " تَبَارَكَ ٱلَّذِي نَزَّلَ ٱلْفُرْقَانَ عَلَىٰ عَبْدِهِ" (25:1), and "[All] praise is [due] to God, who has sent down upon His Servant [Muhammad (r)] the Book" "ٱلْحَمْدُ لِلَّهِ ٱلَّذِي أَنزَلَ عَلَىٰ عَبْدِهِ ٱلْكِتَٰبَ" (18:1). So, He described him Mohammad with the description of servitude in the regard of revealing the book unto him and in the regard of challenging the disbelievers of Mecca, to bring something like the Quran.

And He says: "And that when the Servant [i.e., Prophet] of God stood up supplicating Him, they almost became about him a compacted mass.", "وَأَنَّهُ لَمَّا قَامَ عَبْدُ ٱللَّهِ يَدْعُوهُ كَادُوا۟ يَكُونُونَ عَلَيْهِ لِبَدًا" (72:19), He describes him with servitude in the regard of calling for worshipping Him. And He says "is He who took His Servant [i.e., Prophet Muhammad] by night" "سُبْحَٰنَ ٱلَّذِي أَسْرَىٰ بِعَبْدِهِ لَيْلًا" (17:1), He describes him with servitude in the position of ascension to Him (Night Journey to the Heaven). And it is narrated in the Sahih that the prophet (PBUH) said: "Do not exceed in praising me as the Christians over-praised (Jesus) (That they made him the son of God.) I am a bondsman of God, therefore, call me the bondsman of God and His Rasul (messenger)". And in the (another) narration "I am a servant, eat as a servant eats and sit as a servant sits". And it is narrated in the Sahih of Albukhary that Abdullah ibn Amr ibn Alas) said: I have read in the Torah the description of Mohammad (PBUH) : "Mohammad is the messenger of God, You are my slave and My Apostle, and I have named you Al-Mutawakkil (one who depends upon God). You are neither hard-hearted nor of fierce character, nor one who shouts in the markets. You do not return evil for evil, but excuse and forgive."

God has granted the absolute good tidings only for his servants, so He says: "So give good tidings to My servants Who listen to speech and follow the best of it", " فَبَشِّرْ عِبَادِ ٱلَّذِينَ يَسْتَمِعُونَ ٱلْقَوْلَ فَيَتَّبِعُونَ أَحْسَنَهُ " (39:17-18). And He has made the absolute security only for them, He says; "[To whom God will say], "O My servants, no fear will there be concerning you this Day, nor will you grieve, [You] who believed in Our verses and were Muslims." "يَٰعِبَادِ لَا خَوْفٌ عَلَيْكُمُ ٱلْيَوْمَ وَلَآ أَنتُمْ تَحْزَنُونَ ٱلَّذِينَ ءَامَنُواْ بِـَٔايَٰتِنَا وَكَانُواْ مُسْلِمِينَ" (43:68-69). He has made no power or authority for Satan over them, and made the Satan's authority only be over those who follow him. God says: "Indeed, My servants – no authority will you have over them, except those who follow you of the deviators" سُلْطَنٌ إِلَّا مَنِ ٱتَّبَعَكَ مِنَ ٱلْغَاوِين" (15:42), and He says: "إِنَّ عِبَادِي لَيْسَ لَكَ عَلَيْهِمْ "indeed, there is for him no authority over those who have believed and rely upon their Lord. His authority is only over those who take him as an ally and those who through him associate others with God إِنَّهُ لَيْسَ لَهُ سُلْطَنٌ عَلَى ٱلَّذِينَ ءَامَنُواْ وَعَلَىٰ رَبِّهِمْ يَتَوَكَّلُون إِنَّمَا سُلْطَنُهُ عَلَى ٱلَّذِينَ يَتَوَلَّوْنَهُ وَٱلَّذِينَ هُم بِهِۦ مُشْرِكُون" " (16:99-100). And the prophet (PBUH) has ranked the Ihsan of servitude in the best rank of religion, so he (PBUH) said in the hadeeth of Gabriel when the later asked him about (the meaning of) 'Ihsan': "Ihsan is to worship God as if you see Him, and if you do not see Him, then take it for granted that God sees you.

Chapter

For the requirement of adhering to "It is You we worship and You we ask for help." " إِيَّاكَ نَعْبُدُ وَإِيَّاكَ نَسْتَعِينُ " for every slave until death

God says to His messenger: "And worship your Lord until there comes to you the certainty [i.e., death].", وَٱعْبُدْ رَبَّكَ حَتَّىٰ يَأْتِيَكَ ٱلْيَقِينُ (15:99), and the people of the Hell will say: "And we used to deny the Day of Recompense Until there came to us the certainty [i.e., death]." " وكنا نُكَذِّبُ بِيَوْمِ ٱلدِّينِ حَتَّىٰ أَتَىٰنَا ٱلْيَقِينُ " (74:46-47), and the word "Certainty" here according to most of Qur'an interpretation scholars means the death.

Moreover, it is narrated in the Sahih, in the story of Othman's ibn Madhoun death (may God be pleased with him) that the prophet (PBUH) said: "As for Othman, the 'Yaqin' has come to him from his Lord", i.e. death and what accompanies it. So a servant should never cease worshipping as long as he is still in this life of mandate. Rather, he has another worship in the life of Barzakh , when the two angles asks him "who is the one you used to worship – in the worldly life-? And what are you saying concerning the messenger of God PBUH?, and they will seek answers from him. And he has another worship on the doomsday, on the day- when God will call everyone to prostrate for Him, so the believers will prostrate. But, disbelievers and hypocrites will not be capable of prostrating. And as soon as all people enter the home of reward or punishment (Heaven and Hell), obligations (assignment: orders and prohibitions) there will come to an end.

And this who claims that when he reaches a certain position, concerning his relation with God, the worships and obligations will be cancelled, so he has not to do them then, he a heretic and a disbeliever. In fact he reached no position but the position of disbelief.

On the contrary, the more the servant proceeds in the ranks of servitude, the greater his servitude and worship to God become, and the greater his obligations become, compared to the less worshipper. For this reason, we can see that the obligations upon the Messenger of God (PBUH) rather, upon all messengers, are greater than the obligations of their nations. And the obligations upon (those greater five among messengers, who are: Abraham, Noah, Moses, Jesus and Mohammad) are more than these upon the others.

CHAPTER 13

Dividing Servitude into General & Special

Servitude is of two kinds: General & Special.

The general servitude is: the servitude of the dwellers of the heavens and earth d, all of them; the righteous and the wicked, the believer and the disbeliever. This is the servitude of oppression and dominance. God says: "And they say, "The Most Merciful has taken [for Himself] a son. You have done an atrocious thing. The heavens almost rupture therefrom and the earth splits open and the mountains collapse in devastation. That they attribute to the Most Merciful a son. And it is not appropriate for the Most Merciful that He should take a son. There is no one in the heavens and earth but that he comes to the Most Merciful as a servant. " وَقَالُواْ ٱتَّخَذَ ٱلرَّحْمَٰنُ وَلَدًا لَّقَدْ جِئْتُمْ شَيْئًا إِدًّا تَكَادُ ٱلسَّمَٰوَٰتُ يَتَفَطَّرْنَ مِنْهُ

وَتَنشَقُّ ٱلْأَرْضُ وَتَخِرُّ ٱلْجِبَالُ هَدًّا أَن دَعَوْا لِلرَّحْمَٰنِ وَلَدًا وَمَا يَنۢبَغِي لِلرَّحْمَٰنِ أَن يَتَّخِذَ وَلَدًا إِن (19:88-93), this includes "كُلُّ مَن فِي ٱلسَّمَٰوَٰتِ وَٱلْأَرْضِ إِلَّا ءَاتِي ٱلرَّحْمَٰنِ عَبْدًا all of them; the believer and the disbeliever.

And He, the Exalted, says: "And [mention] the Day He will gather them and that which they worship besides God and will say, "Did you mislead these, My servants" " وَيَوْمَ يَحْشُرُهُمْ وَمَا يَعْبُدُونَ ...""مِن دُونِ ٱللَّهِ فَيَقُولُ ءَأَنتُمْ أَضْلَلْتُمْ عِبَادِي هَٰؤُلَآءِ (25:17). Although their misguidance, He called them 'His servants' but it is an appellation restricted with the signal. As for the –unrestricted- absolute appellation, it does not come to describe except those people of the second type, as we are going to explain later…

Moreover, He says: "Say, "O God, Creator of the heavens and the earth, Knower of the unseen and the witnessed, You will judge between your servants concerning that over which they used to differ" " قُلِ ٱللَّهُمَّ فَاطِرَ ٱلسَّمَٰوَٰتِ وَٱلْأَرْضِ عَٰلِمَ ٱلْغَيْبِ وَٱلشَّهَٰدَةِ أَنتَ تَحْكُمُ بَيْنَ ...""عِبَادِكَ فِي مَا كَانُوا فِيهِ يَخْتَلِفُونَ (39:46). And: "And God wants no injustice for [His] servants", "وَمَا ٱللَّهُ يُرِيدُ ظُلْمًا لِّلْعِبَادِ" (40:31), and He says: "Indeed, God has judged between the servants", " إِنَّ ٱللَّهَ قَدْ حَكَمَ بَيْنَ ٱلْعِبَادِ"(40:48), this deals with both of them; the general and special servitude.

As for the second type: it is the servitude of obedience, love and following the orders. God the Exalted says: "O My servants, no fear will there be concerning you this Day, nor will you grieve," " يُعِبَادِ لَا خَوَفٌ عَلَيْكُمُ ٱلْيَوْمَ وَلَا أَنتُمْ تَحْزَنُونَ " (43: 68). And He says: "So give good tidings to My servants Who listen to speech and follow the best of it", "فَبَشِّرْ عِبَادِ ٱلَّذِينَ يَسْتَمِعُونَ ٱلْقَوْلَ فَيَتَّبِعُونَ أَحْسَنَهُ" (39:17-18). "And the servants of the Most Merciful are those who walk upon the earth easily, and when the ignorant address them [harshly], they say [words of] peace" " وَعِبَادُ ٱلرَّحْمَٰنِ ٱلَّذِينَ يَمْشُونَ عَلَى ٱلْأَرْضِ هَوْنًا وَإِذَا خَاطَبَهُمُ ٱلْجَٰهِلُونَ قَالُوا سَلَٰمًا"...(25:63). And He says about Satan: "and I will mislead them all. Except, among them, Your chosen servants." "وَلَأُغْوِيَنَّهُمْ أَجْمَعِينَ إِلَّا عِبَادَكَ مِنْهُمُ ٱلْمُخْلَصِينَ" (15:39-40), so God says about them: "Indeed, My servants – no authority will you have over them" "إِنَّ عِبَادِي لَيْسَ لَكَ عَلَيْهِمْ سُلْطَٰنٌ"...(15:42). There-fore, the whole mankind are His servants of servitude and slavery, while those people of His obedience and loyalty are His servants of divinity).

As for the describing His servants of servitude "with the word servants": it is not used (in the Quran) except in one of these five ways: the first; as indefinite word, as His saying: "There is no one in the heavens and earth but that he comes to the Most Merciful as a servant.", "إِن كُلُّ مَن فِي ٱلسَّمَٰوَٰتِ وَٱلْأَرْضِ إِلَّا ءَاتِي ٱلرَّحْمَٰنِ عَبْدًا"(19:92). The second: as definite word as His saying, "And God wants no injustice for [His] servants", "وَمَا ٱللَّهُ يُرِيدُ ظُلْمًا لِّلْعِبَادِ" (40:31), and His saying: "Indeed, God has judged between the servants", " إِنَّ ٱللَّهَ قَدْ حَكَمَ بَيْنَ ٱلْعِبَادِ"(40:48). The third: as demonstrative pronoun; as His saying, "Did you mislead these, My servants" " ءَأَنتُمْ أَضْلَلْتُمْ عِبَادِي هَٰؤُلَآءِ"... (25:17). The fourth: to be mentioned generally included in His addressing to all His servants; like His saying "You will judge between your servants concerning that over which they used to differ" "أَنتَ تَحْكُمُ بَيْنَ عِبَادِكَ فِي مَا كَانُوا۟ فِيهِ يَخْتَلِفُونَ"... (39:46). The fifth: attributed to and described with their deeds; like His saying "Say, "O My servants who have transgressed against themselves [by sinning], do not despair of the mercy of God", " قُلْ يَٰعِبَادِيَ ٱلَّذِينَ أَسْرَفُوا۟ عَلَىٰ أَنفُسِهِمْ لَا تَقْنَطُوا۟ مِن رَّحْمَةِ ٱللَّهِ"... (39:53). It may be said: He called them His servants if they do not despair of His mercy, repented and returned back to Him and followed the best of what was revealed to them by their Lord, so they will be among His servants of divinity and obedience.

Here is the reason why the servitude is divided into two categories: special and general, because this word in its origin means: humiliation and submission. But the difference is that God allies are humiliated and submitted to Him by their own, willingly, accepting His orders and prohibitions, while His enemies are submitted to him by force and coercion.

As servitude is divided into special and general, devotion (also) is divided into special and general, and prostration is the same. God says about the special devotion "Is one who is devoutly obedient during periods of the night, prostrating and standing [in prayer], fearing the Hereafter and hoping for the mercy of his Lord" " أَمَّنْ هُوَ قَـٰنِتٌ ءَانَآءَ ٱلَّيْلِ سَاجِدًا وَقَآئِمًا يَحْذَرُ ٱلْءَاخِرَةَ وَيَرْجُواْ رَحْمَةَ رَبِّهِۦٓ " (39:9), and He says about Marry "and she was of the devoutly obedient (people)" " ...وَكَانَتْ مِنَ ٱلْقَـٰنِتِينَ"(66:12), and this kind has many examples in the Quran. And He says about the general devotion "And to Him belongs whoever is in the heavens and earth. All are to Him devoutly obedient.", " وَلَهُۥ مَن فِي ٱلسَّمَـٰوَٰتِ وَٱلْأَرْضِۖ كُلٌّ لَّهُۥ قَـٰنِتُونَ"...(30:26), i.e.: subjected to and humiliated. And He says about the special prostration " Indeed, those who are near your Lord [i.e., the angels] are not prevented by arrogance from His worship, and they exalt Him, and to Him they prostrate" "إِنَّ ٱلَّذِينَ عِندَ رَبِّكَ لَا يَسْتَكْبِرُونَ عَنْ عِبَادَتِهِۦ وَيُسَبِّحُونَهُۥ وَلَهُۥ يَسْجُدُونَ"...(7:206), and He says "When the verses of the Most Merciful were recited to them, they fell in prostration and weeping" " إِذَا تُتْلَىٰ عَلَيْهِمْ ءَايَـٰتُ ٱلرَّحْمَـٰنِ خَرُّواْ سُجَّدًا وَبُكِيًّا"...(19:58)...and many examples for this in the Quran.

And He says about the general prostration "And to Allāh prostrates whoever is within the heavens and the earth, willingly or by compulsion, and their shadows [as well] in the mornings and the afternoons" " وَلِلَّهِ يَسْجُدُ مَن فِي ٱلسَّمَـٰوَٰتِ وَٱلْأَرْضِ طَوْعًا وَكَرْهًا وَظِلَـٰلُهُم بِٱلْغُدُوِّ وَٱلْءَاصَالِ"...(13:15). So this kind of prostration is not like that mentioned in "Do you not see [i.e., know] that to Allāh prostrates whoever is in the heavens and whoever is on the earth and the sun, the moon, the stars, the mountains, the trees, the moving creatures and many of the people?" " أَلَمْ تَرَ أَنَّ ٱللَّهَ يَسْجُدُ لَهُ مَن فِي ٱلسَّمَٰوَٰتِ وَمَن فِي ٱلْأَرْضِ وَٱلشَّمْسُ وَٱلْقَمَرُ وَٱلنُّجُومُ وَٱلْجِبَالُ وَٱلشَّجَرُ وَٱلدَّوَآبُّ وَكَثِيرٌ مِّنَ ٱلنَّاسِ "(22:18). Here, He made prostration special for many of people, but He made it general for all people in the verse mentioned in Surah of Alnahl "And to Allāh prostrates whatever is in the heavens and whatever is on the earth of creatures, and the angels [as well]," "وَلِلَّهِ يَسْجُدُ مَا فِي ٱلسَّمَٰوَٰتِ وَمَا فِي ٱلْأَرْضِ مِن دَآبَّةٍ وَٱلْمَلَٰئِكَةُ "...(16:49), which is the prostration of humiliation and submission, because everyone is subjected to His Lordship, humiliated to His Dignity and forced under His Dominion.

Chapter

**Concerning the ranks of (it is you we worship إِيَّاكَ نَعْبُدُ)
regarding both knowledge and work**

Servitude, regarding both knowledge and work, has many ranks. For knowledge, it has two ranks; the knowledge of God, and the knowledge of His religion.

As for the Knowledge of God, it is of five ranks: to know His Being, His attributes, His deeds, His names and to declare His perfection and to exalt His being far from all that is not appropriate Him.

And the knowledge of His religion is of two ranks: the first is: to know his legal orders which is the straight path that access (us) to Him.

The second is: to know His recompense which includes His reward and punishment, and the knowledge of His angels, His books and His messengers.

Regarding work (the practical ranks), it has two ranks: this of the companions of the right, and that for forerunners who are near to God.

The rank of the companions of the right: is to do the obligations and to avoid the forbidden, but they also consumed the permissible act, some of disliked acts and they left some recommended things.

The rank of those forerunners who are near to God is: to perform the obligations and recommended acts, to avoid the forbidden and disliked things, to become ascetic regarding anything cannot benefit in the Afterlife and to refrain from anything may harm the Afterlife. Among those are some specials, for them the permissible things (like eating, sleeping…) became with intention as worship and devotion, so they will get reward even for these permissible things. Hence, for those there are no permissible things which are of no account, that can be done with no reward or punishment), nay every deed (in life) for those is of reward.

Chapter

Worshipping is based on 15 rules; by following them you fulfill the worshipping integration. Worshipping is by heart, tongue and organs, each has its worships. The provisions of the worshipping are five: obligatory, desirable, unlawful, undesirable and allowed, applied for the heart, the tongue and the organs.

The obligation towards the heart is controverted. Agreed obligations are like sincerity, trust in God, amity, patience, reliance, fear, hope, assent and intention of the worshipping.

Intention of worshipping includes two sections: one is favoring the religious cults to traditions, the other is favoring some of the cults to others.

Sincerity means that you worship only one God.

The nation agreed that these deeds are obligatorily performed by heart. Each of these heart obligations has two sides: one is obligatory, the rank of the companions of the right, the other is desirable, it is the rank of those who are near to God.

Patience is also an obligation with the consent of the whole nation and it also has two sides: one is obligatory and the other is desirable. Patience is mentioned in Qur'an more than ninety times.

However, the contentedness is controverted. Those who obligate it argue that dissatisfaction is forbidden. They are supported by such narration: "whoever has no patience for affliction I send and object my judgment, shall worship another lord". Those who deem contentedness is desirable depend that such concept is not referred to in Qur'an or Sunnah.

Unlike patience which is commanded in many verses in the Quran. God also ordered his worshippers to be reliable upon Him in many verses, He says: "If you have believed in God, then rely upon Him, if you should be Muslims."" إِن كُنتُمْ آمَنتُم بِاللَّـهِ فَعَلَيْهِ تَوَكَّلُوا إِن كُنتُم مُّسْلِمِينَ" (10:84), also He commanded worshippers to be sincere to Him as He says: "And they were not commanded except to worship God, [being] sincere to Him in religion, inclining to truth","وَمَا أُمِرُوا إِلَّا لِيَعْبُدُوا اللَّـهَ مُخْلِصِينَ لَهُ الدِّينَ حُنَفَاءَ" (98:5), be afraid of Him; He says: "So fear them not, but fear Me, if you are [indeed] believers." " "فَلَا تَخَافُوهُمْ وَخَافُونِ إِن كُنتُم مُّؤْمِنِينَ(3:175), also He commanded the truth; He says: "O you who have believed, fear God and be with those who are true." " مَعَ وَكُونُوا اللَّـهَ اتَّقُوا آمَنُوا الَّذِينَ أَيُّهَا يَا الصَّادِقِينَ" (9:119), also He commanded the amity which is the highest obligation.

Contentedness is mentioned in Quran via praising those who are content not as a command. The Prophet (PBUH) said: "If you can be very content, it is good, if not, the patience is the best".

People are classified regarding contentedness with the fate into three; the contentedness, the highest degree; dissatisfaction, the lowest degree; and the patience without contentedness, the intermediate. The first class is for those who has been already near to God, the third class is for the moderate persons and the second class is for the evil doers.

Some scholars refused the existence of contentedness together with

pain as they are contradicting each other and thought they negate each other, but others see that pain does not negate the contentedness. This contradiction regarding the contentedness is only towards His universal destiny but regarding the God, it is agreed upon its obligation; the man is not considered a Muslim except being content with the God, as the unique lord, Islam and Prophet Mohammed (PBUH).

Another example, there is a disagreement among scholars regarding submissiveness during performing the prayers, there are two opinions regarding performing the prayers again for those Satan whispered to them in the prayers. Some scholars said that the prayers must be performed again but others negate that. Those negaters depend on the Messenger's narration, regarding forgetting, as he recommended performing two prostrations of forgetfulness not repeating the prayer. He said: "The Satan comes to any one of you while he is praying and comes between him and his soul, until he does not know whether he has added something or omitted something. If that happens, then he should prostrate twice before the Salam, then he should say the Salam."

The significance is that the deeds - obligatory and desirable - are by heart so that the heart can be the worshipper; worship has to be done by both heart and organs, not only by organs.

The unlawful deeds are like haughtiness, hypocrisy, arrogance, envy, negligence, two-facedness; they are two kinds: atheism and sin.

Atheism is like doubt, two-facedness, polytheism and so on. The are two kinds of the sin: major and minor sins.

Major sins are like hypocrisy, arrogance, haughtiness, despair of mercy of God, despair not relief from God, joy with Muslims harms, gloating over their afflictions, liking the spread of immorality, envy them because of bounty God bestowed them, hoping the cessation of blessings and such sins that are more banned than adultery, drinking alcohol and other known major sins. Neither heart nor body shall be purified unless avoiding the same sins and sticking to repentance.

These sins arise because the heart ignores worshipping. The sins swing between majority and minority, according to its strength, degree and so on.

The minor sins are like the lust for performing unlawful deeds. Lust degree varies according to the desired deeds; lust for atheism and polytheism is atheism, the lust for heretics is immoral action and the lust for major sins is a sin. If the man abandoned doing the sin while he can commit it, he is rewarded but if he abandoned doing it because he cannot commit it after exerting his utmost efforts, he deserves the punishment of the doer. So, the Prophet (PBUH) said: "If two Muslims confront each other with swords, and one kills the other, they will both be in Hell." It was said: "O Messenger of Allah, (we understand about) the killer, but what about the one who is killed?" He said: "He wanted to kill his companion." So, he is rewarded and punished as the same as the doer.

Tongue worship

For the five provisions of the tongue worships, the obligatory worships are like uttering the declarations of faith, reciting some of Quran during prayers, uttering the obligatory reminder of the prayers...etc.

Desirable worships are like reciting Quran, uttering some reminders, studying and so on.

Unlawful deeds are saying what annoying the God and His Messenger like promoting the heretics, cursing, false accusation of adultery, lying, perjury and so on. Undesirable worships are talking about things that it is better not talking about but there is no punishment. There some contradicted views regarding that; some said that any speech deserves punishment and accounting and some said it may be accounted according to the benefit or the harm it causes.

Organs' worship

The worship of the organs is based on fifty-five provisions: senses are five, each has five worships.

Regarding hearing: It is obligatory to listen and hear what God and His messenger commanded like hearing about Islam and its pillars, recitation of Quran and religious speeches. It is unlawful to hear to atheism and heretics except for a possible benefit, listening to others' secrets, and so on. It is desirable to hear and listen to knowledge circles, recitation of Quran and what God likes, there is no obligation, but it is undesirable to hear and listen to the contrary of that, there is no accounting.

The obligatory seeing is like looking at Quran and knowledge books, and looking to discriminate between the lawful and the unlawful and so on. Unlawful seeing is like looking at unlawful women with lust. The desirable seeing is like looking at Quran and knowledge books and pondering over the creation of God. It is undesirable to curiously look at non-beneficial matters. It is allowed to look at anything that is not forbidden or harmful.

The obligatory taste is like eating and drinking when it is necessary to avoid death, if food and drink is abandoned till death, one is sinful. The same also applies to the medicine.

Unlawful taste is like drinking alcohol and poison; and tasting food during fasting. Undesirable is like tasting doubtful food, eating too much, eating from food of the person who is surprised by your coming and so on. Desirable taste is by eating what helps you obeying God, eating together with the guest. Some scholars said that it is obligatory to eat from the food of the marriage banquet. But the allowed taste is by tasting any lawful things.

Regarding smelling, the obligatory is to smell something to know if it is lawful or unlawful; is this thing good or bad? And if this is harmful or beneficial. Unlawful smelling is when you smell perfume while in pilgrimage or the perfume of the unlawful women, lest one shall be fascinated. The desirable smelling is like smelling what help you obey God, strengthen the senses and please your soul to work and learn. The undesirable smelling is like smelling the perfume of the sinners and doers of the doubtful sins and so on. But the allowed smelling is by smelling what God allows.

Regarding the touching sense, the obligatory touching is like touching the wife during sexual intercourse. The unlawful touching is like touching the unlawful women. The desirable touching is like what help you lower your gaze, preventing you from doing the adultery and the same for your wife. Undesirable touching is like touching your wife during pilgrimage, seclusion and fasting for sexual desire, if he cannot control himself. Also, touching the body of the dead person is undesirable except who wash the dead body. The allowed touching is like what is not harmful or contradicts with a religious end.

These five provisions can also be applied on using the hands and walking on feet. For example, earning money to spend on family and oneself or paying debt, helping the needy, throwing pebbles and ablution and tayammum are obligatory. Killing the soul which God has forbidden, robbing the property of the protected by law, striking the weak persons, and gambling are unlawful. Playing, rashness and writing nonsense that is not beneficial for the life or the doomsday are undesirable but writing what is beneficial for the religion or the sake of a Muslim, helping others and so on are desirable. The use of hands is allowed as long as it was not to harm or has to be rewarded. "Woe to them for what their hands have written and woe to them for what they earn." "فَوَيْلٌ لِّلَّذِينَ يَكْتُبُونَ الْكِتَابَ بِأَيْدِيهِمْ ثُمَّ يَقُولُونَ هَٰذَا مِنْ عِندِ اللَّهِ لِيَشْتَرُوا بِهِ ثَمَنًا قَلِيلًا" (2:79) "فَوَيْلٌ لَّهُم مِّمَّا كَتَبَتْ أَيْدِيهِمْ وَوَيْلٌ لَّهُم مِّمَّا يَكْسِبُونَ - 2:79

Also, these five provisions can be applied on walking: walking around Kaaba, between Safa and Marwa Mounts, attending knowledge circles and performing Hajj are obligatory whereas walking to do a sin is unlawful.

These five provisions can also be applied on riding: riding during the war, Jihad and pilgrimage are obligatory. Riding to ask for science, visiting kinship and relatives are desirable. Riding to do sins is unlawful. Riding for playing and amusement or doing things that are more abandoning them are better than doing them are undesirable. Riding for something that does not waste a reward is allowed.

These are 50 provisions applied on ten organs: heart, tongue, ears, eyes, nose, mouth, hands, leg, sexual organs and riding an animal.

Degrees of "It is You we worship" of the heart regarding worshipping of God

First degree of worship is "Awakening"; it is when the heart wakes up from negligence to achieve the other degrees of worship. Then, the degree of "Intention"; intending to leave everything that hinders a servant and following everything to worship God. So, if a servant becomes awake, he reaches the "idea"; which is the insistence of the heart on doing the necessary. Then comes the "Insight"; it is a light in the heart, through which the heart perceives the promise and threat, the Heaven and the Hell. Insight is a light bestowed from the God to see the truth of the messages of the messengers.

The author of "Manazel Assalekeen" conceptualizes the "Insight" in another way. He argues that the insight prevents confusion; you believe in the truth of what the Messenger told as the person who follows the truth does not fear ever. Insight varies among people based on variation of their knowledge and understanding of the prophetic texts and what contradict with them.

Insight regarding commands and prohibitions to be followed without being opposed by explanation, tradition or desire. One's heart shall not contain a conflict between science and God's commands.

Insight regarding promise and punishment. You have to confirm that God accounts the deeds of each soul, sooner or later. Otherwise, you may doubt God, His Existence, His justice and His wisdom. If the mind confirms punishment, it confirms the Oneness of God. The same applies to the doomsday, as denial of it refers to denial refers to denial of God, His Omnipotence and Divinity. So, both call forth blasphemy. In this regard, God says: "And if you are astonished, [O Muhammad] - then astonishing is their saying, "When we are dust, will we indeed be [brought] into a new creation?" Those are the ones who have disbelieved in their Lord, and those will have shackles upon their necks, and those are the companions of the Fire; they will abide therein

eternal", " وَإِن تَعْجَبْ فَعَجَبٌ قَوْلُهُم أَإِذَا كُنَّا تُرَابًا أَإِنَّا لَفِي خَلْقٍ جَدِيدٍ ۗ أُولَٰئِكَ الَّذِينَ كَفَرُوا

بِرَبِّهِمْ ۖ وَأُولَٰئِكَ الْأَغْلَالُ فِي أَعْنَاقِهِمْ ۖ وَأُولَٰئِكَ أَصْحَابُ النَّارِ ۖ هُمْ فِيهَا خَالِدُونَ" (13:5)

Insight is divided into three divisions, whoever achieved them got the deep insight: insight regarding names and attributes; insight regarding commands and prohibitions; and insight regarding promise and punishment.

Insight regarding names and attributes is like that your faith cannot be infected with a doubtful matter that negates an attribute that God ascribed Himself or His Messenger. You have believe that God has many names and ascribed many attributes for Himself, that cannot be argued against.

Intention

If the servant becomes alert and has insight, he gets the intention and the true will; he entirely intended to migrate to God with good faith. "Intention" is divided into three degrees.

The first degree: Intention that prevents hesitation and forsakes the purposes. The second degree: Intention that surpasses causes and paves the way before difficulties. The third degree: Intention to pursue knowledge to be righteous and respond to the religious provisions.

Decision

If your intention is really held, then your decision is held and this decision is accompanied with reliance on God, Exalted is He said: "And when you have decided, then rely upon God" فَإِذَا عَزَمْتَ "فَتَوَكَّلْ عَلَى الله" ِ (3:159).

Decision is the strong intention related to action; starting to do something is because of the decision. During this stage you have to distinguish between what you have to do and what you mustn't do; to follow the commands and stop doing the prohibitions; this is the accounting that is prior to "Repentance" that leads to it at the end. Repentance is the aim and the end of every person. Repentance comes before the accounting as it is a complement for it. In fact, the order is not a matter as they continue to happen together; accounting happens so that repentance can continue, they are based on each other. These stations' order is not based on succession; they are reached status whenever you got, they continue with you. For example, the station of contentedness is the result of patience, but patience is not a step to contentedness. This does not mean that after patience station comes the next station "contentedness"; being content is when you become patient and they continue together. This is applied on all stations.

Also, "Intention" and "Decision" come prior to other stations. Monotheism is the first station as it is the first claim that all the messengers evoke, the Prophet (PBUH) said to Muaz ibn Jabal when he sent him to Yemen: "First of all invite them to worship Allah (alone)"; it is the key of all messengers' invitation and the first obligation be imposed on the servants. For example, this is the first obligation instructed by Noah, he said: "O my people, worship God; you have no deity other than Him" " فَقَالَ يَا قَوْمِ اعْبُدُوا اللَّـهَ مَا لَكُم مِّنْ إِلَهٍ غَيْره" (7:59).

There are stations that have two status or more. Repentance includes the status of accounting and fear. Expectancy includes fear and will, as fear includes expectancy and will. Status of thankfulness includes all statuses of faith. There are two kinds of servants in terms of each status, these who are righteous and those who are near to God, the first kind are the lower status and the second ones are the higher one. The same is the status of faith; their variation and degrees are only counted by God.

Stations of worshipping mentioned in Quran and Sunnah are notable, referring to their limitations and statuses. God described those who did not know them of being ignorant and hypocrite. Exalted is He said: "The Bedouins are stronger in disbelief and hypocrisy and more likely not to know the limits of what [laws] the God has revealed to His Messenger". " الْأَعْرَابُ أَشَدُّ كُفْرًا وَنِفَاقًا وَأَجْدَرُ أَلَّا يَعْلَمُوا حُدُودَ مَا أَنزَلَ اللَّـهُ عَلَىٰ رَسُولِهِ" (9:97). You have to be aware about these limitations and execute them carefully to become faithful and one of these following "It is You we worship and You we ask for help.".

First station for this heedless person is awakening: It is when the heart is shocked because of a great awakening. It is this state that mentioned in His verse: "Say, "I only advise you of one [thing] - that you stand for God, [seeking truth] in pairs and individually" "قُلْ إِنَّمَا أَعِظُكُم بِوَاحِدَةٍ ۖ أَن تَقُومُوا لِلَّـهِ مَثْنَىٰ وَفُرَادَىٰ" (34:46). If he wakes up, his heart is guided by the awakening, then he recognizes bounties of God, intangible or obvious. The more the heart considers these bounties, the more it witnesses their greatness and abundancy. As a result, the heart cannot count and appreciate them. Thus, the servant is just watching favor of God upon him without any return for, then he feels his negligence for thanking God for these bounties. He realizes that he is unable to praise His bounties, and his state is according to "I acknowledge the favors that You have bestowed upon me, and I confess my sins. Pardon me, for none but You has the power to pardon)" and knows that this is the best supplication for seeking forgiveness to be said. Then, he realizes that if God tortured all people of the earth, He is fair for that, there is no salvation but asking for His Mercy.

After that, he realizes that he has committed many sins and he is endangered. God dispraise those who forgot their sins, He said: "And who is more unjust than one who is reminded of the verses of his Lord but turns away from them and forgets what his hands have put forth?" " وَمَنْ أَظْلَمُ مِمَّن ذُكِّرَ بِآيَاتِ رَبِّهِ فَأَعْرَضَ عَنْهَا وَنَسِيَ " "مَا قَدَّمَتْ يَدَاهُ" (18:57). If he realizes his sins, he tries to compensate his negligence and sins, through doing good deeds and repenting. He is not going to enter the Heaven except after reaching this case. The Heaven is pure and only those who are pure can enter it; Exalted is He said: "Peace be upon you; you have become pure; so enter it to abide eternally therein." " سَلَامٌ عَلَيْكُمْ طِبْتُمْ " "فَادْخُلُوهَا خَالِدِينَ" (39:73).

Asking for forgiveness of God on these sins in the world life follows repentance, asking for forgiveness, goods deeds to omit bad ones and expiations. If he fulfilled the same, during his death, the angles give him good tidings "The angels will descend upon them, [saying], "Do not fear and do not grieve but receive good tidings of Paradise, which you were promised. We [angels] were your allies in worldly life and [are so] in the Hereafter. And you will have therein whatever your souls desire, and you will have therein whatever you request [or wish]" " تَتَنَزَّلُ عَلَيْهِمُ الْمَلَائِكَةُ " أَلَّا تَخَافُوا وَلَا تَحْزَنُوا وَأَبْشِرُوا بِالْجَنَّةِ الَّتِي كُنتُمْ تُوعَدُونَ، نَحْنُ أَوْلِيَاؤُكُمْ فِي الْحَيَاةِ الدُّنْيَا وَفِي الْآخِرَةِ وَلَكُمْ فِيهَا مَا تَشْتَهِي أَنفُسُكُمْ وَلَكُمْ فِيهَا مَا تَدَّعُونَ " (41:30-31).

If these four things does not help, he can be forgiven during the life of "Barzakh", by three ways: first, by the funeral prayer performed by righteous people, asking for forgiveness to him and intercession of the righteous people; second, the affliction of the grave and its torture; third, gifts of his Muslim brothers like alms, performing pilgrimage, prayers and fasting on behalf of him - intending their reward be granted to him.

If not, he is to be forgiven while being before God on the doomsday, it's a difficult situation, by intercession and the forgiveness of God. If these three stages do not help, the Hell purifies him, he stays there, so that he can be purified from sins, then he becomes pure and enter the Heaven.

The idea

If he waked up, he gets the idea – the heart turns to the request. There are two kinds of the idea; one related to knowledge and the other related to the request and the intention. The first distinguishes between truth and deceit, the second distinguishes between benefit and harm. Then, there is another idea is to reach the benefit and leave the harm.

Accounting

Back to stations of "It is You we worship; it is You we ask for hep" that servants cannot reach except fulfilling their status. There are four stations: awakening, insight, idea and decision;

these four stations are the basics in the way to the God. A traveler is to wake up first, work his insight second, think how to reach the God's path third, then to decide to reach God's path. After that the servant reaches the station of "Accounting"; which is to distinguish between the rights and the duties, the do's and don'ts.

After station of "Accounting", the servant reaches station of repentance as if he sets accounting for himself, he knows what he must do, leaving this sin; it is the essence of repentance, so accounting comes first before repentance. Correspondingly, accounting can only happen after true repentance, as there are two phases of accounting; one before repentance that necessitates its existence and another after repentance to hold on.

What is intended here is to consider all what you have done saves you from the Hell.

Accounting has three pillars: one of them is to compare between His favor and your sins; comparing between the grace of God bestowed to you and good deeds and worships you offered, also you have to compare between your righteous deeds and sins. Then, you discover that there is no salvation but asking for mercy of God.

This comparison is very hard to do for those who lack three matters: light of wisdom, self-mistrust and distinguishing between grace and temptation. This comparison and accounting based on wisdom's light, it is the light that the God deposits in the hearts of the messengers' followers; through it you can judge various deeds and set the accounting. Light of wisdom is the knowledge by which the slave distinguishes between truth and falsehood, harm and benefit, incompleteness and completeness, goodness and evil; and judges deeds. The stronger the light is, the more perfect the accounting becomes. Self-mistrust is needed as blind trust misguides us, render us realizing bad matters as good and deficits as perfection. Distinguishing between grace and temptation is to know the whole favor of God upon us and not to be tempted with it; not feeling its value and benefit. If you get the three matters, you get happiness and success.

Second pillar of accounting: recognizing obligatory worships, abiding by obedience and avoiding disobedience. You have rights and obligations; fulfill your obligations, then you get your rights. Many people who confuse whether to fulfill or leave the obligations and if they fulfill, they acted as a grace from the doer. Some people misunderstand the worships, for example, they do not marry or eat meat ... as a worship, The Prophet (PBUH) denied that: "There was a group of the Companions of the Prophet, one of whom said: "I will not marry." Another said: "I will not eat meat." Another said: "I will not sleep on a bed." Another said: "I will fast and not break my fast." News of that reached the Messenger of God and he praised God then said: "What is the matter with people who say such and such? But I pray and I sleep, I fast and I break my fast, and I marry. Whoever turns away from my Sunnah is not of me." Another example, there are people who perform

The third pillar of accounting: "Every obedience you fulfill while you are very pleased with it, it counted upon you; every disobedience you disgrace your brother for is counted upon you." The person who neglects his deficits and being ignorant to God and obligatory worships, becomes content with his deeds and has blind trust regarding them. As a result, one commits conceit and haughtiness that are greater than the major sins like adultery and drinking alcohol.

Every disobedience you disgrace your brother for is counted upon you. It is probable that this means you will commit the same sin, according to Hadith narrated by Alturmuzy, quoting the Prophet (PBUH): "If anyone disgraces his brother for a sin, he will not die before committing it himself." Also, the statement connotes gloating; the Messenger of God (PBUH) said, "Do not express pleasure at the misfortune of a (Muslim) brother lest

God should bestow mercy upon him and make you suffer from a misfortune."

If accounting fulfilled properly and the servant reached this station, then he is about to reach "Repentance" station. By accounting, the servant realized his obligations and prohibitions.

Repentance station is the first, middle and the last station; it is the beginning of the servant and his final abode. God, Exalted is He, said: "And turn to God in repentance, all of you, O believers, that you might succeed." " وَتُوبُوا إِلَى اللَّهِ جَمِيعًا أَيُّهَا الْمُؤْمِنُونَ لَعَلَّكُمْ تُفْلِحُونَ" (24:31). In this verse God addressed the faithful Muslims, asking them to repent after their faith, patience, Hijra and Jihad, then He resulted success after repentance. God divided servants into those who are repentant on one side and wrongdoers on the other side, according to the following verse: "And whoever does not repent - then it is those who are the wrongdoers"." وَمَنْ لَمْ يَتُبْ فَأُولَٰئِكَ هُمُ الظَّالِمُونَ" (49:11). The Messenger (PBUH) said: "I swear by God that I seek God's Pardon and turn to Him in repentance more than seventy times a day." The companions counted that the Messenger of the God (PBUH) would say a hundred times during a meeting: "My Lord, forgive me and pardon me; Thou art the Pardoning and forgiving One". It is the Prophet (PBUH) who is the most aware person to the God, His rights, greatness and the best worshipping, so we must go after him and be guided with him.

Repentance is turning to God and leaving the path of those whom God evoked His anger or those who are astray. This only happen when you follow the straight path. You cannot be bestowed His guidance except by His will and testifying the oneness of your Lord, according to Surat Al-Fatihah. Complete guidance to the straight path does not go with ignoring sins or insisting on them. Repentance follows recognizing the sin, confessing and asking for forgiveness.

Joy while disobedience refers to the desire to doing it and ignoring the magnitude of the God, severe punishment and the great danger of sins.

If the sinner is a believer, he becomes miserable and gloomy when he committed a sin. This happens because he fears death before repentance, regrets for what he has done and seriously tries to revoke it by good deeds. Intention and decision to repeat the sin is greater than the first sin and it leads to destruction.

Conditions of the repentance are three: regret, abstention and finding an excuse. Both happen simultaneously with repentance. Repentance is based on regret, abstention of the sin and confessing weakness to resist desire. Such sin is not an underestimation towards God and His warning. Blaming fate is a pretention before God; considering his sin resulted from the fate. Finding an excuse is two-fold: finding an excuse instead of confession, justifying a sin, which is against repentance; and finding an excuse confirming the confession; this is the perfect repentance.

Facts of repentance are three: Confessing that the sin is disgraceful, confirming repentance and finding an excuse for the mankind disobedience. Facts are what is required to prove things and become clear and true. Considering the sin disgraceful results in great regret. This can be achieved through considering the matter tremendous, glorifying the commander and believing in the punishment.

Confirming repentance shall be performed, because it is an obligation and sinner is not sure whether he truly fulfilled it, feeling that it is not accepted. He may repent to maintain his position, fear people or unable to repeat this sin, but he did not repent because he fears the Almighty God. You must confirm your repentance if you find yourself joyfully remembering the sin and feeling secure. Accepted repentance follows turning to be more righteous than before, always fearing God, thus your heart always feels distress for committing this sin. The heart must be broken, humiliated and submissive, then surrendering to God. If you did not find that in your heart, then you must doubt your repentance, as you need to confirm that it is absolutely true.

"Finding an excuse for mankind" is two-faced: one is a praised and the other is rebuked.

The rebuked face: is to find an excuse for mankind's disobedience, with regard to fatalistic judgement and its effectiveness upon them, whether they accept or refuse it, and pardon them for fate. Many fatalists come to the argument that fate is an excuse for any forbidden deed. And this is a very dangerous way which has low benefit and does not rescue from torture by itself.

And this is rebuked because if one pardons enemies of God and those who are against God and his Messengers, he will become against God judgement as God judges to blame them. If he was excused by God, He would never punish him as God is the most Gracious and the Fairest. For this, He sent down Messengers and Holy Books to void mankind excuses.

The one who has an excuse, is a child, a mad, the one ignorant of calling to God, the deaf and blind, they are not tortured for no sin. Instead, on the doomsday, God will examine them by sending a Messenger that commands and forbids them. The one who obeys the Messenger will enter the Heaven while the other who disobeys the Messenger will enter the Hell.

There is no excuse at all for anyone who disobeys God, while he well knows the right and wrong and has the ability to do or stop something forbidden.

God's antagonists see that Man has an excuse for disobeying God as he is falling under fate.

These antagonists complain fate. This is ultimate ignorance and injustice, as God says about Man "indeed, he was unjust and ignorant". "إنه كان ظلومًا جهولاً" (33:72)

This unjust and ignorant Man should know that he is the only one who is responsible for his affliction.

O unjust and ignorant Man, if fate is an excuse for you to neglect God's right, then can it be an excuse for your slave or maid to neglect your right partially? So, how do you consider fate an excuse for you?

In addition, God offers you several blessings; He granted you hearing, sight and heart, made you distinguish between good and evil, sent to you His Messenger and revealed His Holy Quran. He helped you through His angels who guard you and fight your enemy "Satan". However, you follow your enemy and take him as an ally other than your God. God says "And [mention] when We says to the angels, "Prostrate to Adam," and they prostrated, except for Iblees. He was of the jinn and departed from the command of his Lord. Then will you take him and his descendants as allies other than Me while they are enemies to you? Wretched it is for the wrongdoers as an exchange". " وإذ قلنا للملائكة اسجدوا لآدم فسجدوا إلا إبليس كان من الجن ففسق عن أمر ربه أفتتخذونه وذريته أولياء من دوني وهم لكم عدو بئس للظالمين بدلاً". (18:50)

This is one of the two meanings of "finding an excuse for Mankind's disobedience, as one of facts of repentance". It has been made clear to you that finding an excuse for offenses of mankind abolishes repentance.

The other meaning is to find an excuse for mankind's disobedience for doing wrong to you and in this context, you consider fate. So, you pardon them – for fate – for violating your right not God's right. This is true. And this is the case of our Prophet (PBUH) as Aisha (May God be pleased with her) says: "The Messenger of God (PBUH) never took revenge for his own self in any matter presented to him till God's limits were exceeded, in which case he would take revenge for God's sake."

Anas (May God be pleased with him) says: "I remained in the service of the Prophet for ten years. When I did something, he never asked me why did you do so? When I did not do a certain task, he never asked me why I did not do it. And if one of his family blamed me, he says let him because this is fate".

So, look how the Prophet considers fate, when the matter relates to his right and how he executes God's orders when it comes to God's right. For example, the Prophet cut the woman's hands because she robbed, and he did not say that she is under the rule of fate. Also, he lashed the man and the woman who fornicate and did not take fate as an excuse for them.

This other meaning is true, but it is not related to repentance nor it is one of its conditions. If man did not pardon them for their abuse to him, this would not affect his repentance. Becoming angry at someone for his violating God's right is among facts of repentance. Not considering an excuse for mankind if they did not follow do's and don'ts and becoming very angry at such act are signs of magnifying what is forbidden by God. This certainly includes finding an excuse for pagans and idolaters, killers of prophets, Firaun and Haman, Abu Jahl and his friends, Satan and his soldiers, every disbeliever and wrongdoer, whoever transgresses limits of God. They are all under the rule of fate and belong to mankind but finding an excuse for them is not a true repentance.

God, the Almighty, orders to rebel the evil deed (that is under His fate) by the good deed (that is under His fate). Similarly, hunger is under His fate and He orders to get over it by eating that is under His fate. If God's slave submitted to the fate of hunger until he died, in spite of his ability to get over it by the fate of eating, he would die as a sinful. Similarly, coolness, warmness and thirst are all under the fate of God. And He orders to get over them by fates that are opposite to them. The Prophet (PBUH) expressed this clearly as he was asked: "Do you think that the medicines with which we treat ourselves, the Ruqyah by which we seek healing and the means of protection that we seek, change the decree of God? He says: "They are part of the decree of God". In another narration, "Disaster and supplication conflict between the heaven and earth". Hence, if you are doomed to disobedience, and you disobey God because you are falling under fate, repel obligation of fatal disobedience by sincere repentance which is also falling under fate.

Repelling fate by fate has two types:

First: To repel fate that its reasons were concluded – and when it befalls – by other fatal reasons that react against it, so that it does not befall. For example, repel enemy by fighting it, repel coldness and heat and so on.

Second: To repel fate that has befallen by another fate that removes it. For example, to repel the fate of illness by that of healing, to repel the fate of committing a sin by that of repentance and to repel the fate of misdeeds by that of good deeds.

This is the case of people who know God well and this is the matter of fate; not to submit to fate and remain passive and idle because this is called incapacity and God, the Almighty, blames for it.

"There are three secrets of the fact of repentance: distinguishing between piety and honor, obliteration of thought of sin and repenting from repentance. This is because the one who turns to God in repentance is falling within "all of you" that was says by God in His verse: "And turn to God in repentance, all of you, O believers, that you might succeed" " وتوبوا إلى الله جميعًا أيها المؤمنون لعلكم تفلحون" (24:31), i.e. God commanded a repentant to repent".

- distinguishing between piety and honor: means that the intention of repentance should be to achieve piety, fear God, obey His commands and avoid His prohibitions. Man should obey God, hoping for His reward and avoid disobeying Him out of fearing His punishment. He does not seek piety for the purpose of getting honor of obedience.

- Obliteration of the thought of sin: Scholars have different views in this matter. One opinion says that Man should not remember his sin and he has to disregard it. Spending time contemplating God's glory with a serene mood is more deserving and favorable for a repentant. The other opinion says that remembering sin is more deserving for a repentant. He should always bear it in his mind so that he humbles and yields to God.

The right opinion is to make this matter detailed, i.e. if a slave felt self-conceit and forgot grace of God upon him and forgot his reality as an imperfect creature, being in need of God, then remembering his sin will be more favorable for him. If a slave knows well the grace of God upon him and he is in full need of God, longs to meet Him and realizes His vast mercy, most forbearance, oft-pardoning, then, forgetting and disregarding his sin will be favorable.

As for "Repenting from repentance": It is one of the outlines which highlights truth and falsehood. Repentance is one of the greatest deeds, whereas repentance from doing good deeds is one of the most disgraceful evil deeds. Rather, it is a disbelief of God.

If one repented, and became engaged with mentioning God's favors, names and attributes, after that, he turned upside down and became engaged with mentioning his repentance from a previous sin, regarded his sin and engaged with it instead of God, this would be a deficient action from which he had to repent. And this is a repenting from that untrue repentance.

"Secrets of repentance include regarding sin and knowing God's will as He let His slave commit it. God lets a slave commit a sin for two purposes:

First: is to make His slave know the honor of God in His decree, His respite to him for a while, His generosity as He accepted his excuse and His grace as He forgave him for his sin.

Second: is the establishment of God's justice; to punish Man for his sin.

When Man recognizes the honor of God in His decree, God grants him complete degrees of humbleness and yield to Him because a soul has some analogy to Lordship. Humbleness of servitude to God helps the soul to get rid of this analogy. There are four degrees for humbleness of servitude:

First: is common among mankind. It is about humbleness of need of God.

Second: It is humbleness of obedience and servitude. It is an optional humbleness. This degree is just confined to the obedient ones. And it is the secret of servitude.

Third: is the humbleness of God's love. A slave's humbleness to God is as much as his love to Him.

Fourth: is the humbleness of disobedience and sin.

If a slave shows these four degrees, humbleness and yield to God will be more perfect. A slave humbles to God out of fear, love, obedience and need.

When Man pays attention to the best names of God, he will see its effects in the world. For example, God's name of "the [continual] Provider" implies that mankind rely only on God to give provisions to them. God's name of the Most Forgiving implies that He forgives His slaves. The Prophet (PBUH) referred to this as he says: "Were you not to commit sins, God would replace you with a people who would commit sins and then seek forgiveness from God; and God would certainly forgive them". Hence, you cannot assume that there is no sin or fault in the world, nor you can assume that slaves are free of need. So exalted is God Who guides His slaves to Him by a variety of evidence. God says: "that those who perished [through disbelief] would perish upon evidence and those who lived [in faith] would live upon evidence; and indeed, God is Hearing and Knowing".

"ليهلك من هلك عن بينة ويحيى من حي عن بينة وإن الله لسميع عليم". (8:42).

Chapter

Know that God, exalted is He, distinguished Man among His creatures as He honored and preferred him over other creatures. He created Man for Himself and created all other things for Man. He subjected whatever is in the heavens and the earth and in-between to him, whatever is in the earth and that between them. He used even angels (who are the closest to Him) for guarding Man in his sleepiness and waking, his travel and en-campment. He sent down to him His messengers and Holy Books. He chose prophets among mankind and preferred some of them. For instance, He chose a prophet for His friendship "Prophet Abraham", a prophet to whom He spoke directly "Prophet Moses",.. etc. Also, He chose people who are closest to Him and granted them His wisdom and love. Man is the creature preferred by God over other creatures. Man is the creature intended for following do's and don'ts and subjected to reward and punishment of God.

God, Exalted is He, created mankind in order to worship Him. His worship comprehends His love, yield to Him and His obedience. He created the heavens and earth in truth. This is the ultimate purpose of creation and the whole command. Denial of that – as done by enemies of God – is a falsehood. God, Exalted is He, likes to be worshipped and obeyed. He does not care for His mankind, but for their love, obedience and supplication to Him.

He rebuked people who claimed that this is not the purpose of God's creation of mankind. If they were created for purpose other than worshipping and obeying God, then their creation would be fruitless. If a slave deviated from obedience and worship for which he was created, this means that he deviated from the most beloved thing to God and from the ultimate purpose for which mankind are created. He would become as if he was created uselessly. If a slave reconsiders the reason for his creation, he will turn to the ultimate purpose that is the most beloved thing to His Creator and to the wisdom of his creation. Hence, God will ardently love him because God loves those who are constantly repentant and loves those who purify themselves.

God likes that His slave shows enmity to His enemy "Satan" and disobeys him just as He likes His slave to be an ally of his Protector, obey and worship Him. God's love to His slave for worshipping, obeying and turning back to Him is added to His love to him for showing enmity to and disobeying His enemy "Satan". So, His love to a slave becomes greater and this is the reality of God's delight with His slave.

God, exalted is He, rejoices when His slave worships Him by the most beloved thing to Him. For instance, He rejoices when His slave forsakes his bed for reciting His verses.. His delight imply His judgement of granting His slave pleasure and love and refer to His will and attributes.

Chapter

The second purpose of God's letting Man commit a sin is the establishment of God's justice; to punish Man for his sin.

One of the necessities of a slave's faith is to confess that God has provided him with His proof. He sent down His messengers and Holy Books and gave him the ability to know Him whether he tried to know Him or not. Everyone who was able to know God's commands and prohibitions and did not seek to know them, God would punish them. God. The Almighty, does not punish anyone but only after establishing a proof. So, if He punished one for committing sin, He would punish him by His justice for his disobedience. God, the Almighty, says: "And never would We punish until We sent a messenger". "اوما كنا معذبين حتى نبعث رسولاً" (17:15) Also He says: "Every time a company is thrown into it, its keepers ask them, "Did there not come to you a warner? They will say, "Yes, a warner had come to us, but we denied and says, ' God has not sent down anything."

" كلما ألقي فيها فوج سألهم خزنتها ألم يأتكم نذير قالوا بلى قد جاءنا نذير فكذبنا وقلنا ما نزل الله من شيء". (67-8:9) And He says: "And your Lord would not have destroyed the cities unjustly while their people were re-formers". "وما كان ربك ليهلك القرى بظلم وأهلها مصلحون" (11:117)

There are two interpretations for this verse. One of which is: God would not have destroyed cities because of their injustice. The other one is: God would not have destroyed cities out of His injustice.

The meaning of the first interpretation is that: God would not have destroyed people because of their previous injustice, i.e. He would not have destroyed them after they have been re-formed and repented.

The meaning of the second interpretation is that: He had de-stroyed them because they were not reformers but unjust. They are unjust for their disobedience and He is just in destroying them.

The two interpretations are also applied on the verse of Surah Al-An'am: "That is because your Lord would not destroy the cities for wrongdoing while their people were unaware". " ذلك أن لم يكن ربك مهلك القرى بظلم وأهلها غافلون" (6:131)

This verse is interpreted as God would not destroy people for their wrongdoing and polytheism while they were unaware; they were not warned by a messenger. Another interpretation is that God would not destroy people before sending them a messenger warning them, lest He should be unjust to them. God, Exalted is He, does not punish one except for one's sin. A slave would be sinful if he did not follow God's commands and avoid prohibitions. Commands and prohibitions are informed by messengers.

God decreed that sin is a reason for punishment, and obedience is a reason for reward. If a slave committed a sin while he previously knew that it is a reason for his punishment, then he has no argument against God and deserves punishment as a matter of God's just decree.

God, the Almighty, says: "And We did not give Prophet Muhammad, knowledge of poetry, nor is it befitting for him. It is not but a message and a clear Qur'an. To warn whoever is alive and justify the word against the disbelievers". " وما علمناه الشعر وما ينبغي له إن هو إلا ذكر وقرآن مبيّن. لينذر من كان حيًا ويحق القول على الكافرين" (36:69- 70) So, God, Exalted is He, told that Man is divided into two categories: alive (one who accepts warning and avails of it), and dead (one who does not accept warning nor avails of it). The latter deserves God's decree that he would not believe in God even after the revealing of a messenger. God says: "Thus the word of your Lord has come into effect upon those who defiantly disobeyed - that they will not believe". " وكذلك حقت كلمت ربك على الذين فسقوا أنهم لا يؤمنون" (10:33). And he deserves God's decree that he will be punished as God says: "And thus has the word of your Lord come into effect upon those who disbelieved that they are companions of the Fire". "وكذلك حقت كلمت ربك على الذين كفروا أنهم أصحاب النار" (40:6) Also, God, the Almighty, says: "but the word of punishment has come into effect upon the disbelievers". " ولكن حقت كلمت العذاب على الكافرين" (39:71)

Chapter

When a slave commits a sin, he regards four matters:

1- Commands and prohibitions

2- The decree of God

3- The source of sin "his soul, the persistent enjoiner of evil"

4- Satan who commands him of disobedience

The first two matters have been mentioned before. As for the third matter, when Man regards it, he will know that his soul is ignorant and commits wrongdoings. Ignorance and wrongdoings result in every evil sayings and deeds. So, Man must seek propitious knowledge to get over ignorance and seek righteous deeds to get over wrong ones. He should supplicate his Creator to protect him from his own evil, to grant him the sense of piety and purify his soul, as He is the Best to purify it and not to protect him to his fancy. The Prophet says to Husain ibn Amundhir: "Say: O God, inspire me with my guidance and protect me from the evil of my soul". God, the Almighty, says: "And whoever is protected from the stinginess of his soul - it is those who will be the successful" "ومن يوق شح نفسه فأولئك هم المفلحون". (64:16)

God also says: "Indeed, the soul is a persistent enjoiner of evil". "إن النفس لأمارة بالسوء". (12:53)

If Man knew the reality of his soul, he would know that it is the source of evil, but its goodness is a favor of God upon him, not begot by his own soul. God says: "And if not for the favor of God upon you and His mercy, not one of you would have been pure, ever" "ولولا فضل الله عليكم ورحمته ما زكى منكم من أحد أبدًا". (24:21). And He, the Almighty, says: "but God has endeared to you the faith and has made it pleasing in your hearts and has made hateful to you disbelief, defiance and disobedience. Those are the [rightly] guided". "ولكن الله حبب إليكم الإيمان وزينه في قلوبكم وكره إليكم الكفر والفسوق والعصيان. أولئك هم الراشدون". (49:7)

This love to faith and this hatred of disbelief are not in control of the soul but are a grace of God. God says: "[It is] as bounty from God and favor. And God is Knowing and Wise". " فضلاً من الله

(49:8) . "ونعمة والله عليم حكيم"

God is "Knowing" of the one who is good for this grace and is "Wise", who does not grant this grace for someone not deserving it so as not to be wasted.

Another benefit that results when Man knows that his soul is the source of evil is that he will always regard favor of God upon him and defects of his soul and misdeeds. This is the greatest sort of knowledge and the most favorable one for a slave. So, the Prophet says: "The most superior manner of asking for forgiveness is to say: "O God! You are my Lord. None has the right to be worshipped except You. You created me and I am your servant and I abide by your covenant and promise as best I can. I seek refuge in You from the evil, which I have committed. I acknowledge your favor upon me and I acknowledge my sins, so forgive me, for verily none can forgive sin except You". This supplication implies that a slave confesses the Lordship of God and He is his Creator who knows well that His slave will fail to duly worship Him.

Chapter

The fourth matter that a slave should regard when he commits a sin is to bear in mind Satan who urges him to disobey God and lures him. This is favorable to a slave in order to take Satan as an enemy and remain vigilant against him. Satan wants to conquer Man in one of the earlier seven obstacles, some of which are tougher than others. Satan does not downgrade among the hard obstacles but only when he fails to conquer Man in a harder obstacle.

First obstacle: is disbelief of God, His religion, the doomsday, God's perfect attributes and messengers' utterances and commands. If Man goes through this obstacle by guidance of God, Satan tries to allure him through the second obstacle.

Second obstacle: is heresy, whether by thinking that messengers and Holy Books are falsehood or by worshipping what is prohibited by God. The two heresies are often correlated. If Man goes through this obstacle by the guidance of Sunnah, Satan tries to allure him, to deviate to the third obstacle.

Third obstacle: is that of major sins. Satan makes major sins attractive to Man and tries to make him delay repentance. If Man goes through this obstacle by God's protection or sincere repentance, Satan tries to turn him disobedient by the fourth obstacle.

Fourth obstacle: is that of minor sins. Satan encourage Man to insist on minor sins. Insisting on committing a sin is worse than the sin itself.

Fifth obstacle: is that of permissible acts. Satan makes Man engaged with them other than doing much better deeds. Then, Satan makes Man forsake supererogatory deeds and then forsake obligatory deeds. If Man overcomes this obstacle by a full insight and learning of the value of doing much better deeds, Satan tries to fascinate him by the fifth obstacle.

Sixth obstacle: is that of good deeds that are less rewarded. Satan makes Man engaged with these deeds other than others which are more rewarded and more beloved to God. Those who are affected by this obstacle are rare, but the majority have been deviated in the previous obstacles. This obstacle can not be overcome except by those of knowledge and insight.

Seventh obstacle: is that Satan musters his soldiers against Man. This obstacle is inevitable, even messengers and prophets have challenged them. Man cannot get rid of this obstacle but he should always fight the enemy of God "Satan" by seeking God's help. The most beloved thing to God is that His allies "believers" fight His enemies "Satan and disbelievers".

God says: "And whoever emigrates for the cause of God will find on the earth many [alternative] locations and abundance". (4:100) ‏"ومن يهاجر في سبيل الله يجد في الأرض مراغمًا كثيرًا وسعة"‏. God, the Almighty, also says: "It was not [proper] for the people of Madinah and those surrounding them of the bedouins that they remain behind after [the departure of] the Messenger of God or that they prefer themselves over his self. That is because they are not afflicted by thirst or fatigue or hunger in the cause of God, nor do they tread on any ground that enrages the disbelievers, nor do they inflict upon an enemy any infliction but that is registered for them as a righteous deed. Indeed, God does not allow to be lost the reward of the doers of good". "ذلك بأنهم لا يصيبهم ظمأ ولا نصب ولا مخمصة في سبيل الله ولا يطئون موطئًا يغيظ الكفار ولا ينالون من عدو نيلاً إلا كتب لهم به عمل صالح. إن الله لا يضيع أجر المحسنين" . (9:120)

God says about His Messenger (PBUH) and followers: "And their description in the Gospel is as a plant which produces its offshoots and strengthens them so they grow firm and stand upon their stalks, delighting the sowers - so that God may enrage by them the disbelievers". "ومثلهم في الإنجيل كزرع أخرج شطأه فآزره. فاستغلظ. فاستوى على سوقه. يعجب الزراع ليغيظ بهم الكفار" . (48:29)

This grade of worshipping is reached by a few people. If a slave reaching this grade regards Satan when he intends to commit a sin, he will defeat Satan by sincere repentance. This defeat enhances his worshipping.

The Difference between God's Will and Love

It is evidenced that there is a difference between God's will and love by the Holy Qur'an and Sunnah, human mind, natural disposition and consensus of Muslim scholars. God says: "They conceal [their evil intentions and deeds] from the people, but they cannot conceal [them] from God, and He is with them [in His knowledge] when they spend the night in such as He does not accept of speech". " إذ يستخفون من الناس ولا يستخفون من الله وهو معهم يبيتون ما لا يرضى من القول". (4:108)

So, God told that He does not approve their speech that includes slander, false witness and innocence of a guilty. However, all this is under God's will. Muslim scholars agree together that what God wills comes to pass and what He does not will does not come to pass.

All deeds, whether good or evil, are subject to God's will. Some of which are beloved to Him while others are not. God says: "And God does not like corruption". "والله لا يحب الفساد" (2:205). He, the Almighty, also says: "If you disbelieve - indeed, God is Free from need of you. And He does not approve for His servants disbelief. And if you are grateful, He approves it for you". " إن تشكروا فإن الله غني عنكم ولا يرضى لعباده الكفر. وإن تشكروا يرضه لكم" (39:7) So, disbelief and gratitude exist and fall under the will and decree of God. One of which is approved while the other is not. God prohibited polytheism, injustice, immoralities and arrogance. He says about these things: "All that - its evil is ever, in the sight of your Lord, detested". "كل ذلك كان سيئه عند ربك مكروهًا". (17:38) He detests these evil things but they occur under His will and decree.

The Messenger (PBUH) says: "Verily God disapproves three things for you: engaging in gossip, asking too many questions (asking people for money, asking scholars about things which will be of no benefit or will lead to dispute, or asking about people's affairs) and wasting wealth". This is a disapproval for acts occur but falling under God's will. The Messenger (PBUH) was supplicating God: "O God! I seek protection against Your wrath in Your pleasure. I seek protection in Your pardon against Your chastisement and in You from You". So, consider carefully that wrath, pleasure, pardon and chastisement of God are all of God's will.

Repentance of common people

Repentance of common people is for a slave to repent consideration his good deeds as so great, as it is deemed a denial of God's favor upon a slave. One should do much more good deeds without forgetting their evil ones.

The Islamic religion is all about doing plenty of good deeds; for instance, prostrating abundantly, constantly supplicating for forgiveness, performing pilgrimage (Hajj and Umrah) frequently... etc.

The Prophet (PBUH) says to someone who asked him for his company in the Heaven: "Help me for yourself by making prostrations abundantly". And He (PBUH) says to another one: "Make frequent prostrations before God, for you will not make one prostration without raising you a degree because of it, and removing a sin rom you because of it". God, the Almighty, says: " They used to sleep but little of the night, And in the hours before dawn they would ask forgiveness". " كانوا قليلاً من الليل ما يهجعون. " 51:17) ".وبالأسحار هم يستغفرون) – (51:18) The Prophet (PBUH) says: "Perform Hajj and Umrah consecutively; for they remove poverty and sin as the bellows removes impurity from iron". He also says to someone who asked him for a thing to stick to: "Let not your tongue cease to be moist with the remembrance of God".

The most beloved people to God are those who do much better deeds than others. Through the Prophet, God says: "And the most beloved thing with which My slave comes nearer to me is what I have enjoined upon him; and My slave keeps on coming closer to Me through performing Nawafil (voluntary prayers or doing extra deeds besides what is obligatory) till I love him. When I love him, I become his hearing with which he hears, his seeing with which he sees, his hand with which he strikes and his leg with which he walks. And if he asks Me something, I will surely give him, and if he seeks My protection (refuge), I will surely protect him". So, this is God's reward for those performing better deeds more often.

Repentance of moderate people

Repentance of moderate people includes that a slave repents from regarding his sin as insignificant, because this is daring and challenging God. A slave's Regarding his evil deed as insignificant is a sin as well as regarding his good deeds as so great is a sin. The righteous slave is the one who sees his good deeds tiny and his sins disgraceful. The more a slave's good deeds are underestimated, the greater he is to God, unlike a slave's evil deeds. When a slave offer better deeds, he will be closer to God and he will know that his all deeds are insignificant against exaltedness of God. Moderate repentant salves are different from common repentant in that the former always watch out defects of their souls and deeds. Accordingly, they are keen on purifying themselves from evil deeds.

The Elite Repentance

Elite repentance is conductive to overtaking of faultiness.

Elite repentance is conductive to overtaking of faultiness. Time is not wasted in a sin or a falsity. Time is dedicated to religious obligations and duties. If time is wasted, thus elite shall not be so. For Arabs, time is special, as some said it is the truth. Some refer to time dedication to God worship and His oneness declaration. It is said about those who spend their times worshipping God and performing their religious obligations, that they have a time with God.

Thus, such repentance with dedication of some special time to God is valid and true, nothing can desolate it.

Later more lines shall be allocated to Time, distinguishing between the valid and the invalid.

Time shall be spent in overtaking faultiness, as time keeper is looking forward to perfection. If one wastes time, one shall be downgraded. If servants do not proceed, they lag, servants go forward not motionless. Nature and Islamic law do not refer to any motionlessness, as one's life encompasses steps that are conductive to either Heaven or Hell. Some hasten, others fall behind. Yet, no one is still. We all move, but in different directions and speeds. "Indeed, the Fire is of the greatest [afflictions], as a warning to humanity, to whoever wills among you to proceed or stay behind." "إِنَّهَا لَإِحْدَى الْكُبَرِ نَذِيرًا لِّلْبَشَرِ لِمَن شَاءَ مِنكُمْ أَن يَتَقَدَّمَ أَوْ يَتَأَخَّرَ" (74:35-37). In these verses, God stated progress or lagging, not motionlessness, as there are only Heaven and Hell, with no other spots in-between. People can reach only one of these two spots. Whoever does not proceed to reach Heaven through virtues, will lag to the Hell through sins.

However, seekers may halt, then keep on progressing. Those who may halt, are either putting themselves together, or lagging. For the first case, this halt is for much development. The Prophet narrates "for every action, there is a vigor and for every vigor, there is a tepidity.

In the other case, one may halt for lagging and tardiness. If one responds to such tardiness, one must pause and stumble. If so is overtaken, servants can uplift, regretting such lag to keep up. If the servants get attached to such lag, they shall be downgraded, just like a setback after recovery, yet in a more problematic and serious manner.

May God rescue such lagging servants, otherwise they shall be in immortal tardiness.

Controlling and keeping an eye on our deeds highlight worship and knowledge. Wasting time shall miss such control. Whoever can save time worshiping God, manages to maintain a special accompaniment with God. Whoever obeys God, God shall bless him. Yet, if he wastes his time, indeed he shall waste such accompaniment accordingly. In case people do not overtake wasting time, they will be in cul-de-sac, which may last to the Doomsday, on which regret and grief will be uttermost. They will be like those who viewed the Heaven and after being in joy with its pleasure, their faces turned to the Hell. Thus, the elite repentance is achieved through spending time worshipping God.

There is a greater and loftier rank of repentance, discerned only by the elite who dedicated their deeds, life and utterances to their beloved God. They are self-denying and glorifying only God's self. If they dropped God's obedience, they seek repentance as if they perpetrate heinous sins. They are always repenting in a different way from others. "over every possessor of knowledge is one [more] knowing." "وَفَوْقَ كُلِّ ذِي عِلْمٍ عَلِيمٌ" (12:76)

The more is their love to God, the more is their apprehension to Him. Thus, they always feel in default. So, their repentance become greater. What they repent for may be others' bests.

The true repentance is that of God lovers.

Repentance is not complete unless recognizing the action necessitating it and abandoning such action.

Repentance from what is below God means that the servant shall only want what God wants, he worships Him.

This only applies on those whom love of God whelmed. Thus, they ardently appreciate and obey God.

Hence, one shall repent to God, recognize such repentance and its motivating action, and then abandoning such action. This is the ultimate end people seek and it is attainable only by the flower of the elite.

Realization of the mistake that necessities repentance is achieved by God Who helps His servant to do so.

They seek a path at whose end pleasure and joy exist, feeling that this is the perfection they may need. This is more perfect than others' path. Perfection lies where servitude to God is at its best. Yet, Quran and Sunnah do not state the perfection of this case over others.

Quran is calling servants to contemplate its verses and God's creatures. Human shall ponder himself, his life and more particularly his future, he shall ponder God's blessings represented in faith, success and guidance. Pondering shall be followed by thanking and praising God for such blessings.

You can contemplate details of prayer, as it is only valid if you recognize and pay attention to it, otherwise it shall be incomplete.

If the prayer said: "I am intending who created heavens and earth as a true monotheist", this may necessitate obedience of God's instructions and worship of God.

If he said: "My prayer, devotion, life and death is by God", this shall mean that prayers and devotion is intended to God, and if he does not commit thereto, he shall be like who so performs in words not actions. Thus, how this could be more perfect than who perform in actions.

When one said: "It is You we worship and You we ask for help", " إِيَّاكَ نَعْبُدُ وَإِيَّاكَ نَسْتَعِينُ" (1:5), so one shall fully understand the significance of worship and asking for help. One shall so allocate only to God, as it is more perfect to understand and practice than only uttering and repeating.

If the prayer said in bowing: "To You I have bowed, and in You I believe, and to You have I submitted. My hearing, my sight, my brain, my bones and my sinew are humbled to you". So, how can only utterance of the above words be enough or substituting its corresponding action. They cannot only be voices.

God said: "They consider it a favor to you that they have accepted Islam. Say, "Do not consider your Islam a favor to me. Rather, God has conferred favor upon you that He has guided you to the faith, if you should be truthful."" " يَمُنُّونَ عَلَيْكَ أَنْ أَسْلَمُوا (49:17) "قُل لَّا تَمُنُّوا عَلَيَّ إِسْلَامَكُم ۖ بَلِ اللَّهُ يَمُنُّ عَلَيْكُمْ أَنْ هَدَاكُمْ لِلْإِيمَانِ إِن كُنتُمْ صَادِقِينَ". The knower shall apply this in worship, the ignorant cannot notice God's favor.

Repentance of a guilt: a duty

We shall bring epitomes regarding provision of repentance that are direly needed to be known by the servants.

Repentance of a guilt is religious duty shall be fulfilled in immediate and shall not be delayed. And if it is delayed, one shall be disobedient. So, if he repents a certain mistake, another repentance is pending, which is that of delay. This sort of repentance does not cross minds of many repentant people, as they guess that if they repent such mistake, they have nothing to do. To avoid missing a necessary repentance, a general one shall be performed, so servants can repent these mistakes they know and those they do not. Mistakes we do not know are more than those we actually know. It does not work to be ignorant of these mistakes, as one will be guilty, ignoring right actions and knowledge. In Sahih of ibn Haban, the Prophet said: "polytheism in this nation is more invisible than ants creepage." Abu Bakr asked: "How could this be eliminated, Messenger?" One shall say: "O' God, I seek refuge to You, so as not to be a polytheist, at my knowledge, I ask you forgiveness for my ignorance".

This is asking for forgiveness for mistakes God knows, while we do not.

In Sahih of Albukhary, the Messenger (PBUH) was quoted saying: "Forgive my errors, ignorance and immoderation in my affairs. You are better aware of my faults than myself. O God! Forgive my faults which I committed in seriousness or in fun deliberately or inadvertently. O God! Grant me pardon for those sins which I committed in the past and I may commit in future, which I committed in privacy or in public and all those sins of which You are better aware than me. You Alone can send whomever You will to the Heaven, and You Alone can send whomever You will to Hell, and You are Omnipotent".

In another narration, the Messenger (PBUH) said: "O' God, Forgive all my sins, the small and the great, first and the last, the open and the secret".

This generalization and inclusiveness are to let repentance include these mistakes servant know and those they ignore.

Is repentance of a guilt valid while keeping on another?

Scholars are split in this regard. Imam Ahmed ibn Hanbal quoted both opinions.

Such matter is problematic, authoritative confirmation of any of them needs a conclusive proof. Who refers to affirmation, declared that embracing Islam which is a repentance of blasphemy occurs while keeping on a non-repented sin. Thus, repentance of a guilt shall be valid, while keeping on another.

Yet, some so abolish as Islam is a very special matter, as it may be inherited. This religion is powerful, and it may happen unintentionally, but upon treading on heels.

The other opinion suggests that repentance is a return to God and obedience of the Almighty. So, how can the obedience be valid and complete while keeping on several sins?

God welcomes those who repent and look forward to obedience of God, as it is a genuine repentance. Who keeps on similar or greater sins, is not a genuine repentant.

Moreover, it is suggested that the servant, if repents, shall no longer be called "disobedient", similarly to the disbeliever who if embraces Islam, shall no longer be called "disbeliever". Yet, if one persists in performing a sin other than the repented, shall be called "disobedient", as repentance is not valid.

The problem locates in whether the repentance is integral, just like disobedience, thus a person could repent of a sin and persist on another, like faith and Islam.

Most scholars negate repentance integrality, it is matter of quality not quantity. If a servant performs a religious duty and neglects another, so he shall be punished for the neglected. The case is the same when comes to repentance of a sin while keeping on another, as the repentance is due regarding both sins. Thus, negligence of an obligation is not a trigger invaliding the one performed. It is the same for who neglects pilgrimage and performs the religious duties of prayer, fasting and paying Zakat (The obligatory tax that every Muslim must give).

This opinion is refused, because repentance is an integral act, refers to quit and regret acts God abhors. Thus, if repentance is not performed fully, it shall be invalid, it is an integral duty. Partial performance of a religious duty is an incomplete performance of the due duty. In other words, intra-relation of a certain duty is stronger than inter-relation of certain several duties.

Who affirms the validity of the partial repentance suggest that for every sin there is a related repentance, not related to another, as sins are not related.

For this matter, we suggest that a repentance of a sin and keeping on a similar one is not valid, yet repentance of a sin and keeping on a different one is valid. For example, who repents of usury but not alcohol-drinking, repentance is valid. On the other side, who repents of excess usury and not credit or delay usury, this is invalid repentance. The same is with who repents of committing adultery with a woman and keeps on doing so with another, and with who repents drinking vin but keeps on drinking another liquors, thus this kind of repentance is invalid. Shifting between similar sins may be attributed to dominance of one over another.

It is similar to Abu Alataheya's case, who repents of killing and stealing, but neither alcohol-drinking nor adultery, his repentance is valid

Is nonrecurrence of a repented sin a condition for repentance validity?

Some conditions nonrecurrence, referring that if it reoccurs, the repentance is invalid, yet most scholars refer that this not a condition for repentance validity, as it is based on quit and regret of a certain sin.

A question is asked, if a servant repented a sin and then re-committed it, shall he deserve punishment for the previous and later sins?

There are two opinions;

Some said guiltiness of the first sin is incurred, as repentance turns invalid by reoccurrence of the sin.

Repentance of a sin is similar to seeking Islam from blasphemy. If a disbeliever embraces Islam, his Islam shall omit the sin of blasphemy, but if he apostatizes from Islam, he shall incur guiltiness of both previous and later blasphemy (apostasy). This opinion is based on the prophet's narration: "He who did good deeds in Islam would not be held responsible for what he did in the state of ignorance, but he who committed evil (after having come within the fold of Islam) would be held responsible for his previous and later deeds." This is the case for whoever embraces Islam and does bad deeds in his Islam, it is known the apostasy is the worst deed in Islam. If one turns to his deeds in the initial blasphemy, repentance between the previous and later blasphemy, does not omit guiltiness of the previous the coming vices.

Some said repentance is conditional to its continuity, just like embracing Islam. Repentance is due all over one's whole life. It is timed by the life. It is related to the life, just like avoiding actions nullifying fasting on a fasting day. If one fasts the most of a day then seeks actions nullifying such fasting, his earlier fasting on that day shall turn worthless.

This is proven by the true narration: "Verily, a person performs deeds for a long time like the deeds of the people of Paradise. Then his deeds are terminated like the deeds of the people of Hell". This is more general than that the later deed is a blasphemy, it is not said: "to apostatize and leave Islam", but a deed necessitates Hell as a punishment. In another narration, the Prophet said: " A man acts in obedience to God for sixty years, then when he is about to die, he causes injury by their will, so they must go to Hell. In other words, acts are considered by ends.

Nonconformists refer that a person in this way nullifies good deeds by bad ones. Quran and Sunnah refer that good deeds nullify the bad ones, not the contrary. In Quran, God says: "Indeed, good deeds do away with misdeeds", "إِنَّ الْحَسَنَاتِ يُذْهِبْنَ السَّيِّئَاتِ" (11:114). In Sunnah, the Prophet (PBUH) said to Moaz: "Fear Allah wherever you are, do good deeds after doing bad ones, the former will wipe out the latter, and behave decently towards people".

Quran and Sunnah indicate counterbalancing, and that good deeds nullify the bad ones. Quran is not conflicted, and it shall not be riposted out of a nonconformist statement.

For counterbalancing, it is mentioned in surahs of Alaraf, Alanbia, Almoeminin, Alqarea and Alhaqa.

For nullification, God said: "O you who have believed, obey Allah and obey the Messenger and do not invalidate your deeds.", "يَا أَيُّهَا الَّذِينَ آمَنُوا أَطِيعُوا اللَّهَ وَأَطِيعُوا الرَّسُولَ وَلَا تُبْطِلُوا أَعْمَالَكُمْ" , (47:33). Invalidation in this verse refers to apostasy, it is the greatest nullifiers. God also said: "O you who have believed, do not invalidate your charities with reminders or injury" "يَا أَيُّهَا الَّذِينَ آمَنُوا لَا تُبْطِلُوا صَدَقَاتِكُم بِالْمَنِّ وَالْأَذَى" (2:264). If these two actions occur after charity, it will be nullified. God likens this case to a person who spends his wealth, only to be seen by the people. In addition, God's words come as follows: "O you who have believed, do not raise your voices above the voice of the Prophet or be loud to him in speech like the loudness of some of you to others, lest your deeds become worthless while you perceive not." "يَا أَيُّهَا الَّذِينَ آمَنُوا لَا تَرْفَعُوا أَصْوَاتَكُمْ فَوْقَ صَوْتِ النَّبِيِّ وَلَا تَجْهَرُوا لَهُ بِالْقَوْلِ كَجَهْرِ بَعْضِكُمْ لِبَعْضٍ أَن تَحْبَطَ أَعْمَالُكُمْ وَأَنتُمْ لَا تَشْعُرُونَ" (49:2). In another context, the Messenger (PBUH) said: "He who misses the 'Asr Salat (deliberately), his deeds will be rendered null and void". Aisha said to mother of Zaid ibn Arqam, tell Zaid that his seeking God's path is not complete till he repents".

If the Islamic law states that there are vices nullifying good deeds, sin recurrence vice may nullify the blessing of repentance, so it cannot exist anymore.

On the Doomsday, a person whose misdeeds are more than good deeds by only one, shall be punished in the Hell, and whose good deeds are more than misdeeds by only one, shall be awarded the heaven. God says: "So those whose scales are heavy - it is they who will be the successful." " فَمَن ثَقُلَتْ مَوَازِينُهُ فَأُولَٰئِكَ هُمُ الْمُفْلِحُونَ " (7:8).

So shall the major nullify the minor ones, or just nullify the counterpart? And the excess shall prevail?

If good deeds are more than bad ones by one, shall good deeds nullify all the bad, so award shall be done upon all good deeds? Or shall good deeds omit the counter bad ones, so no punishment for the omitted bad deeds or award for the omitting good ones, and then the excess shall remain.

The same is with the bad deeds if they are more than the good one by one, shall this only deed cause the doer to enter the Hell?

For some Jabriyyah scholars, the whole matter is attributed to God's will. For them, God may punish a person with more good deeds and award another with more bad deeds, or two shall be punished in Hell, each in a different level. They negate all reasons, grounds, counterbalance and nullification. Good doer and bad doers are the same, and may be both punished.

The other party who consider that guiltiness of the previous repented sin shall not be assumed when the sin reoccurs, as such guiltiness is cancelled through the first repentance, and the re-occurrence of the sin shall bear a separate guiltiness.

They suggest that repentance validity is not conditional to immoral inerrancy, but if a repentant regrets and quits a sin, guiltiness shall be omitted, and if one is back to such sin, one shall be guilty again.

They point that such case is different from blasphemy that nullify good deeds, as blasphemy is a separate peculiar matter. Thus, reoccurrence of the sin does not nullify the previous good deeds.

Repentance is deemed one of the best good deeds. If it is nullified by reoccurrence of the sin, other good deeds shall be nullified, this is absolutely fallacious. Thus, it is similar to the Dissenters' approach that refer to the blasphemy of the wrong doers and to the Nonconformists' approach that refer to immortality in the Hell out of committing of great sins, even if preceded by thousands of good deeds. Both Dissenters and Nonconformists agree on the immortality of great sinners in Hell, yet they are considered as disbelievers by the Dissenters and wicked by the Nonconformists. Both approaches are mistaken. In Quran, God says: "Indeed, God does not do injustice, [even] as much as an atom's weight; while if there is a good deed, He multiplies it and gives from Himself a great reward.", " إِنَّ اللَّهَ لَا يَظْلِمُ مِثْقَالَ ذَرَّةٍ ۖ وَإِن تَكُ حَسَنَةً يُضَاعِفْهَا وَيُؤْتِ مِن لَّدُنْهُ أَجْرًا عَظِيمًا" (4:40)

Imam Ahmed said, supported by some of the Prophet's narration: "God likes the allured repentant servants".

If a reoccurrence of a sin nullified a repentance, God would not love the repentant servant, as it is a trigger to be abhorred.

God conditioned the validity of the repentance to expiation and willingness to quit the sin, but not to the nonrecurrence. In Quran, God says: "And those who, when they commit an immorality or wrong themselves [by transgression], remember God and seek forgiveness for their sins - and who can forgive sins except God? - and [who] do not persist in what they have done while they know.", " وَالَّذِينَ إِذَا فَعَلُوا فَاحِشَةً أَوْ ظَلَمُوا أَنفُسَهُمْ ذَكَرُوا اللَّهَ فَاسْتَغْفَرُوا لِذُنُوبِهِمْ وَمَن يَغْفِرُ الذُّنُوبَ إِلَّا اللَّهُ وَلَمْ يُصِرُّوا عَلَىٰ مَا فَعَلُوا وَهُمْ يَعْلَمُونَ" (3:135). If a person is insisting on committing such sin whenever the opportunity exists, shall not be forgiven.

It is said that the continuity of the repentance is a condition for its benefit not for its validity. Unlike other religious duties, such as fasting and prayer. It is a whole duty, shall not be deemed valid, unless completely performed. For repentance, it is a separate duty for separate sins, for each sin, there is a necessary repentance. As previously said, if one repents a sin and keeps on another, the kept sin shall not nullify the repentance of the other.

Thus, the initial repentance is a good deed and the reoccurrence of a sin is a vice, that shall not nullify the good deed of repentance.

Sunnis agree that the same servant may obey God in some duties and neglect others. Yet, there is always an outbalancing side. God says: "They were nearer to disbelief that day than to faith" "هُمْ لِلْكُفْرِ يَوْمَئِذٍ أَقْرَبُ مِنْهُمْ لِلْإِيمَانِ" (3:167). "And most of them believe not in Allah except while they associate others with Him." "وَمَا يُؤْمِنُ أَكْثَرُهُم بِاللَّهِ إِلَّا وَهُم مُّشْرِكُونَ" (12:106)

Blasphemy is of two types: implicit and express blasphemy, the first may be forgiven. The latter is not forgiven, but only through repentance.

Who recommits a sin is abhorred by God for reoccurrence of the sin and is approached for repentance ad previous good deeds. God is fair and wise. "And your Lord is not ever unjust to [His] servants." "مَّنْ عَمِلَ صَالِحًا فَلِنَفْسِهِ ۖ وَمَنْ أَسَاءَ فَعَلَيْهَا ۗ وَمَا رَبُّكَ بِظَلَّامٍ لِّلْعَبِيدِ" (41:46)

If new sins overweighed the former good deeds, then are genuinely repented, good deeds shall be awarded. Good deeds performed in one's Islam are greater than those performed in blasphemy, like manumission, charity and kinship ties. Hakim ibn

Hazam said: O' Messenger, I released slaves, was charitable and kept good relations with my kith & kin, so shall I be awarded for this? The Messenger (PBUH), replied: your Islam include your former good deeds. It is meant that sins committed between two good deeds are omitted by repentance.

Another argued condition is if the repentant is prevented from the triggers of the repented sin, shall the repentance be accepted? It is like the liar and defamer. It is like the perjurer, if had his tongue cut, the adulterer if castrated, the thief and the forger if had their hands.

In this regard, people have two opinions:

The first refer that the repentance shall not be valid, as it must be out of the inner willingness to quit sins. It is about the possible not the impossible.

They also refer that repentance is overcoming the inner vain desires and responding to God. In the abovementioned cases, vain desires are absent. Such cases express forcing quit of a sin, unwillingly. Thus, repentance is not valid.

This party also refer to Quran verses that indicating that re-pentance shall be performed willingly, God says: "The repentance accepted by God is only for those who do wrong in ignorance [or carelessness] and then repent soon after. It is those to whom God will turn in forgiveness, and God is ever

Knowing and Wise. But repentance is not [accepted] of those who [continue to] do evil deeds up until, when death comes to one of them, he says, "Indeed, I have repented now," or of those who die while they are disbelievers. For them We have prepared a painful punishment.", " إِنَّمَا التَّوْبَةُ عَلَى اللَّهِ لِلَّذِينَ يَعْمَلُونَ السُّوءَ بِجَهَالَةٍ ثُمَّ يَتُوبُونَ مِن قَرِيبٍ فَأُولَٰئِكَ يَتُوبُ اللَّهُ عَلَيْهِمْ ۗ وَكَانَ اللَّهُ عَلِيمًا حَكِيمًا، وَلَيْسَتِ التَّوْبَةُ لِلَّذِينَ يَعْمَلُونَ السَّيِّئَاتِ حَتَّىٰ إِذَا حَضَرَ أَحَدَهُمُ الْمَوْتُ قَالَ إِنِّي تُبْتُ الْآنَ وَلَا الَّذِينَ يَمُوتُونَ وَهُمْ كُفَّارٌ ۚ أُولَٰئِكَ أَعْتَدْنَا لَهُمْ عَذَابًا أَلِيمًا" (4:17-18). Ignorance referred to above is of action, as one knows about the prohibition.

According to the Prophet, "God accepts the repentance of His slave so long as the death rattle has not yet reached his throat". In another narration: Satan says: "O' God, I will continue fancy Your servant till death", God replied: "I will keep on forgiving them as long as they are repenting." Repentance out of pressing necessity is not valid, it is like repentance after sunrise in the west on the Doomsday.

As sin is a definite willingness to do the prohibited, repentance is a definite willingness to quit such sin.

The second refers that the repentance shall be true and possible, as all conditions of repentance are met, including regret. As regret is repentance, if one regrets a certain sin, repentance shall be valid. Such opinion is concluded from the concept that if one intends to obey God, but becomes unable to do so, obedience shall be accounted, as if it is done.

This is clear in the Messenger's narration "When a slave of God suffers from illness or sets on a journey, he is credited with the equal of whatever good works he used to do when he was healthy or at home". In addition, the Messenger (PBUH) said: "Here are some people in Medina who were with you all the time, you did not travel any portion of the journey nor crossed any valley, but they were with you they (i.e. the people) said, "O' God's Messenger! Even though they were at Medina?" He said, "Yes, because they were stopped by a genuine excuse."

Blight of the sin upon which punishment is resulting appears from insisting on or committing the sin. Trigger of such blight is absent, regarding the incapable person.

How can repentance of a sin be performed through committing the sin? Whoever commits a sin and intends repentance but cannot so made unless after committing the sin partially, is like who becomes in a midst of an unlawfully gained land and intends repentance that only can be done through exit which require more steps thereon. So how can one repent from a sin through a sin? And shall such repentance be accepted?

Such matter is problematic. Thus, some suggest that such partial sin shall not be committed to repent from the sin as a whole, as sin is not a duty. Others suggest that committing such sin is obligatory, as it is a way to repentance. So, it is subject to both reward and punishment.

It is said that prayer in an unlawfully gained land is improper, although it is an obligatory duty.

Indeed, repentance of a sin by partially committing it is not a wrongdoing, yet it is a duty and no duty to God is a wrongdoing. So, a single act can be deemed a sin or a repentance from a sin.

From the provisions of the repentance is that if it includes a human right, the repentant shall complete his repentance through granting such right. If it includes a financial right or felony concerning his wealth or an heir's, a repentant shall disentangle oneself therefrom. The Prophet (PBUH) said: "Whoever has oppressed another person concerning his reputation or anything else, he should beg him to forgive him before the Day of Resurrection when there will be no money (to compensate for wrong deeds), but if he has good deeds, those good deeds will be taken from him according to his oppression which he has done, and if he has no good deeds, the sins of the oppressed person will be loaded on him."

If the sin includes an abuse, backbiting or calumny, so shall repentance necessitate informing the abused of such act, or shall repentance be between God and the servant without informing the abused person? There are different opinions in such matter. Alshafey, Abu Hanifa and Malik necessitate informing of the abused. Who so necessitate, argue that the sin engaged a human right, so repentance shall not be complete unless such sinner is forgiven. Such opinion supporters are sticking to the narration of the Prophet (PBUH), "Whoever has oppressed another person concerning his reputation or anything else, he should beg him to forgive him before the Day of Resurrection". They refer that such sin involves two felonies, one against God, and the other against the abused human. So, the repentance shall be complete upon forgiveness of the human and the regret shall be between the sinner and God.

Hence, the killer's repentance shall be only valid after referring to the people of the murdered, they may take revenge from or absolve the killer.

Another opinion refer that it is not necessary to inform the abused, as repentance shall be between the sinner and God. In addition, the sinner shall praise the insulted wherever he is insulted and abused. He shall mention favors and pros of the abused. Abu Alabbas ibn Taimiyyah.

This opinion supporters view that informing the abused person of such calumny or abuse is a bane bringing about harm, wrath and ire. It may also cause enmity between the abused and the abuser, such enmity may bring an evil greater than that of the abuse or the calumny.

There are differences between such rights and financial ones or body felonies;

First; if a possession is returned to its owner, it shall be a benefit, unlike informing the abused of the guilt committed against him, there is no benefit.

Second; if the owner of the unlawfully taken property is informed of his right in such property, he shall rejoice and be pleased, unlike turning angry upon being informed of the abuse against him.

Such opinion is better and more suitable.

Another provision is if the servant repents a sin, shall he regain the same rank he had before committing such sin?

Some refer that he shall regain the same rank he had before such sin, as repentance omit the sin as a whole, as if it is not committed. High rank is gained upon faith and good deeds, which is regained upon repentance (a good deed).

Repentance is a great blessing and a good deed, if such sin downgraded him, so the good deed of repentance shall re-upgrade him. This is similar to who fell in a will and good friend helped him to ascend. The same is with repentance, as it is a good deed and friend.

Another opinion refers that such sinner if repents, shall not regain his rank, as he was not at halt, he was being upgraded, but with such sin he is downgraded. This case is similar to two men walking on the same road, one of them stopped, and then continue his way, he will never catch the other man.

Ibn Taimiyyah declared that there are types of repentant; one shall not regain his rank and the another shall do and the other shall catch a higher one.

Such is determined upon the path the repentant seeks after repentance. If such path is better than that before committing the repented sin, he will catch a higher rank. If the path is the same, the same rank shall be regained. If the path is poorer than that sought before the repented sin, a lower rank shall be gained.

Such three cases are paraphrased in the following examples. A man is on his way and he found gardens, shelter and water, he is inclined to stop at such charms, yet when he reached there, an enemy appears and was about to cause him bane. But his father rescued him, and warned him about such enemy, instructing that he shall be careful of such enemy and speed up his way to follow him to home. After being rescued, the man had three options; to speed up his way and be careful and watchful of such enemy, so his second steps become quicker than the first ones, that led him to his house quicker. The second option is to neglect his enemy, so fall in the same danger where he was initially. The third option is to recall the gardens, shelter and water, so the man can be lagged.

Another example is that a man went to the mosque to perform prayer, intending the first row of prayers. Another man appears to pull him back in order to impair him from performing prayer, thus the first man has two options;

Either to be wrapped up with him, till he misses the prayer. This is the case for the non-repentant, or to flee him so as not to miss the prayer, after such fleeing, he can:

-    Hurry up and get a move on to redress what he misses upon such stoppage, so he can keep up with his goal or excel.

-    To proceed with his way as initially.

-    To be foiled by such stoppage and miss the first-row prayers.

This should take us to a significant matter; is the non-sinner obedient better than the repentant disobeyer, or vice versa?

This matter is controverted.

Some refer that the non-sinner obedient is superior to repentant disobeyer, arguing that the best servants are the most obeying. In addition, while the disobedient is committing sins, the obedient is doing his best to gain a higher rank. Moreover, the repentance aims at omitting of the wrongdoings, as if they were not committed, thus he neither proceed nor lag, unlike the obedient who seeks progress and higher ranks.

Indeed, God abhors violating and disobedient slaves, as while the disobeyers are immersed in their sins, incurring God's wrath, the obedient ones are gaining God's bless.

Those who overweigh the obedient suggest that the sin is like intaking poison, antidoted by repentance, while obedience is like good health. It stands to reason that permanent good health is better than recovered health after illness.

They also insinuate that the disobeyer is in grave danger, fluctuating between three matters, upon his sin; eternal damnation upon poison intake, power deficiencies and difficulty of regaining the same or improved power. The most likely to take place is the first two matters.

This view supporters see that the obedient has built a well-fenced garden, enemies (sins) cannot penetrate, unlike the disobeyer who creates a lacuna to let enemies reach him.

Sins can overcome the disobeyers, because of his poor knowledge and feeble determination, thus he is called an ignorant. It is said by Qatada that the Prophet's companions agree that the disobeyer is ignorant. God also said of Adam: "And We had already taken a promise from Adam before, but he forgot; and We found not in him determination." " وَلَقَدْ عَهِدْنَا إِلَىٰ آدَمَ مِن قَبْلُ فَنَسِيَ وَلَمْ نَجِدْ لَهُ عَزْمًا" (20:115), and of others: "So be patient, as were those of determination among the messengers" " فَاصْبِرْ كَمَا صَبَرَ أُولُو الْعَزْمِ مِنَ الرُّسُلِ" (46:35).

CHAPTER 20

Chapter of Expiation (seeking forgiveness)

Seeking forgiveness is two-fold: independent; and related to repentance.

The independent is like when Noah said to his people: "And said, 'Ask forgiveness of your Lord. Indeed, He is ever a Perpetual Forgiver. He will send [rain from] the sky upon you in [continuing] showers". "فَقُلْتُ اسْتَغْفِرُوا رَبَّكُمْ إِنَّهُ كَانَ غَفَّارا يُرْسِلِ السَّمَاءَ عَلَيْكُم مِدْرَارا" (71:10-11) and When Saleh said to his people: "Why do you not seek forgiveness of Allah that you may receive mercy?" " لَوْلَا تَسْتَغْفِرُونَ اللَّهَ لَعَلَّكُمْ تُرْحَمُون" (27:46) and when He, the Almighty says: "and ask forgiveness of Allah . Indeed, Allah is Forgiving and Merciful." "وَاسْتَغْفِرُوا اللَّهَ إِنَّ اللَّهَ غَفُورٌ رَحِيمٌ"(2:199).

He says "But Allah would not punish them while you, [O Muhammad], are among them, and Allah would not punish them while they seek forgiveness." " وَمَا كَانَ اللَّهُ لِيُعَذِّبَهُمْ وَأَنْتَ فِيهِمْ وَمَا كَانَ اللَّهُ مُعَذِّبَهُمْ وَهُمْ يَسْتَغْفِرُون" (8:33).

The same when He says "And [saying], "Seek forgiveness of your Lord and repent to Him, [and] He will let you enjoy a good provision for a specified term and give every doer of favor his favor." " وَأَنْ اسْتَغْفِرُوا رَبَّكُمْ ثُمَّ تُوبُوا إِلَيْهِ يُمَتِّعْكُمْ مَتَاعاً حَسَناً إِلَى أَجَلٍ مُسَمًّى وَيُؤْتِ كُلَّ ذِي فَضْلٍ فَضْلَه" (11:3)

And when Hud told his people: "And O my people, ask forgiveness of your Lord and then repent to Him. He will send [rain from] the sky upon you in showers"

(11:52) "وَيَا قَوْمِ اسْتَغْفِرُوا رَبَّكُمْ ثُمَّ تُوبُوا إِلَيْهِ يُرْسِلِ السَّمَاءَ عَلَيْكُمْ مِدْرَارا"

Moreover, Saleh said to his people "He has produced you from the earth and settled you in it, so ask forgiveness of Him and then repent to Him. Indeed, my Lord is near and responsive."" يَا قَوْمِ اعْبُدُوا اللَّهَ مَا لَكُمْ مِنْ إِلَهٍ غَيْرُهُ هُوَ أَنْشَأَكُمْ مِنَ الْأَرْضِ وَاسْتَعْمَرَكُمْ فِيهَا" (11:61) and when Shu'ayb said "فَاسْتَغْفِرُوهُ ثُمَّ تُوبُوا إِلَيْهِ إِنَّ رَبِّي قَرِيبٌ مُجِيب" "And ask forgiveness of your Lord and then repent to Him. Indeed, my Lord is Merciful and Affectionate."

(11:91) "وَاسْتَغْفِرُوا رَبَّكُمْ ثُمَّ تُوبُوا إِلَيْهِ إِنَّ رَبِّي رَحِيمٌ وَدُود"

So the independent expiation appears in repentance. It is the repentance itself, when asking God for forgiveness. It is erasing sins, and its consequences, and avoiding its evil. It is not like some people think; it eliminate misdeeds. God would eliminate mistakes of people that He forgives.

The aim of eliminating mistakes is to be protected from sin including forgiveness, because it keeps the person protected from harm.

Therefore, expiation prevents punishment and God said: "and Allah would not punish them while they seek forgiveness." وَمَا كَانَ اللَّهُ لِيُعَذِّبَهُمْ وَأَنْتَ فِيهِمْ وَمَا كَانَ اللَّهُ مُعَذِّبَهُمْ وَهُمْ يَسْتَغْفِرُون"" (8:33) So, God does not punish a person who seeks forgiveness. However if someone recommits a sin and insisted on it and then he asked God for forgiveness, this cannot be seeking forgiveness and in this case punishment will not be prevented. Expiation includes repentance, which by turn, requires seeking forgiveness and asking for it.

When these two concepts corelate, seeking forgiveness is the demand to be protected from the past evil deeds. Repentance is the demand to be protected from the future evil deeds.

These are two sins; a past sin and asking forgiveness for it is asking for protection from its evil and a possible sin, yet repentance is a determination to avoid that sin. Returning to God can be in two ways: Returning to God to protect you from an evil that was in the past, and returning to God to protect you from future evil that can be the result of bad deeds.

The sinner is like a person that heading to the path that leads to his damnation. It will never make him reach his right destination. Therefore, the sinner is required to ignore this false road and to take salvation road.

There are two must-do matters: leaving the sin and returning to good deeds, in this case the repentance is the step concerned with the returning to God, while seeking forgiveness is concerned with leaving the sin. That is why God says in that specific order: "Seek forgiveness of your Lord and repent to Him" "استغفروا ربكم ثم توبوا إليه" (8:33). So returning to the right path requires leaving the wrong one.

Therefore, seeking forgiveness is seeking to avoid harm, and repentance is to bring goodness. Forgiveness is to be prevented from committing sins, while repentance is that this person gets what he likes after being protected from sins.

Sincere Repentance

This is to explain the truth of the Sincere Repentance. God says: "O you who have believed, repent to Allah with sincere repentance. Perhaps your Lord will remove from you your misdeeds and admit you into gardens beneath which rivers flow"

يَا أَيُّهَا الَّذِينَ آمَنُوا تُوبُوا إِلَى اللهِ تَوْبَةً نَصُوحاً عَسَى رَبُّكُمْ أَنْ يُكَفِّرَ عَنْكُمْ سَيِّئَاتِكُمْ وَيُدْخِلَكُمْ "

" جَنَّاتٍ تَجْرِي مِنْ تَحْتِهَا الأَنْهَار (66:8)

God has made preventing evil related to the vanishment of what the worshiper hates the most, and He related entering the Heaven to the sincere repentance. And "sincere" means that it is pure and not fake or deceitful, reflecting the purest level of belief. So, sincere repentance, worship, and asking for advice result in pure repentance.

The righteous ancestors have different concepts, agreeing on the same principle. Omar ibn Alkhattab and Abu Kaab may God be pleased with them said about sincere repentance: "the person should repent from the sin and never recommit it, like breastfed milk would never go back to the breast." Hasan Albasri said also: "Repentance is that worshiper should regret what he has been done, and determine not to repeat it." Alkalby also said: "seek repentance by words, by heart, and by controlling your actions". Saed ibn Almosaib said: "You shall have a sincere repentance to be sincere to yourself."

People said that it is sincere, meaning that the repentant made it sincere

Mohamed ibn Kaab Alkirathy said: "there are four elements for it: "seeking forgiveness verbally, stop committing sins physically, having the intention to quit sins, and to stay away from bad people."

However, we see that sincere repentance includes 3 main things:

First: Recognizing all sins

Second: Determination without any kind of hesitation

Third: Parting all types of excuses and bad habits for the sake of fearing the only God and seeking His forgiveness and blessings. Not the same for the one who repent to keep his power and money fearing that he might lose them one day. Nor it is the case for the one who repents to show off that in front of people, or lest he should be blamed if he does not repent. Same case for similar excuses that does not make the repentance sincere.

The first one is related to the sin itself, the third is related to God, the middle is related to the repenting persons. So, it is a must that the person has a sincere repentance that includes seeking forgiveness and leads to erasing sins.

Difference between making up for bad deeds and getting forgiveness for sins

The book of the Almighty God indicates these two elements jointly and separately. In the part where they are mentioned jointly, God speaks to the believers: "Our Lord, so forgive us our sins and remove from us our misdeeds and cause us to die with the righteous." (3:193)"رَبَّنَا فَاغْفِرْ لَنَا ذُنُوبَنَا وَكَفِّرْ عَنَّا سَيِّئَاتِنَا وَتَوَفَّنَا مَعَ الْأَبْرَارِ"

and when they are mentioned separately, God says: "And those who believe and do righteous deeds and believe in what has been sent down upon Muhammad - and it is the truth from their Lord - He will remove from them their misdeeds and amend their condition." "وَالَّذِينَ آمَنُوا وَعَمِلُوا الصَّالِحَاتِ وَآمَنُوا بِمَا نُزِّلَ عَلَى مُحَمَّدٍ وَهُوَ الْحَقُّ مِنْ رَبِّهِمْ كَفَّرَ عَنْهُمْ سَيِّئَاتِهِمْ وَأَصْلَحَ بَالَهُم" (47:2)

and when God said about forgiveness : "in which they will have from all [kinds of] fruits and forgiveness from their Lord" "وَلَهُمْ فِيهَا مِنْ كُلِّ الثَّمَرَاتِ وَمَغْفِرَةٌ مِنْ رَبِّهِم" (47:15) and when God says: "Our Lord, forgive us our sins and the excess [committed] in our affairs" "قَالُوا رَبَّنَا اغْفِرْ لَنَا ذُنُوبَنَا وَإِسْرَافَنَا فِي أَمْرِنَا" (3:147).

There are four affairs: sin, bad deeds, forgiveness, and expiation

Sin are major guilts. As for bad deeds which are minor sins; they require seeking forgiveness, however, expiation cannot be applied for murder or for lying under oath for God, according to Ahmed and Abu Hanifa.

The proof that bad deeds are the minor sins, and it can be expiated is when God says: "If you avoid the major sins which you are forbidden, We will remove from you your lesser sins and admit you to a noble entrance [into Paradise]". "إِنْ تَجْتَنِبُوا كَبَائِرَ مَا

"تُنْهَوْنَ عَنْهُ نُكَفِّرْ عَنْكُمْ سَيِّئَاتِكُمْ وَنُدْخِلْكُمْ مُدْخَلاً كَرِيمًا" (4:31) and in Sahih Muslim, Abu Hurayrah said that the prophet (PBUH) said that "The five [daily prescribed] Prayers, and Friday [prayer] to the [next] Friday [prayer], and Ramadan to the next Ramadan, is expiation of the sins committed in between them, so long as major sins are avoided."

The expression "forgiveness" is more integrated than expiation expression. That is why expiation is related to major and minor sins. That is why forgiveness includes protection and observation, and expiation includes eliminating and deleting sins. God said: "will remove from you your lesser sins" so, He almighty speaks about the lesser sins and the major ones, and speaks about deleting it, and being protected from its future evil. While expiation is related to the worst deeds, as God said: "That Allah may remove from them the worst of what they did" "لِيُكَفِّرَ اللَّهُ عَنْهُمْ أَسْوَأَ الَّذِي عَمِلُوا"(39:35)

Sadness, harm, and even a pickle, it will be expiation of his sins" So the crisis are related to being forgiven for sins. It is only by repentance that sins are forgiven, or it can be forgiven by good deeds eventually. It is like a sea that does not get polluted by dead bodies.

Sinners have three main rivers by which they can wash their sins in lifetime. If they do not wash away sins, they will be washed away in a river in hell on the day of judgment: the river of sincere repentance, river of good deeds that caused forgiveness, river of major crises that brings expiation. God would get someone pass in one of these three rivers. And this one will end up, one the day of judgment, forgiven. Thus, one will not need the forth river.

The repentance of a servant is between two repentances from his God

Repentance to God is related to a previous repentance sent by God. And another after it. So it is between two repentance attempts. The repenting worshipper is guided to repent by God who accept his repentance. He the almighty says: "Allah has already forgiven the Prophet and the Muhajireen and the Ansar who followed him in the hour of difficulty after the hearts of a party of them had almost inclined [to doubt], and then He forgave them. Indeed, He was to them Kind and Merciful. And [He also forgave] the three who were left behind [and regretted their error] to the point that the earth closed in on them in spite of its vastness and their souls confined them and they were certain that there is no refuge from Allah except in Him. Then He turned to them so they could repent. Indeed, Allah is the Accepting of repentance, the Merciful." "لَقَدْ تَابَ اللَّهُ عَلَى النَّبِيِّ وَالْمُهَاجِرِينَ وَالأَنصَارِ الَّذِينَ اتَّبَعُوهُ فِي سَاعَةِ الْعُسْرَةِ مِنْ بَعْدِ مَا كَادَ يَزِيغُ قُلُوبُ فَرِيقٍ مِنْهُمْ ثُمَّ تَابَ عَلَيْهِمْ إِنَّهُ بِهِمْ رَءُوفٌ رَحِيمٌ وَعَلَى الثَّلاثَةِ الَّذِينَ خُلِّفُوا حَتَّى إِذَا ضَاقَتْ عَلَيْهِمُ الأَرْضُ بِمَا رَحُبَتْ وَضَاقَتْ عَلَيْهِمْ أَنفُسُهُمْ وَظَنُّوا أَنْ لا مَلْجَأَ مِنَ اللَّهِ إِلاَّ إِلَيْهِ ثُمَّ تَابَ عَلَيْهِمْ لِيَتُوبُوا إِنَّ اللَّهَ هُوَ التَّوَّابُ الرَّحِيمُ" (9:117-118)

God told them that they already forgave them before they repent, this is the reason that made them repent. So this is the proof that they only repent when God already forgave them.

Similar to this: when God guide his worshiper to the right path before he starts to discover the way to it. So the guidance follows a divine guidance by which God support the worshipper. The reward of self-guidance is the divine guidance. And the punishment for aberration, aberration itself. God the almighty said "And those who are guided - He increases them in guidance and gives them their righteousness.""وَالَّذِينَ اهْتَدَوْا زَادَهُمْ هُدًى وَآتَاهُمْ تَقْوَاهُمْ" (47:17)

So, God guided them and then they figured out the right path. The opposite for deviates, as God says: "And when they deviated, Allah caused their hearts to deviate"

(61:5) "فَلَمَّا زَاغُوا أَزَاغَ اللَّهُ قُلُوبَهُم"

This is the fate; the caused and resulted. Worshipper keeps repenting, and God keeps forgiving. This is the repentance of the worshiper to his Lord after making mistakes. God's forgiveness comes in two types: Permission and compromise, acceptance and support.

The start and end of Repentance

Repentance has a start and an end. Its start is to obey God by choosing the right path that God set for His worshippers and that leads to his satisfaction. God ordered to take this path by saying: "And, [moreover], this is My path, which is straight, so follow it; and do not follow [other] ways," " وَأَنَّ هَذَا صِرَاطِي مُسْتَقِيماً فَاتَّبِعُوهُ وَلا تَتَّبِعُوا السُّبُلَ فَتَفَرَّقَ بِكُمْ عَنْ سَبِيلِهِ ذَلِكُمْ وَصَّاكُمْ بِهِ لَعَلَّكُمْ تَتَّقُون" (6:153).

He also says: "And indeed, [O Muhammad], you guide to a straight path"" وَإِنَّكَ لَتَهْدِي إِلَى صِرَاطٍ مُسْتَقِيم" (42:52-53). God says: "And they had been guided [in worldly life] to good speech, and they were guided to the path of the Praiseworthy." " وَهُدُوا إِلَى الطَّيِّبِ مِنَ الْقَوْلِ وَهُدُوا إِلَى صِرَاطِ الْحَمِيد" (22:24).

The end of the repentance is to go back to God and to follow His path to reach the Heaven. Those who return to God through repentance God would reward them in time. God says about this: "And he who repents and does righteousness does indeed turn to Allah with [accepted] repentance."" وَمَنْ تَابَ وَعَمِلَ صَالِحاً فَإِنَّهُ يَتُوبُ إِلَى اللَّهِ مَتَابا" (25:71). Fist repentance is when God says: "he who repents" which means giving up polytheism. And the second is to return to God to be rewarded.

The reward includes the meaning of order, the one that has the intention of repentance, should make it for the sake of God only and no one else but God.

An interpretation refers that the aim should be clear; and the repenting person should recognize what he should abandon, and to whom he should repent. It should be for God only.

Similarly, God says: "O Messenger, announce that which has been revealed to you from your Lord, and if you do not, then you have not conveyed His message"

"يَا أَيُّهَا الرَّسُولُ بَلِّغْ مَا أُنزِلَ إِلَيْكَ مِنْ رَبِّكَ وَإِنْ لَمْ تَفْعَلْ فَمَا بَلَّغْتَ رِسَالَتَهُ" (5:67). It means that he should know the consequences of disobeying orders.

Another interpretation argues that the repentance should be in purpose and with clear intention. So, the intention and the determination should be translated into actions. Similarly when the Prophet (PBUH) said: "Those who immigrate to God and his prophet, will have their immigration to God and his prophet. And those who immigrate to life will have life, or to a woman that he will marry; so whoever intend to go to something will have it".

Sins: minor and major ones

, Sins can be divided into two groups: minors and majors according to Quran, Sunnah and to the agreement of the righteous ancestors. God the Almighty says: "If you avoid the major sins which you are forbidden, We will remove your lesser sins." " إِنْ تَجْتَنِبُوا كَبَائِرَ مَا تُنْهَوْنَ عَنْهُ نُكَفِّرْ عَنْكُمْ سَيِّئَاتِكُمْ وَنُدْخِلْكُمْ مُدْخَلاً كَرِيما" (4:31)

God says: "Those who avoid the major sins and immoralities," "الَّذِينَ يَجْتَنِبُونَ كَبَائِرَ الإِثْمِ وَالْفَوَاحِشَ" (53:32) and in Sahih, the prophet (PBUH) said that "The five [daily prescribed] Prayers, and Friday [prayer] to the [next] Friday [prayer], and Ramadan to the next Ramadan, is expiation of the sins committed in between them, so long as major sins are avoided."

Abu Isaac Alesfaraeiny said : "all sins are major, and there are no minor sins." he does not mean that they are equal in punishment: so that looking to something forbidden is equal to doing it"

Baghawy said: minor sins can be considered major sins. Also there is a hadith saying: "never come close to small minor sins"

So servants should not commit major sins, it was a mistake that the believer is willing not to repeat in his lifetime. So it shall be considered a onetime incident and an exception.

This is what encouraged Abu Isaac to say that "all sins are major" so the exception should not continue or happen again.

However, righteous ancestors agreed on dividing sins to minors and majors.

Then they disagree about two things, first: what are pardonable sins? Second: is there a specific number for major sins, or a certain rule for it.

Pardonable/slight sins

The righteous ancestors said that slight sins are the one that are only done once and the sinner would not repeat, even if it is major. Abdullah ibn Amr ibn Assi said "pardonable sins are all sins except polytheism" Sadi said: Abu Saleh said: "I was asked about God saying "only [committing] slight sins" and I said: "it is the case when a man commit a crime one time and he never repeat" and I said it to ibn Abbas and he told me "a noble angel helped you interpreting it". It is agreed that slight sins are all sins except for major ones.

Alkalby said that slight sins are two-fold; one is the sin that there is no punishment for in life or the afterlife. It is forgiven by the five prayers unless they are not major.

The other is the major sin, the Muslim committing it once in a while so he repents.

Saed ibn Mosaib said: it is what the heart got, which means what it desires.

Husain ibn Fathl said: slight sins are these done unintentionally. Therefore, it will be forgiven. If this person did it again so it is not a slight sin,. Ataa ibn Abbas said: the Prophet (PBUH) said: "Oh God if you forgive the sin, forgive them all, and any worshipper would not do any more slight sins"

A group said that slight sins is what people did in Jahiliya before they convert to Islam. God would not punish them. the non-believers told Muslims that they were working with them before so God said this verse as a reply. This was said by Zaid ibn Thabet and Zaid ibn Aslam.

The correct explanation is what has been agreed on: that slight sins are minor sins, like a look, an eye wink, a kiss etc. The companions of the Prophet (PBUH) agreed on this as well as the successors. This does not contradict with Abu Hurayrah and Ibn Abbas saying; "it is related to the major sin but it does not refer to it"

Major Sins

Abdullah ibn Amr (May God be pleased with them) reported: The Prophet (PBUH) said, "(Of the) major sins are: to ascribe partners to God, disobey parents, murder someone, and to take a false oath (intentionally)". Also, Abu Bakra narrated: The Prophet (PBUH) said thrice, "Should I inform you out the gravest of major sins?" They said, "Yes, O God's Messenger (PBUH)!" He said, "To join others in worship with God and to be undutiful to one's parents." The Prophet (PBUH) then sat up after he had been reclining (on a pillow) and said, "And I warn you against giving a false witness, and he kept on saying that warning till we thought he would not stop".

Abdullah ibn Masoud narrated (May God be pleased with him): I asked God's Messenger (PBUH): "What is the gravest sin in the sight of God?" He said, "To set up rivals unto God though He alone created you." I asked "What next?" He said, "To kill your son being afraid that he may share your food with you." I further asked, "What next?" He said, "To commit illegal sexual intercourse with the wife of your neighbor." God then revealed the following Qur'anic verse in support of the statement of the Prophet (PBUH): "And those who do not invoke with God another deity or kill the soul which God has forbidden [to be killed], except by right, and do not commit unlawful sexual intercourse".

"وَالَّذِينَ لَا يَدْعُونَ مَعَ اللَّهِ إِلَٰهًا آخَرَ وَلَا يَقْتُلُونَ النَّفْسَ الَّتِي حَرَّمَ اللَّهُ إِلَّا بِالْحَقِّ وَلَا يَزْنُونَ".

(25:68)

Abu Hurayrah (May God be pleased with him) narrated: The Prophet (PBUH) said, "Avoid the seven destructive things." It was asked: (by those present): "What are they, O Messenger of God?" He replied, "Associating anyone or anything with God in worship; practising sorcery, killing of someone without a just cause whom God has forbidden, devouring the property of an orphan, eating of usury, fleeing from the battlefield and slandering chaste women who never even think of anything touching chastity and are good believers." Abdullah ibn Amr (May God be pleased with them) narrated: God's Messenger (PBUH) said. "It is one of the gravest sins that a man curses his parents." It was asked (by the people), "O God's Messenger (PBUH)! How does a man curse his parents?" The Prophet (PBUH) said, "The man abuses the father of another man and the latter abuses the father of the former and abuses his mother." In addition, Abu

Hurayrah narrated (May God be pleased with him): The Prophet (PBUH) said: The gravest sin is going to lengths in talking unjustly against a Muslim's honor".

In fact, constantly begging forgiveness from God abolishes major sins and minor ones.

But a slave should not underestimate his sin. Anas (May God be pleased with him) said: "You indulge in bad actions which are more insignificant to you than a hair while we considered them at the time of Messenger of God (PBUH) to be major destroying sins". No one of the companions of the Prophet (PBUH) opposed what he has reported, neither mentally nor emotionally.

Good deeds intercede for their doer till God forgives him. They would save him (under God's will) if he experienced hardship. God, the Almighty, forgave His messenger Jonah when he went off in anger as a result of his people's disobedience to his call to worship God. He says about Jonah who persisted on exalting Him: "And had he not been of those who exalt God. He would have remained inside its belly until the Day they are resurrected". " فَلَوْلَا أَنَّهُ كَانَ مِنَ الْمُسَبِّحِينَ. لَلَبِثَ فِي بَطْنِهِ إِلَى يَوْمِ يُبْعَثُونَ " (37:143-144). On the contrary, Pharaoh had not performed any good deed that would intercede for him. So when he said, while drowning overtook him, "I believe that there is no deity except that in whom the Children of Israel believe" آمَنتُ أَنَّهُ لَا إِلَهَ إِلَّا الَّذِي

"آمَنَتْ بِهِ بَنُو إِسْرَائِيلَ". (10:90), Gabriel replied: "Now? And you had disobeyed [Him] before and were of the corrupters?" " آلْآنَ وَقَدْ عَصَيْتَ قَبْلُ وَكُنتَ مِنَ الْمُفْسِدِينَ" (10:91).

The Prophet (PBUH) said: "What you mention of glory of God, of Tabsih (Subhan-Allah), Takbir (Allahu-Akbar) and Tahmid (Al-Hamdu lillah), revolves around the Throne, buzzing like bees, reminding of the one who said it. Wouldn't any one of you like to have something that reminds of him (in the presence of God)?". Unlike a polytheist, a Muslim will be forgiven for his sins.

Testifying that there is no lord but God nullifies sins, depending on the certainty and sincerity of this testimony. The more sincere it is, the further a Muslim will be from sins and doubtful matters. Monotheism is not only to confess that there is no lord but God, rather, it includes loving God, humbling, yielding, being totally submissive and sincere to Him in every saying and deed.

Accordingly, a servant will avoid committing or insisting on sins. Knowing this, a slave will understand the Prophet's saying: "If anybody said: there is no lord but God, sincerely, with the intention to win God's pleasure, God will protect him from the Hell". Also, the Prophet (PBUH) said: "Whosoever utters: 'Subhan-Allahi wa bihamdihi (God is free from imperfection and His is the praise)' one hundred times a day, his sins will be obliterated even if they are equal to the extent of the foam of the sea".

Chapter

God, the Sovereign, forgives His allies so differently from others who are not in the same position as of the earlier. This applies to His punishment too. God says: "And if We had not strengthened you, you would have almost inclined to them a little. Then [if you had], We would have made you taste double [punishment in] life and double [after] death. Then you would not find for yourself against Us a helper". " وَلَوْلَا أَن ثَبَّتْنَاكَ لَقَدْ كِدتَّ تَرْكَنُ إِلَيْهِمْ شَيْئًا قَلِيلًا. " "إِذًا لَّأَذَقْنَاكَ ضِعْفَ الْحَيَاةِ وَضِعْفَ الْمَمَاتِ ثُمَّ لَا تَجِدُ لَكَ عَلَيْنَا نَصِيرًا" (17:74-75).

God has decreed that if a married man did unlawful sexual intercourse, he would be punished worse than the one who was not granted the favor of marriage. So, Exalted is He, Whose wisdom in His creation, commands and penalty astonishes human mind and makes Man witness that God is the most superior judge.

Kinds of what can be repented from (Disbelief)

Servants cannot become repentant except after getting rid of some prohibitions.

They are twelve: Disbelief, polytheism, hypocrisy, defiance, disobedience, sin, aggression, immortality, misconduct, oppression, saying about God that which you do not know, following a path other than that of believers.

These twelve matters are all what God prohibited and they will destruct those who are not followers of the messengers. The servants may commit one of them or more and they did not realize that; repentance comes true after getting rid of these unlawful matters. Only those who learnt about them can avoid them.

Disbelief is of two kinds: Major and minor disbelief. Major disbelief is resulting in eternal staying in the Hell. But minor disbelief deserves the warning (punishment) temporarily. The Messenger of God (PBUH) said: "Two things are signs of disbelief on the part of those who indulge in them: Slandering one's lineage and wailing over the dead."

The Messenger of God said: 'Whoever has intercourse with a menstruating woman, or with a woman in her rear, or who goes to a fortuneteller and believes what he says, he has disbelieved that which was revealed to Muhammad." God says: "And whoever does not judge by what God has revealed - then it is those who are the disbelievers" "وَمَن لَمْ يَحْكُم بِمَا أَنزَلَ اللَّـهُ فَأُولَـٰئِكَ هُمُ الْكَافِرُونَ" (5:44).

Non-implementation of God's judgments includes the two kinds of disbelief, minor and major; it is according to the state of the judge, if he knows the judgement of God and did its contrary and he is disobedient, this is considered major disbelief. However, ignoring the judgment requires the punishment of the sinners.

All sins are considered as minor disbelief as they are against obeying God; working on the obedience through good deeds.

Major Disbelief

Major Disbelief are of five kinds: disbelief by denial, disbelief by arrogance, disbelief by desertion, disbelief by doubt and disbelief by hypocrisy.

Disbelief by denial means rejection of the messengers and disbelieving their messages. Those disbelievers are rare, as Exalted is He sent signs to support His messengers, He says: "And they rejected them, while their [inner] selves were convinced thereof, out of injustice" " وَجَحَدُوا بِهَا وَاسْتَيْقَنَتْهَا أَنفُسُهُمْ ظُلْمً " (27:14). Exalted is He says to His Prophet (PBUH): "And indeed, they do not call you untruthful, but it is the verses of God that the wrongdoers reject." " فَإِنَّهُمْ لَا يُكَذِّبُونَكَ وَلَـٰكِنَّ الظَّالِمِينَ بِآيَاتِ اللَّـهِ يَجْحَدُونَ " (6:33). It is called disbelief by denial as it is denial by the tongue.

Disbelief by arrogance is like the disbelief of the Satan; he did not deny or reject God's creation, he dealt with it with arrogance. Also like those who refused to believe in the messengers because of arrogance and conceit, as Pharaoh and his people: "They said, "Should we believe two men like ourselves while their people are for us in servitude?" " فَقَالُوا أَنُؤْمِنُ لِبَشَرَيْنِ مِثْلِنَا وَقَوْمُهُمَا لَنَا عَابِدُونَ " (23:47). Nations said to their messengers: "They said, "You are not but men like us" " إِنْ أَنتُمْ إِلَّا بَشَرٌ مِّثْلُنَا " (14:10).

Moreover, disbelief of Jews appears as Exalted is He says: "When there came to them that which they recognized, they disbelieved in it" " فَلَمَّا جَاءَهُم مَّا عَرَفُوا كَفَرُوا بِهِ " (2:89),"Know him as they know their own sons" "يَعْرِفُونَهُ كَمَا يَعْرِفُونَ أَبْنَاءَهُمْ" (2:146), and it is like the disbelief of Abu Taleb who believed the Prophet (PBUH) but he refused to follow him because he did want to testify that his fathers were wrong and abandon their creed.

Disbelief by desertion means turning away by ears and heart; for those who did not believe or disbelieve in the Messenger; they are neither allies nor enemies.

Disbelief by doubt means that servants neither believe nor disbelieve in the messenger but doubt and continue to doubt. This doubt does not continue if they consider the signs of God then believe and become believers.

For disbelief by hypocrisy servants show belief by tongue but they disbelieve by heart.

Chapter

Rejecting is of two kinds regarding disbelief: Absolute disbelief and limited disbelief.

Absolute disbelief: rejecting all what God has revealed, including messengers.

Limited disbelief: willingly rejecting Islam duties, a prohibition, a divine name or a story God told for His messenger. But if this rejection is out of ignorance, one is not considered as a disbeliever.

Polytheism: Major and minor.

Major polytheism is not forgiven by God except by repentance, they are those who worshiped others and considered them similar to God; they love them like their love to God. Exalted is He says: "By God, we were indeed in manifest error. When we equated you with the Lord of the worlds." " تَاللَّـهِ إِن كُنَّا لَفِي ضَلَالٍ مُّبِينٍ. إِذْ نُسَوِّيكُم بِرَبِّ الْعَالَمِينَ" (26:97-98). Along with acknowledging that God is the creator alone, their gods cannot create or provide, bring to life or cause to die; they just love and glorify their idols like God. They feel fury if their idols were criticized but regarding God they do not feel angry.

God recites about the ancestors of those disbelievers: "And those who take protectors besides Him [say], "We only worship them that they may bring us nearer to God in position." Indeed, God will judge between them concerning that over which they differ." " الَّذِينَ اتَّخَذُوا مِن دُونِهِ أَوْلِيَاءَ مَا نَعْبُدُهُمْ إِلَّا لِيُقَرِّبُونَا إِلَى اللَّـهِ زُلْفَىٰ إِنَّ اللَّـهَ يَحْكُمُ بَيْنَهُمْ فِي مَا هُمْ فِيهِ يَخْتَلِفُونَ" (39:3), then God described them of disbelief and telling lies and He deprived them from His guidance: "Indeed, God does not guide he who is a liar and [confirmed] disbeliever." " إِنَّ اللَّـهَ لَا يَهْدِي مَنْ هُوَ كَاذِبٌ كَفَّارٌ" (39:3).

These are the state of those who made allies except God, claiming that they made them near to God. In their hearts, their gods intercede between them and God and this is the real polytheism. God, Exalted is He rebuffed that in Quran and says that intercession is by His will; no one can intercede except by His permit. On the contrary, there are the people of monotheism who did not ask intercession except by God.

Consider the Hadith of the Prophet (PBUH) to Abu Hurayra: "The luckiest person who will have my intercession on the Day of Resurrection will be the one who said sincerely from the bottom of his heart "None has the right to be worshipped but God." Intercession of the Prophet (PBUH) is only attained by testifying that None has the right to be worshipped but God, on the contrary to the polytheists, who believe that the intercession is attained by having allies to be intercessors.

It is an ignorance of the polytheists when they believed that having allies or intercessors will benefit them before God; they did not know that there is no one can intercede with Him except by His permission and only those people who God is pleased with them and their deeds who can be benefited from the intercessor, Exalted is He says: "Who is it that can intercede with Him except by His permission?" "مَن ذَا الَّذِي يَشْفَعُ عِندَهُ إِلَّا بِإِذْنِهِ" (2:255). Also, Intercessors cannot intercede except for those people whom God approves: "They cannot intercede except on behalf of one whom He approves." "وَلَا يَشْفَعُونَ إِلَّا لِمَنِ ارْتَضَىٰ" (21:28). Also, God is not pleased with deeds except monotheism and following the messengers.

Exalted is He does not forgive those people who disbelieve, equating [others] with their Lord, He says: "Then those who disbelieve equating [others] with their Lord." "ثُمَّ الَّذِينَ كَفَرُوا بِرَبِّهِمْ يَعْدِلُونَ" (6:1). Those people equate God and others regarding worships and love, according to this verse: "By God, we were indeed in manifest error. When we equated you with the Lord of the worlds." "تَاللَّهِ إِن كُنَّا لَفِي ضَلَالٍ مُّبِينٍ. إِذْ نُسَوِّيكُم بِرَبِّ الْعَالَمِينَ " (26:97-98). And also, as in this verse: "And [yet], among the people are those who take other than God as equals [to Him]. They love them as they [should] love God." " وَمِنَ النَّاسِ مَن يَتَّخِذُ مِن دُونِ اللَّهِ أَندَادًا يُحِبُّونَهُمْ كَحُبِّ اللَّهِ" (2:163). The polytheists' deeds contradict with their sayings: they say that they did not give them the same love of God, however, they get very angry if their intercessors are abused, unlike the case with God; they feel full joy by listening to their names or being mentioned more than God.

Exalted is He says: "He whom God guides is the [rightly] guided, but he whom He leaves astray - never will you find for him a protecting guide." " مَن يَهْدِ اللَّهُ فَهُوَ الْمُهْتَدِ ۖ وَمَن يُضْلِلْ فَلَن تَجِدَ لَهُ وَلِيًّا مُّرْشِدًا" (18:17), God revoked all reasons that polytheists show; those people who take allies other than God are like the spider that takes a home, the weakest of homes, Exalted is He says: "Say, [O Muhammad], "Invoke those you claim [as deities] besides God." They do not possess an atom's weight [of ability] in the heavens or on the earth, and they do not have therein any partnership [with Him], nor is there for Him from among them any assistant. And intercession does not benefit with Him except for one whom He permits." " قُلِ ادْعُوا الَّذِينَ زَعَمْتُم مِّن دُونِ اللَّهِ ۖ لَا يَمْلِكُونَ مِثْقَالَ ذَرَّةٍ فِي السَّمَاوَاتِ وَلَا فِي الْأَرْضِ وَمَا لَهُمْ فِيهِمَا مِن شِرْكٍ وَمَا لَهُ مِنْهُم مِّن ظَهِيرٍ. وَلَا تَنفَعُ الشَّفَاعَةُ عِندَهُ إِلَّا لِمَنْ أَذِنَ لَهُ" (34:22-23).

Polytheist takes an idol because he believes that it can benefit him. Benefit cannot occur except from those who owns what his slaves want, partner, assistant or intercessor. These four ranks are revoked by God and proved that the intercession is not for a polytheist as it is only for He permits.

Minor Polytheism

Minor polytheism is like pretension, swearing by anyone other than God, the Prophet (PBUH) said: "He, who swears by anyone or anything other than God, has indeed committed an act of Kufr or Shirk." Also, like when a man says, when God and you wish, this is from God and you, I do not have except God and you, I rely on God and you, the Prophet said to a man telling him what God wills and what you want: "Do you equate me with our Lord? Say: God willing only".

Prostration of the person to his elder narrator is polytheism by both of them.

In Musnad, a captive went to the Prophet (PBUH) and said: "O, my Lord, I repent for You, not for Mohammed, the Prophet (PBUH said: He knew the truth." Repentance is a worshipping for God only as prostration and fasting.

Some kinds of polytheism: swearing by others than God; it is polytheism, fear others than God, Reliance on others than God, intending deeds for others than God, returning in repentance for others than God, asking provision from others than God, thanking others than God, dispraise and being angry because a provision was not bestowed to him and so on. Also, asking dead people for needs, asking for their help and turning to them are deemed to be strongest polytheism where the dead cannot harm or benefit themselves, and then they cannot harm or benefit others. The Prophet (PBUH) asked us when visiting the graves of Muslims; to ask God for forgiveness and mercy for them.

Polytheists do on the contrary, visiting them for worshipping, asking for demands, asking for help and taking their graves as idols to be worshipped, they are the worst enemies of messengers and monotheism in every place and time. Prophet Abraham asked God: "And [mention, O Muhammad], when Abraham said, "My Lord, make this city [Makkah] secure and keep me and my sons away from worshipping idols. My Lord, indeed they have led astray many among the people." " وَإِذْ قَالَ إِبْرَاهِيمُ رَبِّ اجْعَلْ هَٰذَا الْبَلَدَ آمِنًا وَاجْنُبْنِي وَبَنِيَّ أَن نَّعْبُدَ الْأَصْنَامَ. رَبِّ إِنَّهُنَّ أَضْلَلْنَ كَثِيرًا مِّنَ النَّاسِ" (14:35-36).

Only those who worshipped God only, take polytheists as enemies, become near to God by hating them, love God, fear God, rely on God, ask God for help and being sincere while turning to God, they are saved from major polytheism.

Hypocrisy

Hypocrisy is also of two types: Major and minor hypocrisy.

Major hypocrisy necessitates eternal staying in the most painful stages of the Hell; hypocrites pretends before Muslims that they believe in God, His angles, His messengers, His books and the doomsday but internally they does not believe in all of that.

God revealed manners and secrets of hypocrites in Quran so that Muslims can be aware for them. God talks about hypocrites in thirteen verses because their kinds are many and their affliction is severe upon Islam and Muslims. They ascribed for Islam but they are its enemies in fact. Exalted is He says: "Unquestionably, it is they who are the corrupters, but they perceive [it] not." "أَلَا إِنَّهُمْ هُمُ الْمُفْسِدُونَ وَلَكِن لَّا يَشْعُرُونَ" (2:12) and "They want to extinguish the light of God with their mouths, but God will perfect His light, although the disbelievers dislike it." " يُرِيدُونَ لِيُطْفِئُوا نُورَ اللَّهِ

(61:8). "بِأَفْوَاهِهِمْ وَاللَّهُ مُتِمُّ نُورِهِ وَلَوْ كَرِهَ الْكَافِرُونَ" They agreed upon contradicting the revelation, Exalted is He says: "But the people divided their religion among them into sects - each faction, in what it has, rejoicing." "فَتَقَطَّعُوا أَمْرَهُم بَيْنَهُمْ زُبُرًا ۖ كُلُّ حِزْبٍ بِمَا لَدَيْهِمْ فَرِحُونَ" (23:53), "Inspiring to one another decorative speech in delusion." "يُوحِي بَعْضُهُمْ إِلَىٰ بَعْضٍ زُخْرُفَ الْقَوْلِ غُرُورًا" (6:112) thus, "Indeed my people have taken this Qur'an as [a thing] abandoned." " اتَّخَذُوا هَٰذَا الْقُرْآنَ مَهْجُورًا" (25:30).

They pretended that they are people of faith but they are not, Exalted is He says: "And of the people are some who say, "We believe in God and the Last Day," but they are not believers." "وَمِنَ النَّاسِ مَن يَقُولُ آمَنَّا بِاللَّهِ وَبِالْيَوْمِ الْآخِرِ وَمَا هُم بِمُؤْمِنِينَ" (2:8). They are full of deceit, plot, telling lies and treachery, Exalted is He says: "They [think to] deceive God and those who believe, but they deceive not except themselves and perceive [it] not." " يُخَادِعُونَ اللَّهَ وَالَّذِينَ آمَنُوا وَمَا يَخْدَعُونَ إِلَّا أَنفُسَهُمْ وَمَا يَشْعُرُونَ " (2:9).

They are afflicted with doubtful deeds, desires, bad intention and determination, Exalted is He says: "In their hearts is disease, so God has increased their disease; and for them is a painful punishment because they [habitually] used to lie." " فِي قُلُوبِهِم مَّرَضٌ فَزَادَهُمُ اللَّهُ مَرَضًا ۖ وَلَهُمْ عَذَابٌ أَلِيمٌ بِمَا كَانُوا يَكْذِبُونَ" (2:10).

Their corruption on Earth is huge but most people are igno-rant for them, Exalted is He says: "And when it is said to them, "Do not cause corruption on the earth," they say, "We are but reformers. Unquestionably, it is they who are the corrupters, but they perceive [it] not." " وَإِذَا قِيلَ لَهُمْ لَا تُفْسِدُوا فِي الْأَرْضِ قَالُوا إِنَّمَا نَحْنُ مُصْلِحُونَ. أَلَا إِنَّهُمْ هُمُ الْمُفْسِدُونَ وَلَكِن لَّا يَشْعُرُونَ" (2:11-12).

Exalted is He says: "And when it is said to them, "Believe as the people have believed," they say, "Should we believe as the foolish have believed?" Unquestionably, it is they who are the foolish, but they know [it] not." " قِيلَ لَهُمْ آمِنُوا كَمَا آمَنَ النَّاسُ قَالُوا أَنُؤْمِنُ كَمَا آمَنَ السُّفَهَاءُ أَلَا إِنَّهُمْ هُمُ السُّفَهَاءُ وَلَكِن لَّايَعْلَمُونَ" (2:13).

They have two states, one when deal with believers and the other one is for their followers, Exalted is He says: "And when they meet those who believe, they say, "We believe"; but when they are alone with their evil ones, they say, "Indeed, we are with you; we were only mockers."" " وَإِذَا لَقُوا الَّذِينَ آمَنُوا قَالُوا آمَنَّا وَإِذَا خَلَوْا إِلَى شَيَاطِينِهِمْ قَالُوا إِنَّا مَعَكُمْ إِنَّمَا نَحْنُ مُسْتَهْزِئُونَ" (2:14).

They turn away from Quran and Sunnah and they mocked the people of Quran and Sunnah, Exalted is He says: "[But] God mocks them and prolongs them in their transgression [while] they wander blindly." " اللَّـهُ يَسْتَهْزِئُ بِهِمْ وَيَمُدُّهُمْ فِي طُغْيَانِهِمْ يَعْمَهُونَ" (2:15).

They sought the unsold trade through seas of darkness, God says: "Those are the ones who have purchased error [in exchange] for guidance, so their transaction has brought no profit, nor were they guided." " أُولَٰئِكَ الَّذِينَ اشْتَرَوُا الضَّلَالَةَ بِالْهُدَىٰ فَمَا رَبِحَت تِّجَارَتُهُمْ وَمَا كَانُوا مُهْتَدِينَ" (2:16).

They are offered the light of faith and have insight to see guidance and error, God says: "Their example is that of one who kindled a fire, but when it illuminated what was around him, God took away their light and left them in darkness [so] they could not see." " مَثَلُهُمْ كَمَثَلِ الَّذِي اسْتَوْقَدَ نَارًا فَلَمَّا أَضَاءَتْ مَا حَوْلَهُ ذَهَبَ اللَّهُ بِنُورِهِمْ وَتَرَكَهُمْ فِي ظُلُمَاتٍ لَّا يُبْصِرُونَ" (2:1).

Their hearing is blocked, they cannot listen, their eyes are covered with veil; they cannot grasp facts and truth from Quran, God says: "Deaf, dumb and blind - so they will not return [to the right path]." " صُمٌّ بُكْمٌ عُمْيٌ فَهُمْ لَا يَرْجِعُونَ" (2:18).

They considered the revelation as some commands and prohibitions so they put their fingers in their ears, covered themselves with their garments, God says: "Or [it is] like a rainstorm from the sky within which is darkness, thunder and lightning. They put their fingers in their ears against the thunderclaps in dread of death. But God is encompassing of the disbelievers." " أَوْ كَصَيِّبٍ مِّنَ السَّمَاءِ فِيهِ ظُلُمَاتٌ وَرَعْدٌ وَبَرْقٌ يَجْعَلُونَ أَصَابِعَهُمْ فِي آذَانِهِم مِّنَ الصَّوَاعِقِ حَذَرَ الْمَوْتِ ۚ وَاللَّهُ مُحِيطٌ بِالْكَافِرِينَ" (2:19).

Their insights cannot perceive meanings and lights and their ears failed to listen to His promise, commands and prohibitions so God says: "Every time it lights [the way] for them, they walk therein; but when darkness comes over them, they stand [still]. And if God had willed, He could have taken away their hearing and their sight. Indeed, God is over all things competent." " لَّمَا أَضَاءَ لَهُم مَّشَوْا فِيهِ وَإِذَا أَظْلَمَ عَلَيْهِمْ قَامُوا ۚ وَلَوْ شَاءَ اللَّـهُ لَذَهَبَ بِسَمْعِهِمْ وَأَبْصَارِهِمْ ۚ إِنَّ اللَّـهَ عَلَىٰ كُلِّ شَيْءٍ قَدِيرٌ" (2:20).

They have some characteristics illustrated in Quran and Sunnah, clear for those who can contemplate, like pretention and double-dealing, the worst state of human beings; they are very lazy regarding commands of God and it is very hard for them to be sincere, Exalted is He says: "Indeed, the hypocrites [think to] deceive God, but He is deceiving them. And when they stand for prayer, they stand lazily, showing [themselves to] the people and not remembering God except a little." " وَإِذَا قَامُوا إِلَى الصَّلَاةِ قَامُوا كُسَالَى يُرَاءُونَ النَّاسَ وَلَا يَذْكُرُونَ اللَّهَ إِلَّا قَلِيلً" (4:142).

Some of them are not bias; they do not belong to the right side or the left one, exalted is He says: "Wavering between them, [belonging] neither to the believers nor to the disbelievers. And whoever God leaves astray - never will you find for him a way." " مُّذَبْذَبِينَ بَيْنَ ذَٰلِكَ لَا إِلَىٰ هَـٰؤُلَاءِ وَلَا إِلَىٰ هَـٰؤُلَاءِ وَمَن يُضْلِلِ اللَّهُ فَلَن تَجِدَ لَهُ سَبِيلًا" (4:143).

They wait and watch if people of Quran and Sunnah will gain a victory from God. If you wanted to learn about their characteristics, learn from Quran, exalted is He says: "Those who wait [and watch] you. Then if you gain a victory from God, they say, "Were we not with you?" But if the disbelievers have a success, they say [to them], "Did we not gain the advantage over you, but we protected you from the believers?" God will judge between [all of] you on the Day of Resurrection, and never will God give the disbelievers over the believers a way [to overcome them]." " الَّذِينَ يَتَرَبَّصُونَ بِكُمْ فَإِنْ كَانَ لَكُمْ فَتْحٌ مِنَ اللَّهِ قَالُوا أَلَمْ نَكُنْ مَعَكُمْ وَإِنْ كَانَ لِلْكَافِرِينَ نَصِيبٌ قَالُوا أَلَمْ نَسْتَحْوِذْ عَلَيْكُمْ وَنَمْنَعْكُمْ مِنَ الْمُؤْمِنِينَ فَاللَّهُ يَحْكُمُ بَيْنَكُمْ يَوْمَ الْقِيَامَةِ وَلَنْ يَجْعَلَ اللَّهُ لِلْكَافِرِينَ عَلَى الْمُؤْمِنِينَ سَبِيلًا" (4:141).

Their speech may please you, yet God witnesses their lies in their hearts as Exalted is He describes them: "And of the people is he whose speech pleases you in worldly life, and he calls God to witness as to what is in his heart, yet he is the fiercest of opponents." " وَمِنَ النَّاسِ مَنْ يُعْجِبُكَ قَوْلُهُ فِي الْحَيَاةِ الدُّنْيَا وَيُشْهِدُ اللَّهَ عَلَى مَا فِي قَلْبِهِ وَهُوَ أَلَدُّ الْخِصَامِ" (2:204).

They ask their followers to cause corruption for countries and people, Exalted is He says: "And when he goes away, he strives throughout the land to cause corruption therein and destroy crops and animals. And God does not like corruption." " وَإِذَا تَوَلَّى سَعَى فِي الْأَرْضِ لِيُفْسِدَ فِيهَا وَيُهْلِكَ الْحَرْثَ وَالنَّسْلَ وَاللَّهُ لَا يُحِبُّ الْفَسَادَ" (2:205).

They are very similar to each other, they enjoin what is wrong and forbid what is right. They are stingy regarding spending money seeking the path of God. God always reminds them with His bounties but they turn way from His reminder. Exalted is He says: "The hypocrite men and hypocrite women are of one another. They enjoin what is wrong and forbid what is right and close their hands. They have forgotten God, so He has forgotten them [accordingly]. Indeed, the hypocrites - it is they who are the defiantly disobedient." "الْمُنَافِقُونَ وَالْمُنَافِقَاتُ بَعْضُهُمْ مِنْ بَعْضٍ يَأْمُرُونَ بِالْمُنْكَرِ وَيَنْهَوْنَ عَنِ الْمَعْرُوفِ وَيَقْبِضُونَ أَيْدِيَهُمْ نَسُوا اللَّهَ فَنَسِيَهُمْ إِنَّ الْمُنَافِقِينَ هُمُ الْفَاسِقُونَ" (9:67).

If you ask them to follow what God has revealed, they turn away; if you call them to the provisions of Quran and Sunnah, they also turn way. If you can perceive truth and reality of them, you find them very away from guidance; not following revelation, Exalted is He says: "And when it is said to them, "Come to what God has revealed and to the Messenger," you see the hypocrites turning away from you in aversion."" "وَإِذَا قِيلَ لَهُمْ تَعَالَوْا إِلَى مَا أَنْزَلَ اللَّهُ وَإِلَى الرَّسُولِ رَأَيْتَ الْمُنَافِقِينَ يَصُدُّونَ عَنْكَ صُدُودًا" (4:61).

How can they attain success and guidance after their minds and religions were corrupted? How can they get rid of astray and illness while they changed their faith to atheism? Exalted is He says: "So how [will it be] when disaster strikes them because of what their hands have put forth and then they come to you swearing by God, "We intended nothing but good conduct and accommodation."" فَكَيْفَ إِذَا أَصَابَتْهُمْ مُصِيبَةٌ بِمَا قَدَّمَتْ أَيْدِيهِمْ ثُمَّ جَاءُوكَ يَحْلِفُونَ "بِاللَّهِ إِنْ أَرَدْنَا إِلَّا إِحْسَانًا وَتَوْفِيقًا" (4:62).

Their hearts are full of doubtful matters and suspension, Exalted is He says: "Those are the ones of whom God knows what is in their hearts, so turn away from them but admonish them and speak to them a far-reaching word."" أُولَئِكَ الَّذِينَ يَعْلَمُ اللَّهُ مَا فِي قُلُوبِهِمْ "فَأَعْرِضْ عَنْهُمْ وَعِظْهُمْ وَقُلْ لَهُمْ فِي أَنْفُسِهِمْ قَوْلًا بَلِيغًا" (4:63).

They are very away from truth of Faith; Exalted is He swears in His Quran, its essence is known by people of insight, He says warning those hypocrites: "But no, by your Lord, they will not [truly] believe until they make you, [O Muhammad], judge concerning that over which they dispute among themselves and then find within themselves no discomfort from what you have judged and submit in [full, willing] submission."" فَلَا وَرَبِّكَ لَا يُؤْمِنُونَ " حَتَّى يُحَكِّمُوكَ فِيمَا شَجَرَ بَيْنَهُمْ ثُمَّ لَا يَجِدُوا فِي أَنْفُسِهِمْ حَرَجًا مِمَّا قَضَيْتَ وَيُسَلِّمُوا تَسْلِيمًا (4:65).

Hypocrites always swear, even without claim, as they know that the people of faith do not trust them because of bad thought regarding them, Exalted is He says: "They have taken their oaths as a cover, so they averted [people] from the way of

God. Indeed, it was evil that they were doing." اتَّخَذُوا أَيْمَانَهُمْ جُنَّةً فَصَدُّوا

(63:2). " عَنْ سَبِيلِ اللَّهِ إِنَّهُمْ سَاءَ مَا كَانُوا يَعْمَلُونَ

Hypocrites realized faith and when they found it is hard to be achieved, they preferred enjoying their state and pleasure of sleeping in their homes; they rejected the guidance and they become blind after they have sight to truth, Exalted is He says: "That is because they believed, and then they disbelieved; so their hearts were sealed over, and they do not understand" ذَلِكَ

(63:3). " بِأَنَّهُمْ آمَنُوا ثُمَّ كَفَرُوا فَطُبِعَ عَلَى قُلُوبِهِمْ فَهُمْ لَا يَفْقَهُونَ

Their appearances are the best, having the most fluent tongues, the coolest talk but with the most evil hearts; they are like pieces of wood, Exalted is He says: "And when you see them, their forms please you, and if they speak, you listen to their speech. [They are] as if they were pieces of wood propped up - they think that every shout is against them. They are the enemy, so beware of them. May God destroy them; how are they deluded?"" وَإِذَا رَأَيْتَهُمْ تُعْجِبُكَ أَجْسَامُهُمْ وَإِنْ يَقُولُوا تَسْمَعْ لِقَوْلِهِمْ كَأَنَّهُمْ خُشُبٌ مُسَنَّدَةٌ يَحْسَبُونَ

(63:4). " كُلَّ صَيْحَةٍ عَلَيْهِمْ هُمُ الْعَدُوُّ فَاحْذَرْهُمْ قَاتَلَهُمُ اللَّهُ أَنَّى يُؤْفَكُونَ

They perform prayer later not in its set time; they perform Dawn prayer with sun rise. They perform prayer by their bodies not by their hearts and they never perform it during a gathering. Whenever they quarrel, they behave in a very imprudent, evil and insulting manner; whenever they make a covenant, they prove treacherous; whenever they speak, they tell a lie; and whenever they are entrusted, they betray. Exalted is He says: "O Prophet, strive against the disbelievers and the hypocrites and be harsh upon them. And their refuge is Hell, and wretched is the destination.""" يَاأَيُّهَا النَّبِيُّ جَاهِدِ الْكُفَّارَ وَالْمُنَافِقِينَ وَاغْلُظْ عَلَيْهِمْ وَمَأْوَاهُمْ جَهَنَّمُ وَبِئْسَ الْمَصِيرُ" (66:9), and: "And they swear by God that they are from among you while they are not from among you; but they are a people who are afraid.""" وَيَحْلِفُونَ بِاللَّهِ إِنَّهُمْ لَمِنْكُمْ وَمَا هُمْ مِنْكُمْ وَلَكِنَّهُمْ قَوْمٌ يَفْرَقُونَ" (9:56).

If people of Quran and Sunnah gain health, victory or dominance, these hypocrites are in distress and if these people are afflicted by distress from God to remove their sins, hypocrites are in joy and pleasure, Exalted is He says: "If good befalls you, it distresses them; but if disaster strikes you, they say, "We took our matter [in hand] before," and turn away while they are rejoicing. Say, "Never will we be struck except by what God has decreed for us; He is our protector. And upon God let the believers rely.""" إِنْ تُصِبْكَ حَسَنَةٌ تَسُؤْهُمْ وَإِنْ تُصِبْكَ مُصِيبَةٌ يَقُولُوا قَدْ أَخَذْنَا أَمْرَنَا مِنْ قَبْلُ "وَيَتَوَلَّوْا وَهُمْ فَرِحُونَ. قُلْ لَنْ يُصِيبَنَا إِلَّا مَا كَتَبَ اللَّهُ لَنَا هُوَ مَوْلَانَا وَعَلَى اللَّهِ فَلْيَتَوَكَّلِ الْمُؤْمِنُونَ" (9:50-51). Their plot does not harm you, Exalted is He says: "If good touches you, it distresses them; but if harm strikes you, they rejoice at it. And if you are patient and fear God, their plot will not harm you at all. Indeed, God is encompassing of what

إِنْ تَمْسَسْكُمْ حَسَنَةٌ تَسُؤْهُمْ وَإِنْ تُصِبْكُمْ سَيِّئَةٌ يَفْرَحُوا بِهَا وَإِنْ تَصْبِرُوا وَتَتَّقُوا لَا "."they do

يَضُرُّكُمْ كَيْدُهُمْ شَيْئًا إِنَّ اللَّهَ بِمَا يَعْمَلُونَ مُحِيطٌ " .(3:120).

God hates their obedience because of their evil hearts and bad intentions; God disliked their being obedient. God disliked them being near to Him simultaneously with turning to His enemies. They left His revelation, then God left them; hardening their lives and He decided that they are not going to reach success except after they return to Him in repentance, Exalted is He says: "And if they had intended to go forth, they would have prepared for it [some] preparation. But God disliked their being sent, so He kept them back, and they were told, "Remain [behind] with those who remain."" وَلَوْ أَرَادُوا الْخُرُوجَ لَأَعَدُّوا لَهُ عُدَّةً وَلَكِنْ كَرِهَ "

اللَّهُ انْبِعَاثَهُمْ فَثَبَّطَهُمْ وَقِيلَ اقْعُدُوا مَعَ الْقَاعِدِينَ" .(9:46).

God kept them back and sent them away because of His kindness to his allies to please them, Exalted is He says: "Had they gone forth with you, they would not have increased you except in confusion, and they would have been active among you, seeking [to cause] you fitnah. And among you are avid listeners to them. And God is Knowing of the wrongdoers."" لَوْ خَرَجُوا فِيكُمْ مَا

"زَادُوكُمْ إِلَّا خَبَالًا وَلَأَوْضَعُوا خِلَالَكُمْ يَبْغُونَكُمُ الْفِتْنَةَ وَفِيكُمْ سَمَّاعُونَ لَهُمْ وَاللَّهُ عَلِيمٌ بِالظَّالِمِينَ (9:47). They felt struggle with scripture, so they disliked it and abandoned following Sunnah. God has already exposed them, so that His allies be aware of them, Exalted is He says: "That is because they disliked what God revealed, so He rendered worthless their deeds."" ذَلِكَ بِأَنَّهُمْ كَرِهُوا مَا أَنْزَلَ اللهُ فَأَحْبَطَ أَعْمَالَهُمْ " (47:9).

They concealed hypocrisy but God discovers it, Exalted is He says: "That is because they said to those who disliked what God sent down, "We will obey you in part of the matter. "And God knows what they conceal. Then how [will it be] when the angels take them in death, striking their faces and their backs? That is because they followed what angered God and disliked [what earns] His pleasure, so He rendered worthless their deeds."" ذَلِكَ بِأَنَّهُمْ قَالُوا لِلَّذِينَ كَرِهُوا مَا نَزَّلَ اللهُ سَنُطِيعُكُمْ فِي بَعْضِ الْأَمْرِ وَاللهُ يَعْلَمُ إِسْرَارَهُمْ. فَكَيْفَ إِذَا تَوَفَّتْهُمُ الْمَلَائِكَةُ يَضْرِبُونَ وُجُوهَهُمْ وَأَدْبَارَهُمْ. ذَلِكَ بِأَنَّهُمُ اتَّبَعُوا مَا أَسْخَطَ اللهَ وَكَرِهُوا رِضْوَانَهُ فَأَحْبَطَ أَعْمَالَهُمْ " (47:26-28).

They concealed their hypocrisy but God makes it clear upon their faces so that the people of faith and insight can recognize them; they conceal their atheism and pretend being believers. How are they on the doomsday and the mask will be removed and they are invited to prostration but they are not able, Exalted is He says: "Their eyes humbled, humiliation will cover them. And they used to be invited to prostration while they were sound."" خَاشِعَةً أَبْصَارُهُمْ تَرْهَقُهُمْ ذِلَّةٌ وَقَدْ كَانُوا يُدْعَوْنَ إِلَى السُّجُودِ وَهُمْ سَالِمُونَ " (68:43)

What is their state when they are before the Hell passing its bridge which would be thinner even than the hair and sharper than the sword, no body passes except by guidance of God. Then, a wall will be placed with a door, thereafter mercy locates, but therebefore is torment, God says: "Wait for us that we may acquire some of your light." "انْظُرُونَا نَقْتَبِسْ مِنْ نُوركُمْ" (57:13). It was said to them "Go back behind you and seek light."" "قِيلَ ارْجِعُوا وَرَاءَكُمْ" (75:13). They say: "Were we not with you?"" "فَالْتَمِسُوا نُورًا مَعَكُمْ" (75:14). They will say "We were fasting, praying, reading, giving alms and performing Haj as you". "Yes, But you were hypocrites", Exalted is He says: "But you afflicted yourselves and awaited [misfortune for us] and doubted, and wishful thinking deluded you until there came the command of God. And the Deceiver deceived you concerning God. So today no ransom will be taken from you or from those who disbelieved. Your refuge is the Fire. It is most worthy of you, and wretched is the destination." "وَلَكِنَّكُمْ فَتَنْتُمْ أَنْفُسَكُمْ وَتَرَبَّصْتُمْ وَارْتَبْتُمْ وَغَرَّتْكُمُ الْأَمَانِيُّ حَتَّى جَاءَ أَمْرُ اللَّهِ وَغَرَّكُمْ بِاللَّهِ الْغَرُورُ ـ فَالْيَوْمَ لَا يُؤْخَذُ مِنْكُمْ فِدْيَةٌ وَلَا مِنَ الَّذِينَ كَفَرُوا مَأْوَاكُمُ النَّارُ هِيَ مَوْلَاكُمْ وَبِئْسَ الْمَصِيرُ" (57:14-15).

Description and characteristics of those people (Hypocrites) are much; unmentioned description is much more than the expressed.

Most companions of the Prophet (PBUH) feared being among hypocrites; their hearts were full of faith and certainty but their fear from hypocrisy was great.

Hypocrisy is based on two pillars: Telling lies and showing of (good deeds); they resulted from weakness of insight and determination. Their deeds are to be uncovered on the Day when secrets will be put on trial, the contents of the graves are scattered, then they will know if their deeds were out of hypocrisy and they are in vain, Exalted is He says: "But those who disbelieved - their deeds are like a mirage in a lowland which a thirsty one thinks is water until, when he comes to it, he finds it is nothing but finds God before Him, and He will pay him in full his due; and God is swift in account. "" يَحْسَبُهُ الظَّمْآنُ مَاءً حَتَّى إِذَا جَاءَهُ لَمْ يَجِدْهُ شَيْئًا وَوَجَدَ اللَّهَ عِنْدَهُ فَوَفَّاهُ حِسَابَهُ وَاللَّهُ سَرِيعُ الْحِسَابِ" (24:39).

Their hearts are very distracted away from doing good deeds, their organs are seeking hypocrisy if they listened to the truth, their hearts were very distant from truth and faith, but regarding falsehood and saying it, their hearts and ears were open and aware.

Whenever hypocrites talk, they tell a lie; whenever they make a promise, they break it; whenever they make a covenant, they are treacherous; and whenever they quarrel, they behave impudently in an evil insulting manner. If they to say, they are unjust;

if they are asked to obey, they delay and when it is said to them: "Come to what God has revealed and to the Messenger," the hypocrites turning away in aversion. If their desires urged them to do something, they hastened, so let them choose upon their desires, choosing disgrace and loss in the world. Do not trust their pledges or be secure for their promises, they are liars, Exalted is He says: "And among them are those who made a covenant with God, [saying], "If He should give us from His bounty, we will surely spend in charity, and we will surely be among the righteous." But when he gave them from His bounty, they were stingy with it and turned away while they refused. So He penalized them with hypocrisy in their hearts until the Day they will meet Him - because they failed God in what they promised Him and because they [habitually] used to lie."" وَمِنْهُمْ مَنْ عَاهَدَ اللَّهَ لَئِنْ آتَانَا مِنْ فَضْلِهِ لَنَصَّدَّقَنَّ وَلَنَكُونَنَّ مِنَ الصَّالِحِينَ. فَلَمَّا آتَاهُمْ مِنْ فَضْلِهِ بَخِلُوا بِهِ وَتَوَلَّوْا وَهُمْ مُعْرِضُونَ. فَأَعْقَبَهُمْ نِفَاقًا فِي قُلُوبِهِمْ إِلَى يَوْمِ يَلْقَوْنَهُ بِمَا أَخْلَفُوا اللَّهَ مَا وَعَدُوهُ وَبِمَا كَانُوا يَكْذِبُونَ" (9:75-77).

Defiance

Defiance is labeled in two kinds in Quran: general defiance and disobedience-related defiance.

General defiance is binary: defiance of disbelief that gets someone out of Islam and defiance that does not get someone out of Islam.

Disobedience-related defiance is like saying of Exalted is He: "But God has endeared to you the faith and has made it pleasing in your hearts and has made hateful to you disbelief, defiance and disobedience. Those are the [rightly] guided." " وَلَٰكِنَّ اللَّهَ حَبَّبَ إِلَيْكُمُ الْإِيمَانَ وَزَيَّنَهُ فِي قُلُوبِكُمْ وَكَرَّهَ إِلَيْكُمُ الْكُفْرَ وَالْفُسُوقَ وَالْعِصْيَانَ أُولَٰئِكَ هُمُ الرَّاشِدُونَ" (49:7).

General defiance (That gets out of Islam) is like saying of Exalted is He: "He misleads many thereby and guides many thereby. And He misleads not except the defiantly

يُضِلُّ بِهِ كَثِيرًا وَيَهْدِي بِهِ كَثِيرًا وَمَا يُضِلُّ بِهِ إِلَّا الْفَاسِقِينَ الَّذِينَ يَنْقُضُونَ disobedient.""

"عَهْدَ اللَّهِ (2: 26), Exalted is He says: "And We have certainly revealed to you verses [which are] clear proofs, and no one would deny them except the defiantly disobedient." " وَلَقَدْ أَنْزَلْنَا إِلَيْكَ آيَاتٍ

بَيِّنَاتٍ وَمَا يَكْفُرُ بِهَا إِلَّا الْفَاسِقُونَ" (2:99) and His saying: "But as for those who defiantly disobeyed, their refuge is the Fire. Every time they wish to emerge from it, they will be returned to it."" وَأَمَّا الَّذِينَ فَسَقُوا

فَمَأْوَاهُمُ النَّارُ كُلَّمَا أَرَادُوا أَنْ يَخْرُجُوا مِنْهَا أُعِيدُوا فِيهَا" (32:20), these all is of the defiance of disbelief.

But regarding defiance that (Does not get someone out of Islam) is expressed in the saying of Exalted is He: "If you do so, indeed, it is [grave] disobedience in you."" إِنْ تَفْعَلُوا فَإِنَّهُ فُسُوقٌ بِكُمْ "

(2:282) and: "O you who have believed, if there comes to you a disobedient one with information, investigate."" يَاأَيُّهَا الَّذِينَ آمَنُوا إِنْ

جَاءَكُمْ فَاسِقٌ بِنَبَإٍ" (49:6).

Information has to be investigated to decide if it is a truth or not; Exalted is He commands that you have to verify the truth of any information told by people of defiance. If there are evidences for the truth of this information, so it is true. If their narration is rejected, most rights can be delayed and much news is nullified, especially people whose defiance results from their beliefs and opinions.

Defiance that requires repentance is of two kinds: deeds-related defiance and belief-related defiance.

Deeds-related defiance is sub-divided into: disobedience and general defiance of deeds.

This of disobedience is committing what God prohibited, disobedience is to contravene God, Exalted is He says: "They do not disobey God in what He commands" "لَا يَعْصُونَ اللَّه مَا أَمَرَهُمْ" (66:6), also like when Moses said to his brother Aaron, May God be pleased with them: "[Moses] said, "O Aaron, what prevented you, when you saw them going astray. From following me? Then have you disobeyed my order?" " مَا مَنَعَكَ إِذْ رَأَيْتَهُمْ ضَلُّوا أَلَّا تَتَّبِعَنِ أَفَعَصَيْتَ أَمْرِي" (20:92-93).

Committing prohibitions is related to defiance, Exalted is He says: "For if you do so, indeed, it is [grave] disobedience in you." "وَإِنْ تَفْعَلُوا فَإِنَّهُ فُسُوقٌ بِكُمْ" (2:282). Disobeying the command is noncompliance, Exalted is He says: "Except for Iblees. He was of the jinn and departed from the command of his Lord." " إِلَّا إِبْلِيسَ كَانَ مِنَ الْجِنِّ فَفَسَقَ عَنْ أَمْرِ رَبِّهِ" (18:50); Exalted is He called abandoning God's commands a defiance. Exalted is He called doing the prohibited deeds disobedience; He says: "Adam disobeyed his Lord and erred" " وَعَصَى آدَمُ رَبَّهُ فَغَوَى" (20:121).

Piety comes by giving up prohibited deeds, then repentance comes true when abandoning defiance and disobedience; the servant has to obey God, expecting God's reward, forsaking dis-obedience and fearing God's punishment.

Defiance regarding belief is like the defiance of the heretics who believe in God, His messenger, the doomsday and forbid what God forbids but they negates some matters that God and His messenger proved whether because of their ignorance or misinterpretation, They are the same as most dissenters and re-jecters of faith.

Repentance from defiance is by confirming what God and His messenger proved.

Those people of defiance have to repent from these spoiled beliefs by following Sunnah, also they have to show and illustrate the corruption of what they followed, Exalted is He says: "In-deed, those who conceal what We sent down of clear proofs and guidance after We made it clear for the people in the Scripture - those are cursed by God and cursed by those who curse. Except for those who repent and correct themselves and make evident [what they concealed]. Those - I will accept their repentance, and I am the Accepting of repentance, the Merciful. "" إِنَّ الَّذِينَ يَكْتُمُونَ مَا أَنْزَلْنَا مِنَ الْبَيِّنَاتِ وَالْهُدَى مِنْ بَعْدِ مَا بَيَّنَّاهُ لِلنَّاسِ فِي الْكِتَابِ أُولَئِكَ يَلْعَنُهُمُ اللَّهُ وَيَلْعَنُهُمُ اللَّاعِنُونَ - إِلَّا الَّذِينَ تَابُوا وَأَصْلَحُوا وَبَيَّنُوا فَأُولَئِكَ أَتُوبُ عَلَيْهِمْ وَأَنَا التَّوَّابُ الرَّحِيمُ (2:159-160).

The guilty of heretics is greater than those people who conceal the truth as heretics concealed the truth and invited people to act against such truth.

The hypocrites have to be sincere on repentance, Exalted is He says: "Indeed, the hypocrites will be in the lowest depths of the Fire - and never will you find for them a helper - Except for those who repent, correct themselves, hold fast to God, and are sincere in their religion for God, for those will be with the believers. And God is going to give the believers a great reward."" إِنَّ الْمُنَافِقِينَ فِي الدَّرْكِ الْأَسْفَلِ مِنَ النَّارِ. إِلَّا الَّذِينَ تَابُوا وَأَصْلَحُوا وَاعْتَصَمُوا بِاللَّهِ وَأَخْلَصُوا دِينَهُمْ لِلَّهِ فَأُولَٰئِكَ مَعَ الْمُؤْمِنِينَ وَسَوْفَ يُؤْتِ اللَّهُ الْمُؤْمِنِينَ أَجْرًا عَظِيمًا" (4:145-146).

Sin And Aggression

Sin and aggression are corelated, Exalted is He says: "And cooperate in righteousness and piety, but do not cooperate in sin and aggression." "وَتَعَاوَنُوا عَلَى الْبِرِّ وَالتَّقْوَى وَلَا تَعَاوَنُوا عَلَى الْإِثْمِ وَالْعُدْوَانِ" (5:2). Every sin is an aggression; committing what God prohibited or leaving what God commanded. Every aggression is a sin; the doer is sinner.

The sin is all what is prohibited like telling lies, adultery, drinking alcohol and so on.

Aggression is encroachment upon the lawful limit like aggression while restoring dues from the debtors via violating their property, body or honor.

This aggression is binary: aggression against God's right and aggression against the servant's right. For aggression against God's right is when having joy from unlawful property and women than what God makes lawful, Exalted is He says: "And they who guard their private parts. And they who guard their private parts - But whoever seeks beyond that, then those are the transgressors." " وَالَّذِينَ هُمْ لِفُرُوجِهِمْ حَافِظُونَ إِلَّا عَلَى أَزْوَاجِهِمْ أَوْ مَا مَلَكَتْ أَيْمَانُهُمْ فَإِنَّهُمْ غَيْرُ مَلُومِينَ فَمَنِ ابْتَغَى وَرَاءَ ذَلِكَ فَأُولَئِكَ هُمُ الْعَادُون" (23:5-7). Also, when the servant encroach upon the limits God set. Sin and aggression are like sin and oppression but oppression is related to the rights of servants.

Immortality and misconduct

Immortality is like adultery and buggery but misconduct means any conduct which is hateful and repulsive.

Missaying about God

Missaying about God is the most unlawful deeds and the greatest sin.

Unlawful matters are two-fold: permanent prohibitions and temporary prohibitions. Exalted is He says about those are prohibited by themselves: "Say, "My Lord has only forbidden immoralities - what is apparent of them and what is concealed" "قُلْ إِنَّمَا حَرَّمَ رَبِّيَ الْفَوَاحِشَ مَا ظَهَرَ مِنْهَا وَمَا بَطَنَ" (7:33), then He moves to what is greater: "Sin, and oppression without right" "وَالْإِثْمَ وَالْبَغْيَ بِغَيْرِ الْحَقِّ"(7:33), Then the greater: "And that you associate with God that for which He has not sent down authority." "وَأَن تُشْرِكُوا بِاللَّهِ مَا لَمْ يُنَزِّلْ بِهِ سُلْطَانًا" (7:33), then the greatest: "And that you say about God that which you do not know." "وَأَن تَقُولُوا عَلَى اللَّهِ مَا لَا تَعْلَمُونَ" (7:33).

This is the greatest prohibition and the one of most hateful sin; it includes telling lies about God, negating what He proved, proving what He negates and denies, making true what He con-siders false, making false what He considers true, having His enemies allies and having His allies enemies, loving what He hates and hating what He likes, describing Him in a detestable way, and negating His merits, sayings and deeds, Exalted is He says: "And do not say about what your tongues assert of untruth, "This is lawful and this is unlawful," to invent falsehood about God." "وَلَا تَقُولُوا لِمَا تَصِفُ أَلْسِنَتُكُمُ الْكَذِبَ هَذَا حَلَالٌ وَهَذَا حَرَامٌ لِتَفْتَرُوا عَلَى اللَّهِ الْكَذِبَ" (16:116).

The origin of atheism and polytheism is to missay about God; the polytheist claims that his idol makes him nearer to God, in-tercedes for him and meets his needs. Those who tell lies upon the Prophet (PBUH) will enter the Hell, Exalted is He says: "And who is more unjust than one who invents about God a lie or denies His verses?" " وَمَنْ أَظْلَمُ مِمَّنِ افْتَرَى عَلَى اللَّهِ كَذِبًا" (6:21). Heretics are from the people who missay about God; there is no accepted repentance except after repenting from these heresies. Servants have to migrate to God and His Messenger by their hearts, seeking help from God, being sincere and migrating to His Messenger, applying his Sunnah and following him.

Repentance Provisions

How is the repentance of someone who could not compensate the right that he violated?

Regarding God's rights, like the servant who abandoned prayer intentionally without excuse, although he knows that it is obligatory, then he repents, scholars disagreed regarding this matter:

Some said: his repentance comes true by regret, executing the required ordinances and missed ones, this is the opinion of the four Imams and others.

Others said: his repentance comes true by executing the required ordinances in the future as he cannot compensate the missed ordinances.

First group of people has evidence: The Prophet (PBUH) said: "There is no negligence when one sleeps, rather negligence is when one is awake. If anyone of you forgets a prayer or sleeps and misses it, let him pray it when he remembers it."

They said if it is obligatory that the sleepy and forgetter have to pray when they remember, thus the negligent person has to pray what are missed.

Chapter

Servants' Rights

Regarding servants' rights; they are described in many aspects:

First: someone took some property, then he repented but he cannot give it back to its real owner or his heirs because he cannot reach them or they died, people disagreed regarding the repentance of this person:

Some said: No repentance comes true except by giving these rights back to their real owners. If he cannot do that, repentance also cannot come true. They said it is a right for a servant and Exalted is He never wastes rights of servants; He always revokes injustice.

Others referred that repentance is available by giving dues in charity on behalf of the real owner.

Second: If someone is compensated through an unlawful act like adulterer, singer, seller of alcohol, perjurer and so on then he repents. Some said these people have to pay back such compensation to the real owner, others said repentance comes true when compensation is spent in charity.

If someone stole money and he wanted to repent but he finds it hard to get the money back to the real owner and heirs, he has to give this money for charity so that they can benefit from its reward.

Chapter

Is there any sin that there is no accepted repentance for

People disagreed:

The majority said: repentance is for any sin and is always accepted.

Few said: there is no repentance for the killer; this is the doctrine of ibn Abbas when his people said did not God say: "And those who do not invoke with God another deity or kill the soul which God has forbidden [to be killed], except by right." " وَالَّذِينَ لَا يَدْعُونَ مَعَ اللَّهِ إِلَهًا آخَرَ وَلَا يَقْتُلُونَ النَّفْسَ الَّتِي حَرَّمَ اللَّهُ إِلَّا بِالْحَقِّ" (25:68), then: "Except for those who repent, believe and do righteous work. For them God will replace their evil deeds with good. And ever is God Forgiving and Merciful."" إِلَّا مَنْ تَابَ وَآمَنَ وَعَمِلَ عَمَلًا صَالِحًا فَأُولَئِكَ يُبَدِّلُ اللَّهُ سَيِّئَاتِهِمْ حَسَنَاتٍ وَكَانَ اللَّهُ غَفُورًا رَحِيمًا" (25:70), He said this verse regarding Ignorance Era, where polytheists who killed and having adultery came to the Messenger (PBUH)and said: "What you invite to is good except if you told us that there is repentance on what we committed," It has been revealed: "And those who do not invoke with God another deity." " "وَالَّذِينَ لَا يَدْعُونَ مَعَ اللَّهِ إِلَهًا آخَرَ (25:68). But regarding the verse: "But whoever kills a believer intentionally - his recompense is Hell, wherein he will abide eternally, and God has become angry with him and has cursed him and has prepared for him a great punishment." " "وَمَنْ يَقْتُلْ مُؤْمِنًا مُتَعَمِّدًا فَجَزَاؤُهُ جَهَنَّمُ خَالِدًا فِيهَا وَغَضِبَ اللَّهُ عَلَيْهِ وَلَعَنَهُ وَأَعَدَّ لَهُ عَذَابًا عَظِيمً (4:93) if the man entered Islam and become acquainted with its rules and provisions then he killed, his punishment is the Hell.

Those people said that the repentance cannot be accepted from who intentionally killed a human being because it is impossible to get the soul back in the body as the repentance regarding the right of a human being only come true after remedy of the sin and it is impossible for the killer, thus there is no repentance for him.

It is said there is no sin greater than the sin of polytheism and it can be repented; this repentance can be accepted by God as it is a God's right but regarding the human being's right, repentance is restricted by remedy of the sin.

Exalted is He says: "Say, "O My servants who have transgressed against themselves [by sinning], do not despair of the mercy of God. Indeed, God forgives all sins. Indeed, it is He who is the Forgiving, the Merciful. And he who associates others with

God has certainly fabricated a tremendous sin." " قُلْ يَاعِبَادِيَ الَّذِينَ أَسْرَفُوا عَلَى أَنْفُسِهِمْ لَا تَقْنَطُوا مِنْ رَحْمَةِ اللَّهِ إِنَّ اللَّهَ يَغْفِرُ الذُّنُوبَ جَمِيعًا إِنَّهُ هُوَ الْغَفُورُ الرَّحِيمُ " (39:53).

This verse focuses on the right of God and His saying: "Indeed, God does not forgive association with Him, but He forgives what is less than that for whom He wills." " إِنَّ اللَّهَ لَا يَغْفِرُ أَنْ يُشْرَكَ بِهِ وَيَغْفِرُ مَا دُونَ ذَلِكَ لِمَنْ يَشَاءُ " (4:48).

Exalted is He says: "But indeed, I am the Perpetual Forgiver of whoever repents and believes and does righteousness and then continues in guidance." " وَإِنِّي لَغَفَّارٌ لِمَنْ تَابَ وَآمَنَ وَعَمِلَ صَالِحًا ثُمَّ اهْتَدَى" (20:82), if the killer repents, believes and does the righteous actions, then God will forgive him.

The Prophet (PBUH) said while a group of his companions were around him, "Swear allegiance to me for:

1. Not to worship any but God.

2. Not to steal.

3. Not to commit unlawful sexual intercourse.

4. Not to kill children.

5. Not to accuse an innocent person (to spread such an accusation among people).

6. Not to be disobedient (when ordered) to do good deeds"

The Prophet (PBUH) added: "Whoever among you fulfills his pledge will be rewarded by God. And whoever indulges in any one of them (except the ascription of partners to God) and gets the punishment in this world, that punishment will be expiation for that sin. And if one indulges in any of them, and God conceals his sin, it is up to Him to forgive or punish him (in the Hereafter)." 'Ubada bin As-Samit added: "So we swore allegiance for these."

They said: the Prophet (PBUH) narrated: "God has said: 'O Son of Adam, as long as you invoke Me and ask of Me, I shall forgive you for what you have done, and I shall not mind. O Son of Adam, were your sins to reach the clouds of the sky and you then asked forgiveness from Me, I would forgive you. O Son of Adam, were you to come to Me with sins nearly as great as the Earth, and were you then to face Me, ascribing no partner to Me, I would bring you forgiveness nearly as great as it [too]."

Also, the Prophet said: "If anyone's last words are "There is no lord but God" he will enter Paradise."

And said: "God has forbidden the Hell for those who testify that none has the right to be worshipped but God, seeking God's pleasure." In Hadith of Intercession: "God will order those who have had faith equal to the weight of a grain of mustard seed to be taken out from Hell."

The Prophet quoted God, Exalted is He saying: "Then God will say, 'By my Power, and my Majesty, and by My Supremacy, and by My Greatness, I will take out of Hell (Fire) whoever said: 'None has the right to be worshipped except God" Furthermore, there are many texts that refer to that there is no one of people of monotheism will eternally stay in the Fire.

Chapter

The killer repents and surrenders to be killed for his deed, does he has any commitment towards the killed on the doomsday.

Scholars disagreed regarding the killer who repented and surrendered to be killed, is the killed still to be compensated by the killer?

Some said there is nothing as the retaliation is a prescribed penalty and the prescribed penalties are expiatory; the heirs got the right of their inheritor, they have the same rights.

Some said the killed person still cannot regain his right; thus there is no benefit acquired by the killed person.

They said killing encroaches upon three rights: God's right, killed person's right and the heir's right; God's right can be fulfilled by the repentance, the right of the heir is fulfilled by the prescribed penalty, through three options: retaliation, free forgiving or for a blood-money, so if the killer chooses one of them, the right of the killed is not fulfilled, as one of the three options is not enough for fulfillment of the killed right.

The right saying, God knows more: if the killer repents and surrenders to the heirs to get their right, then just two rights are fulfilled but the right of the killed person will be compensated by God and the killer is not punished because of his real repentance. Exalted is He says: "Indeed, your Lord will judge between them by His [wise] judgment. And He is the Exalted in Might, the Knowing."" إِنَّ رَبَّكَ يَقْضِي بَيْنَهُمْ بِحُكْمِهِ وَهُوَ الْعَزِيزُ الْعَلِيمُ" (2:78).

Chapter

Creatures Sin Scenes

Creatures Sin Scenes are thirteen:

1- Scene of bestiality and sensuality.

2- Scene of prerequisites of human creation

3- Scene of people of subjugation

4- Scene of those people who negate fate

5- Scene of wisdom

6- Scene of success and desertion

7- Scene of monotheism

8- Names and merits

9- Boost of faith, having multiple evidences

10- Scene of mercy

11- Scene of disability and weakness

12- Scene of humility, submission and need for God, Exalted is He

13- Scene of worshipping, love and passion for His meeting

The first four scenes related to the misdemeanants, then the following eight scenes for those people of integrity and the best of them is the tenth scene.

Chapter

First Scene: Bestiality and Sensuality

Scene of bestiality and sensuality is the scene of those ignorant people whom there is no difference between them and the animals except being with upright form and articulation of the tongue; their interests are only meeting desires with whatever ways.

Like animals, their states differ.

Some of them are like the dog who finds a corpse that is big enough to feed thousand dogs but he rejects and fights others to get his stomach full, regardless the kind of this food; good or bad, lawful or unlawful and so on. They include who are bestowed knowledge and God's Qur'an verses but they avoid them and follow their desires.

Additionally, some of them are like donkeys; they are only created for labor and food, the lowest insight they are. They are like the person who received Quran but does not realize it or work accordingly.

Some of them are like the wild beast; they have fierce soul, their intention is always to be hostile with people and oppressive to them.

Some have souls like these of snakes, scorpions and others. Exalted is He says: "And there is no creature on [or within] the earth or bird that flies with its wings except [that they are] communities like you. We have not neglected in the Register a thing. Then unto their Lord they will be gathered." " وَمَا مِنْ دَابَّةٍ فِي الْأَرْضِ وَلَا طَائِرٍ يَطِيرُ بِجَنَاحَيْهِ إِلَّا أُمَمٌ أَمْثَالُكُمْ مَا فَرَّطْنَا فِي الْكِتَابِ مِنْ شَيْءٍ" (6:38).

Some of them are like peacocks; that give themselves airs, but their souls are ineffective. Exalted is He prohibited eating the meat of the wild animals, so that the souls of people cannot be infected with these bad characteristics.

Chapter

Second Scene

Prerequisites of human creation scene is observed in heretics who claim that this is from the prerequisites of the human nature; they say that if the humans are sane and have enforced soul, then they do not need superior power to command or prevent them.

Chapter

Third Scene

Scene of people of subjugation: They acknowledge that they are forced to perform their deeds; occurred against their will, these deeds are not theirs at all. They see that all their deeds are obedience, good or evil, as these deeds are in accord with the fate.

Chapter

Fourth Scene

Scene of people negating fate: they acknowledge that their deeds were committed by their own will, not according to God's will, Exalted is He, does not create their deeds, He can guide none; they believe that creatures are those who create and invent their deeds.

Chapter

Fifth Scene

One of the scenes of those people of integrity: scene of wisdom, those people acknowledge that God does not create things in vain and He has absolute wisdom behind every fate and destiny, good or evil, obedience or disobedience...etc. It is very fascinating wisdom that minds cannot perceive or the tongues can express. They believe that there is nothing in the world beyond His will, Exalted is He says: "Unquestionably, His is the creation and the command; blessed is God, Lord of the worlds.""

(7:54). "أَلَا لَهُ الْخَلْقُ وَالْأَمْرُ تَبَارَكَ اللَّهُ رَبُّ الْعَالَمِينَ

The Angels said to Him: "Will You place upon it one who causes corruption therein and sheds blood, while we declare Your praise and sanctify You?" " أَتَجْعَلُ فِيهَا مَنْ يُفْسِدُ فِيهَا وَيَسْفِكُ الدِّمَاءَ وَنَحْنُ نُسَبِّحُ بِحَمْدِكَ وَنُقَدِّسُ لَكَ " (2:30), Exalted is He says: "Indeed, I know that which you do not know." " إِنِّي أَعْلَمُ مَا لَا تَعْلَمُونَ " (2:30). Then they said: "Our Lord, You did not create this aimlessly; exalted are You [above such a thing]."" "رَبَّنَا مَا خَلَقْتَ هَذَا بَاطِلًا سُبْحَانَكَ" (3:191).

Chapter

Sixth Scene

Scene of monotheism: The servant acknowledges and testify the Oneness of God regarding creation and ruling; whatever He wills, it will be, whatever He does not will, it will not be; all creatures are under His dominance; all hearts are in His hand, He guides whatever He wishes by His mercy and favor, Exalted is He says: "He is not questioned about what He does, but they will be questioned."" " لَا يُسْأَلُ عَمَّا يَفْعَلُ وَهُمْ يُسْأَلُونَ " (21:23).

Ibn Abbas said: believing in fate is the basis of monotheism; who rejects the fate, his belief is falsified and who believes in the fate, his belief of monotheism is true.

During this scene, the station of "It is You we worship and You we ask for help." "إِيَّاكَ نَعْبُدُ وَإِيَّاكَ نَسْتَعِينُ" (1:5) comes true by knowledge and becomes a status. If the servant is sure and certain that harm, benefit, giving, hindering, guidance, going stray, happiness and distress are all only by His will.

In this scene, one acquires the station of "It is You we worship", Exalted is He says: "And if you asked them who created them, they would surely say, "God." So how are they deluded? " "وَلَئِنْ سَأَلْتَهُمْ مَنْ خَلَقَهُمْ لَيَقُولُنَّ اللَّهُ فَأَنَّى يُؤْفَكُونَ " (43:78), "Say, [O Muhammad], "To whom belongs the earth and whoever is in it, if you should know?". They will say, "To God." Say, "Then will you not remember?" " "قُلْ لِمَنِ الْأَرْضُ وَمَنْ فِيهَا إِنْ كُنْتُمْ تَعْلَمُونَ. سَيَقُولُونَ لِلَّهِ قُلْ أَفَلَا تَذَكَّرُونَ " (23:85).

They know that God is the Lord of Earth and creatures thereon; He is their Lord, Exalted is He says: "Say, "Who is Lord of the seven heavens and Lord of the Great Throne?" They will say, "[They belong] to God." Say, "Then will you not fear Him?" Say, "In whose hand is the realm of all things - and He protects while none can protect against Him - if you should know? " " "قُلْ مَنْ رَبُّ السَّمَاوَاتِ السَّبْعِ وَرَبُّ الْعَرْشِ الْعَظِيمِ. سَيَقُولُونَ لِلَّهِ قُلْ أَفَلَا تَتَّقُونَ. قُلْ مَنْ بِيَدِهِ مَلَكُوتُ كُلِّ شَيْءٍ وَهُوَ يُجِيرُ وَلَا يُجَارُ عَلَيْهِ " (23:86-88) and in Surah of An-Naml: "Say, [O Muhammad], "Praise be to God, and peace upon His servants whom He has chosen. Is God better or what they associate with Him? [More precisely], is He [not best] who created the heavens and the earth and sent down for you rain from the sky, causing to grow thereby gardens of joyful beauty which you could not [otherwise] have grown the trees thereof? Is there a deity with God? [No], but they are a people who ascribe equals [to Him]." " أَمَّنْ خَلَقَ السَّمَاوَاتِ وَالْأَرْضَ وَأَنْزَلَ لَكُمْ مِنَ السَّمَاءِ مَاءً فَأَنْبَتْنَا بِهِ حَدَائِقَ ذَاتَ بَهْجَةٍ مَا كَانَ لَكُمْ أَنْ تُنْبِتُوا شَجَرَهَا أَإِلَهٌ مَعَ اللَّهِ بَلْ هُمْ قَوْمٌ يَعْدِلُونَ قُلِ الْحَمْدُ لِلَّهِ وَسَلَامٌ عَلَى عِبَادِهِ الَّذِينَ اصْطَفَى آللَّهُ خَيْرٌ أَمَّا يُشْرِكُونَ " (2:59-60).

There is no lord but our God. Therefore, when it is proved that there is no lord who act like our God, then how they can consider those who do not create but created, Exalted is He says: "Or have they attributed to God partners who created like His creation so that the creation [of each] seemed similar to them?" Say, "God is the Creator of all things, and He is the One, the Prevailing." " أَمْ جَعَلُوا لِلَّهِ شُرَكَاءَ خَلَقُوا كَخَلْقِهِ فَتَشَابَهَ الْخَلْقُ عَلَيْهِمْ قُلِ اللَّهُ خَالِقُ كُلِّ شَيْءٍ وَهُوَ الْوَاحِدُ الْقَهَّارُ " (13:16), and His saying: "This is the creation of God. So show Me what those other than Him have created."" هَذَا خَلْقُ اللَّهِ فَأَرُونِي مَاذَا خَلَقَ " (31:11), His saying: "Then is He who creates like one who does not create?"" أَفَمَنْ يَخْلُقُ كَمَنْ لَا يَخْلُقُ الَّذِينَ مِنْ دُونِهِ " (16:17), and His saying: "And those they invoke other than God create nothing, and they [themselves] are created."" وَالَّذِينَ يَدْعُونَ مِنْ دُونِ اللَّهِ لَا يَخْلُقُونَ شَيْئًا وَهُمْ يُخْلَقُونَ " (16:20),

God also says: "But they have taken besides Him gods which create nothing, while they are created."" وَاتَّخَذُوا مِنْ دُونِهِ آلِهَةً لَا يَخْلُقُونَ شَيْئًا وَهُمْ يُخْلَقُونَ " (25:3).

In this scene, the servant recognizes and sees sins and evils according to His fate, no protector against His anger and fury but He; only you can obey Him after being given His help; the sources and outcomes of matters are by God; no reliance except on Him, so Shu'ayb said: "And my success is not but through God. Upon him I have relied, and to Him I return."" وَمَا تَوْفِيقِي إِلَّا بِاللَّهِ عَلَيْهِ تَوَكَّلْتُ "وَإِلَيْهِ أُنِيبُ" (11:88).

Chapter

Seventh Scene

Scene of success and desertion

Success happens when God supports your soul but desertion is when God forsakes your soul; the servant lives upon success God offers, then obeys and worships God. Then by God's desertion, he disobeys and commits sins. God offers the servant success upon His mercy and desertion upon His justice and wisdom; God is only whom the servant has to praise for everything..

If the servant lives this scene, he knows his urgent need for God's help and support every time and his faith and monotheism are also supported only by God. Then, his tongue continues saying "O changer of the hearts, make my heart firm upon Your religion". In this scene he witnesses the support and desertion of God. Success occurs by the will of God that His servant does what pleases God and hates what God hates, Exalted is He says: "But

God has endeared to you the faith and has made it pleasing in your hearts and has made hateful to you disbelief, defiance and disobedience. Those are the [rightly] guided. [It is] as bounty from God and favor. And God is Knowing and Wise."" وَلَكِنَّ اللَّه حَبَّبَ إِلَيْكُمُ الإِيمَانَ وَزَيَّنَهُ فِي قُلُوبِكُمْ وَكَرَّهَ إِلَيْكُمُ الْكُفْرَ وَالْفُسُوقَ وَالْعِصْيَانَ أُولَئِكَ هُمُ الرَّاشِدُونَ - فَضْلًا مِنَ اللَّهِ وَنِعْمَةً وَاللَّهُ عَلِيمٌ حَكِيمٌ" (49:8). Exalted is He is the Most-Knower of those people who deserve His favor, so He confers them all His favor and Mercy, and does not bestow the same for people who are ineligible for; Exalted is He says this verse after saying: "And know that among you is the Messenger of God. If he were to obey you in much of the matter, you would be in difficulty"" "وَاعْلَمُوا أَنَّ فِيكُمْ رَسُولَ اللَّهِ لَوْ يُطِيعُكُمْ فِي كَثِيرٍ مِنَ الأَمْرِ لَعَنِتُّمْ" (49:7).

Your love for faith is not achieved only upon your will; it is by God's support who rooted this in your hearts, so servants follows the Messenger. It is God who makes you keep om faith, as He is the Most-Knower about the interests of His servants. If the Messenger follows what you want, it will be uphill for you and your interests perish you, while you are heedless. It is not your souls that make you love faith and want the guidance and righteousness for you, if you followed your souls, they would lead you to stray.

Chapter

Eighth Scene

Names and merits

This scene is about that the existence of creation is related to the most beautiful names of God and the highest merits; the whole world is based on them. This is the most glorified knowledge; each name has its merit, His names are merits of praise and perfection.

It is not possible to separate between names and merits; or to separate between descriptions and resulted deeds. His fate cannot be separated from His deeds, His deeds cannot be separated from His merits, His merits cannot be separated from His names and His names cannot be separated from His Divinity and Self.

His description is perfection, His deeds are wisdom and interest and His names are the most beautiful. Those who reject His commands, prohibitions, reward and punishment, they attribute to Him what is not suitable for Him.

For those people who ascribed to Him what He disintegrates himself from; those who rejected prophecy and sending messengers and revealing books, Exalted is He says: "And they did not appraise God with true appraisal when they said, "God did not reveal to a human being anything."" وَمَا قَدَرُوا اللَّهَ حَقَّ قَدْرِهِ إِذْ قَالُوا مَا أَنْزَلَ اللَّهُ عَلَى بَشَرٍ مِنْ شَيْءٍ " (6:91) and says regarding those who reject the doomsday, Reward and punishment: "They have not appraised God with true appraisal, while the earth entirely will be [within] His grip on the Day of Resurrection, and the heavens will be folded in His right hand."" وَمَا قَدَرُوا اللَّهَ حَقَّ قَدْرِهِ وَالْأَرْضُ جَمِيعًا قَبْضَتُهُ يَوْمَ الْقِيَامَةِ وَالسَّمَاوَاتُ مَطْوِيَّاتٌ بِيَمِينِهِ" (39:67).

He says regarding those people who ascribe to God that He shall equate between both believers and disbelievers or righteous and wicked people: "Or do those who commit evils think We will make them like those who have believed and done righteous deeds - [make them] equal in their life and their death? Evil is that which they judge."" أَمْ حَسِبَ الَّذِينَ اجْتَرَحُوا السَّيِّئَاتِ أَنْ نَجْعَلَهُمْ كَالَّذِينَ آمَنُوا وَعَمِلُوا الصَّالِحَاتِ سَوَاءً مَحْيَاهُمْ وَمَمَاتُهُمْ سَاءَ مَا يَحْكُمُونَ" (45:21) and He says regarding those people who have thought and account for God that negate His names and merits: "Then did you think that We created you uselessly and that to Us you would not be returned?"" أَفَحَسِبْتُمْ أَنَّمَا خَلَقْنَاكُمْ عَبَثًا وَأَنَّكُمْ إِلَيْنَا لَا تُرْجَعُونَ فَتَعَالَى اللَّهُ الْمَلِكُ الْحَقُّ لَا إِلَهَ إِلَّا هُوَ رَبُّ الْعَرْشِ الْكَرِيمِ" (23:115).

God, Exalted is He, appreciated his merits and 99 names; He is the Great Forgiver as He likes forgiveness; The Pardoner as he likes repentance and His servant's repentance pleases him. His forgiveness is the perfection of his ability; He is not who forgives because of inability or does not recognize His right but He is the

Most Knower and the Omnipotent to restore His right, Jesus said: "If You should punish them - indeed they are Your servants; but if You forgive them - indeed it is You who is the Exalted in Might, the Wise."" "إِنْ تُعَذِّبْهُمْ فَإِنَّهُمْ عِبَادُكَ وَإِنْ تَغْفِرْ لَهُمْ فَإِنَّكَ أَنْتَ الْعَزِيزُ الْحَكِيمُ" (5:118). Who follows the ends of these names and merits, knows how to praise and glorify Him well in a way that is very relevant to His Divinity.

Each name He attributed to Himself has to be worshiped in a way that is different from the worship of the other names; these worships for His names do not prevent each other. Worshipping by His names is taken from Quran, Exalted is He says: "And to God belong the best names, so invoke Him by them."" وَلِلَّهِ الْأَسْمَاءُ الْحُسْنَى فَادْعُوهُ بِهَا" (7:180).

God is the Most Knower and He likes people of knowledge; He is The Source of all goodness and He likes the righteous people. He is the Grateful and He likes people who thank Him.

Obedience and monotheism are liked by Him leading to good conduct and reward but disobedience and polytheism are hated.

Chapter

Ninth Scene

Boost of faith and having multiple evidences

It is a scene related to knowledge. How is faith boosted by sins and disobedience? This happens when the servant knows the sins, disobedience and results thereof. Messengers of God commanded the servants with what benefit them and prohibited them from the corruption of their life. They told them about What God loves and hates and if the servant obeys God and praises Him, God bestows provision, bounties and health. If the servant disobeys God, God gives him scarcity, weakness, humility, disgrace and lack of provision, Exalted is He says: "Whoever does righteousness, whether male or female, while he is a believer - We will surely cause him to live a good life, and We will surely give them their reward [in the Hereafter] according to the best of what they used to do."" مَنْ عَمِلَ صَالِحًا مِنْ ذَكَرٍ أَوْ أُنْثَى وَهُوَ مُؤْمِنٌ "فَلَنُحْيِيَنَّهُ حَيَاةً طَيِّبَةً وَلَنَجْزِيَنَّهُمْ أَجْرَهُمْ بِأَحْسَنِ مَا كَانُوا يَعْمَلُونَ" (16:97), also, "And it will be said to those who feared God, "What did your Lord send down?" They will say, "[That which is] good." For those who do good in this world is good; and the home of the Hereafter is better. And how excellent is the home of the righteous"" وَقِيلَ لِلَّذِينَ "اتَّقَوْا مَاذَا أَنْزَلَ رَبُّكُمْ قَالُوا خَيْرًا لِلَّذِينَ أَحْسَنُوا فِي هَذِهِ الدُّنْيَا حَسَنَةٌ وَلَدَارُ الْآخِرَةِ خَيْرٌ" (16:30), " And [saying], "Seek forgiveness of your Lord and repent to Him, [and] He will let you enjoy a good provision for a specified term and give every doer of favor his favor. But if you turn away, then indeed, I fear for you the punishment of a great Day."" وَأَنِ اسْتَغْفِرُوا رَبَّكُمْ ثُمَّ تُوبُوا إِلَيْهِ يُمَتِّعْكُمْ مَتَاعًا حَسَنًا إِلَى أَجَلٍ مُسَمًّى وَيُؤْتِ كُلَّ "ذِي فَضْلٍ فَضْلَهُ" (11:3) and: "And whoever turns away from My remembrance - indeed, he will have a depressed life, and We will gather him on the Day of Resurrection blind."" وَمَنْ أَعْرَضَ عَنْ ذِكْرِي "فَإِنَّ لَهُ مَعِيشَةً ضَنْكًا وَنَحْشُرُهُ يَوْمَ الْقِيَامَةِ أَعْمَى" (20:124). "Depressed life" is interpreted to be the torture of grave and it is in the worldly life and Barzakh. Those who turn away from His remainder that He has revealed, they live depressed life with misery living, stinginess and fatigue.

People of heretics, ignorance, disobedience are in hellfire in the world before the Hell of the Afterlife and the righteous people are in pleasure then the Heaven, Exalted is He says: "Indeed, the righteous will be in pleasure. And indeed, the wicked will be in Hellfire."" "إِنَّ الْأَبْرَارَ لَفِي نَعِيمٍ وَإِنَّ الْفُجَّارَ لَفِي جَحِيمٍ" (82:13-14), " And indeed, for those who have wronged is a punishment before that""وَإِنَّ لِلَّذِينَ ظَلَمُوا عَذَابًا دُونَ ذَلِكَ" (52:47) and Exalted is He says: "And they say, "When is [the fulfillment of] this promise, if you should be truthful?". Say, "Perhaps it is close behind you - some of that for which you are impatient."" وَيَقُولُونَ مَتَى هَذَا الْوَعْدُ إِنْ كُنْتُمْ صَادِقِينَ قُلْ "عَسَى أَنْ يَكُونَ رَدِفَ لَكُمْ بَعْضُ الَّذِي تَسْتَعْجِلُونَ" (27:71-72).

Exalted is He makes for the good deeds and obedience a good effect and much pleasure than the disobedience and makes for the sins and evils hateful effects. Ibn Abbas said: good deeds guide hearts, shine up faces, perk up the provision and amity in the creatures' hearts. The evil results in darkness of hearts, weakness in the body, shortage of provision and hatred; this is known by people of insight, as they can watch this results.

What happens for the servant is the result of his sins, Exalted is He says: "And whatever strikes you of disaster - it is for what your hands have earned; but He pardons much."" وَمَا أَصَابَكُمْ مِنْ مُصِيبَةٍ فَبِمَا كَسَبَتْ أَيْدِيكُمْ وَيَعْفُو عَنْ كَثِيرٍ (42:30) but He says for righteous servants and the messengers' companions: "Why [is it that] when a [single] disaster struck you [on the day of Uhud], although you had struck [the enemy in the battle of Badr] with one twice as great, you said, "From where is this?" Say, "It is from yourselves." Indeed, God is over all things competent."" أَوَلَمَّا أَصَابَتْكُمْ مُصِيبَةٌ قَدْ أَصَبْتُمْ مِثْلَيْهَا قُلْتُمْ أَنَّى هَذَا قُلْ هُوَ مِنْ عِنْدِ أَنْفُسِكُمْ (3:165) and: "What comes to you of good is from God, but what comes to you of evil, [O man], is from yourself. And We have sent you"" مَا أَصَابَكَ مِنْ حَسَنَةٍ فَمِنَ اللَّهِ وَمَا أَصَابَكَ مِنْ سَيِّئَةٍ فَمِنْ نَفْسِكَ (4:79).

What is meant by the good and the evil are bounties and disasters that occur to the servant; each shortage and disaster in the world life and the Afterlife results from sins and violating God's commands.

The impacts of goods and evils on hearts, bodies and properties are known in the world; every righteous man and sinner knows. Exalted is He says: "Then is He who is a maintainer of every soul, [knowing] what it has earned, [like any other]? But to God they have attributed partners."" "أَفَمَنْ هُوَ قَائِمٌ عَلَى كُلِّ نَفْسٍ بِمَا كَسَبَتْ" (13:33) and His saying: "God witnesses that there is no deity except Him, and [so do] the angels and those of knowledge - [that He is] maintaining [creation] in justice. There is no deity except Him, the Exalted in Might, the Wise."" "شَهِدَ اللَّهُ أَنَّهُ لَا إِلَهَ إِلَّا هُوَ وَالْمَلَائِكَةُ وَأُولُو الْعِلْمِ قَائِمًا بِالْقِسْطِ لَا إِلَهَ إِلَّا هُوَ الْعَزِيزُ الْحَكِيمُ" (3:18). All what you watch in the world regarding evil, pain, punishment, shortage, lack of your provision and others, is an expression for the justice of God even if He uses a tyrant to perform that, Exalted is He says for those who spoiled the Earth: "We sent against you servants of Ours - those of great military might, and they probed [even] into the homes"" "بَعَثْنَا عَلَيْكُمْ عِبَادًا لَنَا أُولِي بَأْسٍ شَدِيدٍ فَجَاسُوا خِلَالَ الدِّيَارِ" (17:5).

When the servant experiences shortage, hatred and misery, if he disobeys God; he shall stop disobedience to see honor after disgrace, richness after poverty, pleasure after sadness; thus his faith increases and the evidences of faith strengthen inside his heart after experiencing the difference between obedience and disobedience. Exalted is He says: "That God may remove from them the worst of what they did and reward them their due for the best of what they used to do."" لِيُكَفِّرَ اللَّهُ عَنْهُمْ أَسْوَأَ الَّذِي عَمِلُوا وَيَجْزِيَهُمْ

أَجْرَهُمْ بِأَحْسَنِ الَّذِي كَانُوا يَعْمَلُونَ" (39:35).

Chapter

Tenth Scene

Scene of mercy

When the servant commits the sin, his heart becomes full of abruptness, cruelty and anger; the same anger towards those who committed a sin. These people wish if they can prevent sinners from disobeying God. Their hearts do not have mercy for the sinners but when they are destined to commit the same sin and live the same state, they ask God for forgiveness and acceptance of their repentance, then their cruelty against sinners changes to be mercy and they ask God to forgive them.

Eleventh Scene

Scene of disability and weakness

The servant is the most disable to keep his soul and the most weakest; he does not have ability or strength except by his Lord, then he sees himself like a feather on earth moving to the right or left by act of wind; he is ruled by fate and destiny. The servant is unable to cause harm or benefit for himself, cause death or bring to life. It is the state of the servant, he is between two strengths: strength of his Lord and that of his enemies; If his Lord forsakes him, he will be controlled by his soul.

In this scene, he knows himself and his God well; if he knows that he is weak, he realizes the power of his God; if he knows that he is unable, he realizes the ability of his God. Whenever the servant realizes his deficits and needs, his knowledge of his Lord and His perfection is increased. Whenever the servant knows His powers and praised merits, he knows that who created him is the most perfect; how the servant has life, hearing, speaking and insight and owns his choice and will while his creator is not having the same and more? In this scene, the servant knows that he is weak, then he knows that he does not have control on anything.

Twelfth Scene

Scene of humility, submission and need for God, Exalted is He

In this scene, the servant sees that he does not deserve little or much from his God; he finds that every good happens for him is much for him and he does not deserve it, only the mercy of his God covered him. The servant sees that his sins are very many and his good deeds are very few. He stands before his God lowering his head because of his modesty and embarrassment.

Thirteenth Scene

Scene of worshipping, love and passion for His meeting

It is the scene of worshipping, love and passion for His meeting; it is the end and destination of worshippers. They have passion of meeting their God; having happiness and pleasure for that. Then the servant's heart becomes full of love to God, his tongue is always remembering his Lord; his wish is to be nearer to him and his organs find it easy to worship his God. Then, the servant finds himself on the straight path of God.

It is enough stating all of that about repentance, its provisions and outcomes but there is a need to know about it, its provisions and outcomes.

CHAPTER 27

Returning in repentance Station

After the servant reaches the repentance station and acquires its status, he reaches the return station. Exalted is He commanded it in His verses: "And return [in repentance] to your Lord" "وَأَنِيبُوا إِلَىٰ رَبِّكُمْ" (39:53) and "Indeed, Abraham was forbearing, grieving and [frequently] returning [to God]." "إِنَّ إِبْرَاهِيمَ لَحَلِيمٌ أَوَّاهٌ مُّنِيبٌ" (11:75). Only people of returning in repentance are bestowed the insight to realize His signs. He says: "Have they not looked at the heaven above them - how We structured it and adorned it and [how] it has no rifts?" "أَفَلَمْ يَنظُرُوا إِلَى السَّمَاءِ فَوْقَهُمْ كَيْفَ بَنَيْنَاهَا وَزَيَّنَّاهَا وَمَا لَهَا مِن فُرُوجٍ" (50:6) to the verse: "Giving insight and a reminder for every servant who turns [to God]." "تَبْصِرَةً وَذِكْرَىٰ"

‏"لِكُلِّ عَبْدٍ مُّنِيبٍ‏" (50:8). Exalted is He says that His reward and Heaven are for the people who return to Him in repentance, He says: "And Paradise will be brought near to the righteous, not far, [It will be said], "This is what you were promised - for every returner [to God] and keeper [of His covenant]. Who feared the Most Merciful unseen and came with a heart returning [in repentance]. Enter it in peace" ‏"وَأُزْلِفَتِ الْجَنَّةُ لِلْمُتَّقِينَ غَيْرَ بَعِيدٍ. هَذَا مَا تُوعَدُونَ‏ -50:31) ‏". لِكُلِّ أَوَّابٍ حَفِيظٍ. مَّنْ خَشِيَ الرَّحْمَنَ بِالْغَيْبِ وَجَاءَ بِقَلْبٍ مُّنِيبٍ. ادْخُلُوهَا بِسَلَامٍ‏ 34). Exalted is he told that the good tidings are for those who return to God in repentance, He says: "But those who have avoided Taghut, lest they worship it, and turned back to God - for them are good tidings." ‏"وَالَّذِينَ اجْتَنَبُوا الطَّاغُوتَ أَن يَعْبُدُوهَا وَأَنَابُوا إِلَى اللَّـهِ لَهُمُ الْبُشْرَىٰ‏" (39:17).

Returning to God in repentance is two-fold: one is the returning of all His creatures; believer or disbeliever, righteous or sinner, Exalted is He says: "And when adversity touches the people, they call upon their Lord, turning in repentance to Him." ‏"وَإِذَا مَسَّ النَّاسَ ضُرٌّ دَعَوْا رَبَّهُم مُّنِيبِينَ إِلَيْهِ‏" (30:33). The second one is of His Allies. This returning includes four matters: Loving Him, submission to Him, Turning to Him and turning away of anything except Him; no return except by fulfilling the four matters. Returning in repentance to God comes true only when the servant abides by and fulfills all commitments, Exalted is He says: "And he who fulfills that which he has promised God - He will give him a great reward." "وَمَنْ أَوْفَىٰ بِمَا عَاهَدَ عَلَيْهُ اللَّـهَ فَسَيُؤْتِيهِ أَجْرًا عَظِيمًا" (48:10) and "And fulfill [every] commitment. Indeed, the commitment is ever [that about which one will be] questioned." " وَأَوْفُوا بِالْعَهْدِ ۖ إِنَّ الْعَهْدَ كَانَ مَسْئُولًا" (17:34). Fulfilling the commitments towards God is achieved by being sincere, faithful and obedient as well as their commitments towards living creatures.

Returning to God in repentance is achieved only by three matters: repentance from all sins, feeling pain for committing the sin and realizing what worships he has missed. Repentance from all sins that one committed against the right of God and meeting the creatures' rights. Feeling pain for committing sins whether the sins committed by him or by his Muslim brother. Realizing what worships he has missed and trying to compensate for them by doing good deeds.

Returning to God in repentance comes true after getting rid of pleasure of the sin, not despising people of negligence and living in good hopes, questioning the reasons of worshipping.

After getting rid of pleasure of the sin and becoming full of pain when remembering it or even thinking in it, one return to God in good faith. The soul has three states regarding the sins: committing the sin, regarding it, then being secure to God and returning to Him wholly, the last state is the best one. The worship of a repentant who fight against his soul regarding pleasure of sin and desire may be more difficult than the worship of a believer who is secure and returned to God.

Not despising people of negligence and living in good hopes is a sign of returning to God in repentance. Do not ask for the mercy for you and fear the torture for the people of negligence but ask for the mercy for them and fear being you who is punished. You can hate the people of negligence but hate more yourself being negligent after getting the insight.

Questioning reasons of worshipping; question your worship, is it for yourself or is it for God? Some deeds are thought to be for God but there are many blocks that hinder them to be for God like targeting these deeds for some personal ends like self-conceit, pride, arrogance and so on, or for the sake of other creatures.

Return to God in repentance becomes a state by three things: Feeling despair because of your deeds, discovering that you must turn to God and realizing the kindness of God upon you. Feeling despair because of your deeds through considering two matters: First, who helps you to do good deeds is your Lord and second, you are not going to be saved by your deeds but by mercy and favor of God. The Prophet (PBUH) said: "The deeds of anyone of you will not save you (from the (Hell) Fire)." They said,

"Even you (will not be saved by your deeds), O Messenger of God (PBUH)?" He says, "No, even I (will not be saved) unless and until God bestows His Mercy on me." Then, he realizes that you must turn to God as you are always in dire need for Him. Regrading realizing the kindness of God upon servants, one have to admit that all what deeds you have done are achieved by the help of God and one is in dire need for His kindness to have your hopes and demands answered

Remembrance Station

The heart reaches the station of remembrance, it follows the returning to God in Repentance station. Exalted is He says: "But none will remember except he who turns back [in repentance]." "وَمَا يَتَذَكَّرُ إِلَّا مَن يُنِيبُ" (40:13) and "Giving insight and a reminder for every servant who turns [to God]." "تَبْصِرَةً وَذِكْرَىٰ لِكُلِّ عَبْدٍ مُّنِيبٍ" (50:8). Remembrance is one of the characteristics of people of understanding, Exalted is He says: "Only they will remember [who are] people of understanding." "إِنَّمَا يَتَذَكَّرُ أُولُو الْأَلْبَابِ" (39:9).

Contemplation is using insight to realize the quest. Remembrance and contemplation result in knowledge and facts of faith and benevolence. Contemplation is to reach ends of the things, using insight to reach them. Only people of insight who contemplate the signs of the God; the remainder of God is directed only for them – those are the people of thought. Exalted is He says: "Have they not looked at the heaven above them - how We structured it and adorned it and [how] it has no rifts? And the earth - We spread it out and cast therein firmly set mountains and made grow therein [something] of every beautiful kind, giving insight and a reminder for every servant who turns [to God]."

" أَفَلَمْ يَنظُرُوا إِلَى السَّمَاءِ فَوْقَهُمْ كَيْفَ بَنَيْنَاهَا وَزَيَّنَّاهَا وَمَا لَهَا مِن فُرُوجٍ. وَالْأَرْضَ مَدَدْنَاهَا وَأَلْقَيْنَا فِيهَا رَوَاسِيَ وَأَنبَتْنَا فِيهَا مِن كُلِّ زَوْجٍ بَهِيجٍ. تَبْصِرَةً وَذِكْرَىٰ لِكُلِّ عَبْدٍ مُّنِيبٍ." (50:6,7,8)

Insight and remembrance are only for those who return to God in repentance as when the servant return to God, he is bestowed insight to realize lessons and signs. Exalted is He says: "And how many a generation before them did We destroy who were greater than them in [striking] power and had explored throughout the lands. Is there any place of escape? Indeed in that is a reminder for whoever has a heart or who listens while he is present [in mind]." " وَكَمْ أَهْلَكْنَا قَبْلَهُم مِّن قَرْنٍ هُمْ أَشَدُّ مِنْهُم بَطْشًا فَنَقَّبُوا فِي الْبِلَادِ هَلْ مِن مَّحِيصٍ. إِنَّ فِي ذَٰلِكَ لَذِكْرَىٰ لِمَن كَانَ لَهُ قَلْبٌ أَوْ أَلْقَى السَّمْعَ وَهُوَ شَهِيدٌ " (50:36-37). There are three categories of people regarding this previous verse: A category with a dead heart, this verse is not a remainder for it, the second one is with busy and ignorant heart that cannot realize this verse and the third one is with a live heart ready to listen and consider this verse.

If the heart with light of insight listens to verses of God, it has more light, Exalted is He says: "And those who have been given knowledge see that what is revealed to you from your Lord is the truth, and it guides to the path of the Exalted in Might, the Praiseworthy." " وَيَرَى الَّذِينَ أُوتُوا الْعِلْمَ الَّذِي أُنزِلَ إِلَيْكَ مِن رَّبِّكَ هُوَ الْحَقَّ وَيَهْدِي إِلَىٰ صِرَاطِ الْعَزِيزِ الْحَمِيدِ " (34:6).

Stages of the remembrance are three: Benefiting from the lesson, having insight by the lesson and gaining idea of the lesson. Benefiting from the lesson comes after the heart is full of fear and hope, then it works so that it can get rid of this fear and achieve what is hoped and desired. Lesson is the command or the prohibition that accompanied with invitation and intimidation. Lesson is two kinds: Heard and watched lesson. Heard lesson is like benefit from hearing guidance and advices revealed by the messengers. Watched lesson is to benefit from what you watch in the world like fate or the signs of God that were revealed to His messengers. Having insight by the lesson is increasing the insight through acquiring the lesson. Gaining the idea of the lesson is by working according to it. Thus, the good deeds are the outcome of beneficial knowledge gained by contemplation.

Lesson is benefited after occurrence of three things: dire need for it, forgetting about the deficits of the lesson's teller and remembering the promise and the punishment. Dire need for the lesson, invitation and intimidation, is when the servant returns to God and remembers Him with weak heart. Those who return to God in repentance urgently need to be reminded with the commands and the prohibition, those who are negligent urgently need invitation and intimidation and those who are opponent and sinner are in a dire need for argument, Exalted is He says: "Invite to the way of your Lord with wisdom and good instruction, and argue with them in a way that is best." "ادْعُ إِلَىٰ سَبِيلِ رَبِّكَ بِالْحِكْمَةِ وَالْمَوْعِظَةِ الْحَسَنَةِ ۖ وَجَادِلْهُم بِالَّتِي هِيَ أَحْسَنُ" (16:125). This verse is revealed to describe these three categories of people.

Forgetting about the deficits of the lesson's teller; if the person considered these deficits, he cannot benefit from the lesson as he becomes a bad model for you. But remembering the promise and the punishment results in fear of God and warns Him. Exalted is He says: "Indeed in that is a warning for whoever would fear [God]." "إِنَّ فِي ذَٰلِكَ لَعِبْرَةً لِّمَن يَخْشَىٰ" (79:26). Believing in the promise and the punishment is a condition to benefit from the lesson and signs.

Lesson is acquired by insight through three things: active mentality, realizing the fact of life and getting rid of ends and purposes. Lesson is realized and acquired through active mentality, which is the rational awareness and strong understanding.

Realizing the fact of life means that you realize that your life is short, it is briefed in breathes, so one has to spend it obeying God doing righteous deeds. Getting rid of ends and purposes, by not following one's desires and soul. Following the desires blocks the mind's light, the heart's insight and getting one apart from the straight path. If the servant follows his desires, his mind and opinion divert from the straight path.

Outcome of the idea is got by three things: Short-term aims; reflecting on Quran and leaving the distracting relationships. Realizing that death is not far results in short-term aims; urging to realize what worships that we have missed, thus we become less inclined to this world and cling to the hereafter life and get rid of desires related to this world. Exalted is He says: "And on the Day when He will gather them, [it will be] as if they had not remained [in the world] but an hour of the day, [and] they will know each other." " وَيَوْمَ يَحْشُرُهُمْ كَأَن لَّمْ يَلْبَثُوا إِلَّا سَاعَةً مِّنَ النَّهَارِ يَتَعَارَفُونَ بَيْنَهُمْ" (10:45) and "It will be, on the Day they see it, as though they had not remained [in the world] except for an afternoon or a morning thereof." "كَأَنَّهُمْ يَوْمَ يَرَوْنَهَا لَمْ يَلْبَثُوا إِلَّا عَشِيَّةً أَوْ ضُحَاهَا" (79:46). Short-term aims come true when we are sure that the world is not forever but the hereafter lasts forever, so you set your hopes and dreams according to that. Messenger of God (PBUH) said: "Behold! The world, in relation to what has passed of it, shall not remain except as what remains of this day of yours, in relation to what has passed of it."

Reflecting on Quran is through considering meanings in Quran by heart and working the mind to think and ponder over it. Exalted is He says: "[This is] a blessed Book which We have revealed to you, [O Muhammad], that they might reflect upon its verses and that those of understanding would be reminded."

(38:29).   "كِتَابٌ أَنزَلْنَاهُ إِلَيْكَ مُبَارَكٌ لِّيَدَّبَّرُوا آيَاتِهِ وَلِيَتَذَكَّرَ أُولُو الْأَلْبَابِ"

Reflecting on Quran is the most beneficial worship for the servant, realizing its ideas and meanings. You can recognize the limits of the good and the evil, justice and favor of God, His straight Path, the path to the Hell and the Heaven and so on. On the contrary, you realize what Satan invites to and the punishment of those who follow him. This gives you insight to distinguish between the good and the evil, the truth and untruth and the guidance and going astray. Meanings of Quran are based on monotheism and its evidences and signs, names and merits of God, messengers, angels ...etc.

Corruption-makers of the heart are five: Having distracting relationships, wishing, clinging to things other than God, intaking and sleeping.

These five things block the way between the heart and God resulting in illness of the heart. Having distracting relationships fills the heart with their affairs, being busy to meet their demands and desires that divert it to get away from turning to God.

Exalted is He says: "And the Day the wrongdoer will bite on his hands [in regret] he will say, "Oh, I wish I had taken with the Messenger a way. Oh, woe to me! I wish I had not taken that one as a friend. He led me away from the remembrance after it had come to me." " وَيَوْمَ يَعَضُّ الظَّالِمُ عَلَىٰ يَدَيْهِ يَقُولُ يَا لَيْتَنِي اتَّخَذْتُ مَعَ الرَّسُولِ سَبِيلًا. يَا وَيْلَتَىٰ لَيْتَنِي لَمْ أَتَّخِذْ فُلَانًا خَلِيلًا. لَقَدْ أَضَلَّنِي عَنِ الذِّكْرِ بَعْدَ إِذْ جَاءَنِي" (25:27-29).

Co-existing with people can be beneficial during prayers on Fridays, congregational prayers, feasts and Hajj, learning, Jihad and so on, yet get away of them when they bring evil. If you are obliged to co-exist with evil people, do not act like them.

Second corruption-maker of the Heart: Wishing

There are people who spend their lives wishing joys of the world, wealth, power, women …etc. Those people find themselves, at the end, have nothing to save them from the accounting on the doomsday. On the other hand, there are people all their wishes are turning to knowledge and faith; the deeds that make them near to God. The Prophet (PBUH) praised those people who wish the good; he told that the person who wishes doing the good, may get the same reward as the doer. The Prophet (PBUH) said: 'The likeness of this nation is that of four people: A man to whom God gives wealth and knowledge, so he acts according to his knowledge with regard to his wealth, spending it as it should be spent; a man to whom God gives knowledge, but he does not give him wealth, so he says: "If I had been given (wealth) like this one, I would have done what (the first man) did." The Messenger of God (PBUH) said: 'They will be equal in reward. And a man to whom God gives wealth but does not give knowledge, so he squanders his wealth and spends it in inappropriate ways; and a man to whom God gives neither knowledge nor wealth, and he says: "If I had (wealth) like this one, I would do what (the third man) did." The Messenger of God (PBUH) said: 'They are equal in their burden (of sin).'"

Third corruption-maker of the heart: Clinging to things other than God

Clinging to things other God is the worst corruption ever. If the person clings things other than God, He helps him to pursue his quest and finally he fails to reach it. Then, he losses being near to God and reaching his quest, Exalted is He says: "And they have taken besides God [false] deities that they would be for them [a source of] honor. No! Those "gods" will deny their worship of them and will be against them opponents [on the Day of Judgement]." " وَاتَّخَذُوا مِن دُونِ اللَّـهِ آلِهَةً لِّيَكُونُوا لَهُمْ عِزًّا. كَلَّا ۚ سَيَكْفُرُونَ بِعِبَادَتِهِمْ وَيَكُونُونَ عَلَيْهِمْ ضِدًّا." (19:81-82). The severe forsaking is for those who clang to anything other than God. Exalted is He says: "Do not make [as equal] with God another deity and [thereby] become censured and forsaken." " لَّا تَجْعَلْ مَعَ اللَّهِ إِلَـٰهًا آخَرَ فَتَقْعُدَ مَذْمُومًا مَّخْذُولً " (17:22). Those have the worst state being censured and forsaken.

Fourth corruption-maker of the Heart: Fullness (Food)

This corruption-maker is divided into two matters: First corruption-maker includes forbidden acts, they, in turn are subdivided into: deeds forbidden by God like eating dead animals, blood, flesh of swine, fanged beasts of prey and birds having talons; and deeds forbidden for saving the servants' rights like robbing, violation and what things taken without the consent of its owner. Second, things corrupt if they exceed their value or quantity like exceeding limits of lawful matters, extra fullness that hinder doing worships, those who eat much food, drink much water and sleep more time, the Prophet (PBUH) said: "No man fills a container worse than his stomach. A few morsels that keep his back upright are sufficient for him. If he has to, then he should keep one-third for food, one-third for drink and one-third for his breathing."

Fifth corruption-maker of the Heart: Sleeping

Much sleeping causes death to the heart, exhausts the body, wastes time and brings on negligence and lethargy. The most beneficial sleeping is after hard work, at the beginning of night and at the midday.

Station of Firmly Holding and Seeking Protection

This station is sub-divided into: Holding to God and holding to the rope of God. Exalted is He says: "And hold firmly to the rope of God all together and do not become divided." " وَاعْتَصِمُوا بِحَبْلِ اللَّـهِ جَمِيعًا وَلَا تَفَرَّقُوا" (3:103) and "And hold fast to God . He is your protector; and excellent is the protector, and excellent is the helper." " "وَاعْتَصِمُوا بِاللَّـهِ هُوَ مَوْلَاكُمْ ۖ فَنِعْمَ الْمَوْلَىٰ وَنِعْمَ النَّصِيرُ" (22:78).

The world and hereafter pleasures are based on holding to God and His rope. Holding to his rope prevents from going astray and holding to God prevents from destruction. Holding to the rope of God enforces the servant to go on the straight path and following the evidence. Holding to God gives him power. The Prophet (PBUH) said: "It is the firm rope of God, it is the wise remembrance, it is the straight path, and it is the one that the desires cannot distort, nor can tongues twist it, nor can the scholars ever have enough of it, it guides to the Right Path, whoever acts according to it he is rewarded, whoever judges by it he has judged justly, and whoever invites to it then he guides to the Straight Path."

Holding to the rope of God is by keeping his obedience to fulfill His commands. You have to fulfill His commands based on your faith and expecting to His reward.

Holding to God: Relying on Him, and seeking and asking for His protection. Defending the servant is the outcome of the holding to God; God defends him against incorrect desires, lusts, enemies, evil and doubtful matters.

Fleeing to God Station

Exalted is He says: "So flee to God." "ففروا إلى الله". (51:50). There are two kinds of fleeing: Fleeing of the prosperous and wretched people. Fleeing of the prosperous people is to God but the fleeing of the wretched people is from God.

Fleeing from Him to Him is to keep obedience; fleeing from His torture to His reward by faith and obedience. There are three degrees of fleeing: Fleeing of commons from ignorance to knowledge, from laziness to activeness by hard work and determination and from narrowness to vastness by trust and expectation.

Ignorance is two-fold: Ignoring the beneficial knowledge and not working according it. Moses said: "He says, "I seek refuge in God from being among the ignorant." " قَالَ أَعُوذُ بِاللَّـهِ أَنْ أَكُونَ مِنَ الْجَاهِلِينَ" After they said to him: "They said, "Do you take us in ridicule?" " قَالُوا أَتَتَّخِذُنَا هُزُوًا" (2:67). Ignorant means ridiculous person.

Josef said: "And if You do not avert from me their plan, I might incline toward them and [thus] be of the ignorant." " وَإِلَّا تَصْرِفْ عَنِّي كَيْدَهُنَّ أَصْبُ إِلَيْهِنَّ وَأَكُن مِّنَ الْجَاهِلِينَ" (12:33). Ignorant means who do adultery. Exalted is He says: "The repentance accepted by God is only for those who do wrong in ignorance" " إِنَّمَا التَّوْبَةُ عَلَى اللَّـهِ لِلَّذِينَ يَعْمَلُونَ السُّوءَ بِجَهَالَةٍ" (4:17). All companions of the Prophet agreed that every disobedience is an ignorance; sinners are ignorant.

Fleeing is from laziness to activeness by hard work and determination.

Fleeing is from the motives of laziness to the motives of activeness by hard work and determination. Hard work means sincere work and determination means true intention. Exalted is He says: "Take what We have given you with determination" " خُذُوا مَا آتَيْنَاكُم بِقُوَّةٍ" (2:63), "And We wrote for him on the tablets [something] of all things - instruction and explanation for all things, [saying], "Take them with determination" " وَكَتَبْنَا لَهُ فِي الْأَلْوَاحِ مِن كُلِّ شَيْءٍ مَّوْعِظَةً وَتَفْصِيلًا لِّكُلِّ شَيْءٍ فَخُذْهَا بِقُوَّةٍ" (7:145), and He says: "O John, take the Scripture with determination." " يَا يَحْيَىٰ خُذِ الْكِتَابَ بِقُوَّةٍ" (19:12).

Fleeing from narrowness to vastness by trust and expectation.

Fleeing from worry, sadness and fears in the world to trust in God, Exalted is He says: "And whoever fears God - He will make for him a way out. And will provide for him from where he does not expect." "وَمَن يَتَّقِ اللَّهَ يَجْعَل لَّهُ مَخْرَجًا. وَيَرْزُقْهُ مِنْ حَيْثُ لَا يَحْتَسِبُ" (65:2-3). This includes all distresses of the world. As long as the servant has good thought in God, good expectation and reliance on Him, God never disappoints him.

As long as the person has good thought in God, and expects good from Him, and is sincere in trust in Him, God does not disappoint him at all, He does not waste the good deeds of a servant.

There is a kind of fleeing includes that of special people from the action to the evidence of the action. For example, Abraham, May God be pleased with him, asked God: "And [mention] when Abraham said, "My Lord, show me how You give life to the dead." [God] said, "Have you not believed?" He says, "Yes, but [I ask] only that my heart may be satisfied." " وَإِذْ قَالَ إِبْرَاهِيمُ رَبِّ أَرِنِي " كَيْفَ تُحْيِي الْمَوْتَىٰ ۖ قَالَ أَوَلَمْ تُؤْمِن ۖ قَالَ بَلَىٰ وَلَٰكِن لِّيَطْمَئِنَّ قَلْبِ" (2:260).

Exercises Station

Where the soul does exercises on truth and sincerity. Exercises on accepting the truth includes two matters: accepting the truth and applying it through deeds, sayings and will and accepting the truth from the person who is telling it. Exalted is He says: "And the one who has brought the truth and [they who] believed in it - those are the righteous." " وَالَّذِي جَاءَ بِالصِّدْقِ وَصَدَّقَ بِهِ

أُولَٰئِكَ هُمُ الْمُتَّقُونَ ".(39:33)

Exercise station is of three degrees: Exercises for commons; morals governed by knowledge, deeds refined by sincerity and keeping rights of the servants.

Morals governed by knowledge means being in consistence with knowledge; your deeds are always according to Sharia.

Deeds refined by sincerity means being sure that your deeds are always for the Sake of God not something else; having one purpose to be for God.

Keeping rights of the servants means fulfilling all rights upon you whether for God or His servants. As long as these three matters are hard to be fulfilled, so those matters need an exercise to be fulfilled fully so that you acquire them as habits then become morals.

Exercises for special people: Get rid of separation, stop looking back and keep up acquiring more knowledge.

Getting rid of separation means getting away from what divert your heart away from the path of God; turning to Him with your heart.

Stop looking back means not spending time thinking in every status reached while acquiring knowledge; you have to turn to

God and exert no efforts for more knowledge to reach the following status.

Keeping up learning and acquiring knowledge means pursue places and quests of collecting knowledge. These matters are hard to be fulfilled except by people of determination, so they need exercises to acquire and fulfill these matters so they can be habits then become morals.

Exercises for very special people: Not turning to anything but God, getting away from separation claims, not accepting contradictions against God's will, intending your deeds for God not for His reward; your quest has to be for God and becoming among those who are near to Him.

Station of Listening

Exalted is He praised the people of hearing and told that they have good news, He says: "And fear God and listen" " واتقوا الله (5:108), "and listen and obey" "واسمعوا وأطيعوا" (64:16) , "واسمعوا "And if they had said [instead], "We hear and obey" and "Wait for us [to understand]," it would have been better for them and more suitable." " وَلَوْ أَنَّهُمْ قَالُوا سَمِعْنَا وَأَطَعْنَا وَاسْمَعْ وَانظُرْنَا لَكَانَ خَيْرًا لَهُمْ وَأَقْوَمَ " (4:46), "So give good tidings to My servants. Who listen to speech and follow the best of it. Those are the ones God has guided, and those are people of understanding." " فَبَشِّرْ عِبَادِ. الَّذِينَ "يَسْتَمِعُونَ الْقَوْلَ فَيَتَّبِعُونَ أَحْسَنَهُ ۚ أُولَٰئِكَ الَّذِينَ هَدَاهُمُ اللَّـهُ ۖ وَأُولَٰئِكَ هُمْ أُولُو الْأَلْبَابِ

(39:17-18), "So when the Qur'an is recited, then listen to it and pay attention that you may receive mercy." " وَإِذَا قُرِئَ الْقُرْآنُ فَاسْتَمِعُوا لَهُ وَأَنصِتُوا لَعَلَّكُمْ تُرْحَمُونَ" (7:204) and "And when they hear what has been revealed to the Messenger, you see their eyes overflowing with tears because of what they have recognized of the truth." " "وَإِذَا سَمِعُوا مَا أُنزِلَ إِلَى الرَّسُولِ تَرَىٰ أَعْيُنَهُمْ تَفِيضُ مِنَ الدَّمْعِ مِمَّا عَرَفُوا مِنَ الْحَقِّ" (5:83).

Listening is evidence for those where goodness locates, Exalted is He says: "Had God known any good in them, He would have made them hear. And if He had made them hear, they would [still] have turned away, while they were refusing." " وَلَوْ "عَلِمَ اللَّـهُ فِيهِمْ خَيْرًا لَّأَسْمَعَهُمْ ۖ وَلَوْ أَسْمَعَهُمْ لَتَوَلَّوا وَّهُم مُّعْرِضُونَ" (8:23).

Exalted is He described His enemies those who refused to listen and commanded others not listen too, He says: "And those who disbelieve say, "Do not listen to this Qur'an and speak noisily during [the recitation of] it that perhaps you will overcome." "قَالَ الَّذِينَ كَفَرُوا لَا تَسْمَعُوا لِهَٰذَا الْقُرْآنِ" وَالْغَوْا فِيهِ لَعَلَّكُمْ تَغْلِبُونَ " (41:26).

Listening is that brings the faith to the heart, Exalted is He says: "So have they not traveled through the earth and have hearts by which to reason and ears by which to hear?" " أَفَلَمْ يَسِيرُوا "فِي الْأَرْضِ فَتَكُونَ لَهُمْ قُلُوبٌ يَعْقِلُونَ بِهَا أَوْ آذَانٌ يَسْمَعُونَ بِهَا" (22:49).

Listening is the founder of mind and the basis of faith; it is to alarm the heart against what can harm it.

People of listening are many kinds: those who listen to their desires and moods, they benefit only from what are relevant to them; those who listen to their hearts, faith and minds, they reach the sense of speech; those who listen to their God according to the Divine Hadith: "By me he listens and has sight"

Speech are three kinds: Speech that pleases God and His messenger; He commanded His servants and praised those who say it; speech that is hated by God and His Messenger, he prohibited it and praised those who get away of it; speech is allowed and not prohibited, He does not like or hate it.

First kind: Listening that God praised in His Book; command and praise its people, Exalted is He says: "And they will say, "If only we had been listening or reasoning, we would not be among the companions of the Blaze."" " وَقَالُوا لَوْ كُنَّا نَسْمَعُ أَوْ نَعْقِلُ مَا كُنَّا فِي أَصْحَابِ السَّعِيرِ" (67:10), listening to the His verses that were recited by His Messengers; this listening is the core of faith. This kind is subdivided into three types: Listening by ears to realize and recognize, listening by mind to understand and listening by heart to accept and obey.

Listening for realizing is like His verse, Exalted is He says: "And said, 'Indeed, we have heard an amazing Qur'an. It guides to the right course, and we have believed in it." " إِنَّا سَمِعْنَا قُرْآنًا عَجَبًا. يَهْدِي

إِلَى الرُّشْدِ فَآمَنَّا بِهِ" (72:1-2), "indeed we have heard a [recited] Book revealed after Moses" "إِنَّا سَمِعْنَا كِتَابًا أُنزِلَ مِن بَعْدِ مُوسَىٰ" (46:30).

Listening by mind to realize which is not bestowed by God for people of negligence, Exalted is He says: "So indeed, you will not make the dead hear, nor will you make the deaf hear the call" "فَإِنَّكَ لَا تُسْمِعُ الْمَوْتَىٰ وَلَا تُسْمِعُ الصُّمَّ الدُّعَاءَ" (30:52) and "Indeed, God causes to hear whom He wills, but you cannot make hear those in the graves." "إِنَّ اللَّهَ يُسْمِعُ مَن يَشَاءُ ۖ وَمَا أَنتَ بِمُسْمِعٍ مَّن فِي الْقُبُورِ" (35:22). Listening has to be for understanding, Exalted is He says: "Had God known any good in them, He would have made them hear. And if He had made them hear, they would [still] have turned away, while they were refusing." "وَلَوْ عَلِمَ اللَّهُ فِيهِمْ خَيْرًا لَّأَسْمَعَهُمْ ۖ وَلَوْ أَسْمَعَهُمْ لَتَوَلَّوا وَّهُم مُّعْرِضُونَ" (8:23), If God knows that those people of polytheism will accept, He bestowed them understanding so they listened to realize only. Exalted is He says if he had made them hear, they have would turned away and not benefited from what they heard.

Listening by heart to accept and obey: Exalted is He recites that His believers say: "We hear and we obey." "سمعنا وأطعنا"(2:285), it is listening to obey, resulting in obedience.

Listening of those people who are near to God are those who listen to Quran to realize and understand, reflect on and obey; it is every listening that God praises and commands His allies.

Second Kind of Listening

Speech that God and His messenger hate, as they praise those who get away from it; it is by listening to any speech that harms the servant's heart like listening to falsehood speech and listening to ill speech, Exalted is He says: "And when they hear ill speech, they turn away from it" " وَإِذَا سَمِعُوا اللَّغْوَ أَعْرَضُوا عَنْهُ " (28:55), and His saying: "And when they pass near ill speech, they pass by with dignity." " وَإِذَا مَرُّوا بِاللَّغْوِ مَرُّوا كِرَامًا " (25:72).

Decent voice is a bounty. Exalted is He, dispraises the clamorous voice and says: "Indeed, the most disagreeable of sounds is the voice of donkeys." " إِنَّ أَنكَرَ الْأَصْوَاتِ لَصَوْتُ الْحَمِيرِ " (31:19), God described pleasure of the Heaven, He says: "They will be in a garden [of Paradise], delighted." " فِي رَوْضَةٍ يُحْبَرُون " (15:30). The Prophet (PBUH) praised the voice of Abu Musa while reciting Quran and said: "If you were to see me, as I was listening to your recitation (of the Qur'an) yester-night (you would have felt delighted). You are in fact endowed with a sweet voice like that of David himself." And he (PBUH) said: "Make your voices beautiful when you recite Quran." The meaning highlights not the voice but the content of the speech. The Prophet said: "I prohibited two foolish immoral voices: A voice during a calamity while clawing at one's face and tearing one's clothes, and Satan's scream."

Listening is of three degrees: Common listening; it includes three matters: Responding to the shout of warning out of desire, responding to the promise out of efforts, considering God's favor out of insight.

The warning (punishment) is to be on abandoning the commands and doing the prohibitions and this happens only through obedience. Out of desire means with contentedness; willingly not forcibly.

Responding to the promise out of efforts means responding to the matter, in order to reach the promised.

Considering God's favor out of insight means that the listener realizes that all what he recognize is by God's favor, Exalted is He says: "They consider it a favor to you that they have accepted Islam. Say, "Do not consider your Islam a favor to me. Rather, God has conferred favor upon you that He has guided you to the faith, if you should be truthful." " يَمُنُّونَ عَلَيْكَ أَنْ أَسْلَمُوا ۖ قُل لَّا تَمُنُّوا عَلَيَّ إِسْلَامَكُم ۖ بَلِ اللَّـهُ يَمُنُّ عَلَيْكُمْ أَنْ هَدَاكُمْ لِلْإِيمَانِ إِن كُنتُمْ صَادِقِينَ (49:17). Also, considering what God prevents His servants to do is a favor.

Listening of elite people: Realizing God, seeking the intended purpose and end of speech and having pleasure by listening to different speeches.

Realizing God; all speeches that are to be listened to are to realize God, Exalted and Glorified is He; His names, merits, deeds, rules, promise, warning, commands, prohibitions, justice and His favor.

Seeking the intended purpose and end of speech means pursuing speeches aiming at realizing God Exalted is He, He says: "And that to your Lord is the finality" " وَأَنَّ إِلَى رَبِّكَ الْمُنتَهَى " (53:42), every quest except God is useless.

Status of Grief

The status of grief is not one of the required stations on the way to God. Grief is not stated in the Holy Qur'an but prohibited or negated. Grief is prohibited as God, the Almighty, says: "So do not weaken and do not grieve""ولا تهنوا ولا تحزنوا" (3:139), also He says in many positions: "And do not grieve over them". " ولا تحزن عليهم" (16:127) and says in another verse: "Do not grieve; indeed God is with us". "لا تحزن إن الله معنا"(9:40). Grief is mentioned as negated where God says: "there will be no fear concerning them, nor will they grieve". " فلا خوف عليهم ولا هم يحزنون". (2:38), (5:69), 7:35) ,(6:48)), (46:13)

The reason for this is that grief has no benefit for heart. The most beloved thing for Satan is to make a slave grieve to obstruct him on his way to God. God, the Almighty, says: "Private conversation is only from Satan that he may grieve those who have believed". "إنما النجوى من الشيطان ليحزن الذين آمنوا" (58:10). The Prophet (PBUH) said: "When three persons are together, then no two of them should hold secret counsel excluding the third person, for that would grieve him".

The Prophet (PBUH) supplicated God: "I seek refuge with You from worry and grief". Worry is connected to grief. The difference between them is that worry is about the future whereas grief is about the past. Both weaken heart and determination to worship God in the best manner.

But experiencing grief is inevitable as evidenced by reality. So, when the people of the Heaven enter it will say: "Praise to God, who has removed from us [all] sorrow". "الحمد لله الذي أذهب عنا الحزن" (35:34). This indicates that they have experienced grief in the world.

God says: "Nor [is there blame] upon those who, when they came to you that you might give them mounts, you said, "I can find nothing for you to ride upon." They turned back while their eyes overflowed with tears out of grief that they could not find something to spend [for the cause of God]. "ولا على الذين إذا ما أتوك لتحملهم، قلت لا أجد ما أحملكم عليه، تولوا وأعينهم تفيض من الدمع حزنًا ألا يجدوا ما ينفقون". (9:92). This verse does not mean that they were praised for grief itself. Rather, they were praised for their strong belief indicated by their grief out of not accompanying the Messenger (PBUH) [to strive] because of their poverty. As for the Prophet's saying: "Never a believer is stricken with worry, discomfort or grief that his sins are not expiated for him", it indicates that grief is a disaster by which God strikes a slave to nullify his sins. It does not indicate that grief should be sought. On the contrary, the Prophet (PBUH) was always smiling.

As for God's saying about His prophet Israel: "and his eyes became white from grief, for he was [of that] a suppressor". "وابيضت عيناه من الحزن فهو كظيم" (12:84), He tells about disaster of losing his beloved son. It is a trial by God to Israel's patience.

Definitely, grief is a trial by God, which is equal to sickness, worry and distress. But it is not one of the stations on the way to God at all.

Station of Fearing God

The station of "fearing God" is one of the greatest stations on the way to God and the most favorable one to heart. It is obligatory. God, the Almighty, says: "So fear them not, but fear Me, if you are [indeed] believers". " فَلَا تَخَافُوهُمْ وَخَافُونِ إِن كُنتُم مُّؤْمِنِينَ " (3:175). And He, the Almighty, says: "and be afraid of [only] Me". " وَإِيَّايَ فَارْهَبُونِ"(2:40). Also, He says: " So do not fear the people but fear Me". "فَلَا تَخْشَوُا النَّاسَ وَاخْشَوْنِ"(5:44). God praises believers in His Holy Book as He says: "Indeed, they who are apprehensive from fear of their Lord" "إِنَّ الَّذِينَ هُم مِّنْ خَشْيَةِ رَبِّهِم مُّشْفِقُونَ"ـ (23:57) until He says: "It is those who hasten to good deeds, and they outstrip [others] therein". "أُولَٰئِكَ يُسَارِعُونَ فِي الْخَيْرَاتِ وَهُمْ لَهَا سَابِقُونَ". (23:61). It was narrated that Aisha said: "I said: 'O Messenger of God, 'And those who give that (their charity) which they give (and also do other good deeds) with their hearts full of fear." [23:60] Is this the one who commits adultery, steals and drinks alcohol?' He said: 'No, O daughter of Abu Bakr' – O daughter of Siddiq – rather it is a man who fasts and gives charity and prays, but he fears that those will not be accepted from him".

A sincere and praised fear prevents a slave from violating God's prohibitions.

Fear is to always remember promise and warning of God. This includes three degrees:

First degree: is about fearing punishment of God. This kind of fear makes a slave's belief true.

Second degree: is about fearing the loss of delight of faith.

Third degree: is about fearing the magnitude of God. It is the degree of special (strong) believers.

Station of Caution

The station of "caution" is one of the stations on the way to God. God, the Almighty, says: " Who fear their Lord unseen, while they are of the Hour apprehensive". " الَّذِينَ يَخْشَوْنَ رَبَّهُم بِالْغَيْبِ وَهُم مِّنَ السَّاعَةِ مُشْفِقُونَ" (21:49). Also He says: "And they will approach one another, inquiring of each other. They will say, "Indeed, we were previously among our people fearful [of displeasing Allah].

So Allah conferred favor upon us and protected us from the punishment of the Scorching Fire". " وَأَقْبَلَ بَعْضُهُمْ عَلَىٰ بَعْضٍ يَتَسَاءَلُونَ. قَالُوا إِنَّا كُنَّا قَبْلُ فِي أَهْلِنَا مُشْفِقِينَ. فَمَنَّ اللَّـهُ عَلَيْنَا وَوَقَانَا عَذَابَ السَّمُومِ". (52:25), (52:26), (52:27)

Caution is a continual carefulness combined with pleading for mercy of God. It includes three degrees:

First degree: is the caution that the soul may deviate to the way of disobedience. And a caution that good deeds may not be accepted, i.e.: a slave is afraid that his deeds may not be rewarded because they were not for the sake of God only and did not follow God's Law and Sunnah. God says about this: "And We will regard what they have done of deeds and make them as dust dispersed". "وَقَدِمْنَا إِلَىٰ مَا عَمِلُوا مِنْ عَمَلٍ فَجَعَلْنَاهُ هَبَاءً مَّنثُورًا" (25:23)

Second degree: is that a slave is cautious that time may be wasted in things other than those pleasing God. One may be cautious about lusts and doubtful matters that negatively affect heart. He is also cautious that his certainty about God may be not stable.

Third degree: is the caution that protects a slave from seeking conceitedness and antagonizing people. It preserves his seeking pleasure of God. Conceitedness nullifies good deeds. Antagonizing people corrupts moral character. Seeking God's satisfaction is interrupted by useless amusement and diversion away from

God. If a slave's deed and moral character are good and his seeking for God's satisfaction is sincere, then his heart and behaviors will be on the straight path.

Station of Humility

The station of "humility" is one of the stations on the way to God. God, the Almighty, says: "Has the time not come for those who have believed that their hearts should become humbly submissive at the remembrance of Allah and what has come down of the truth?". "ألم يأن للذين آمنوا أن تخشع قلوبهم لذكر الله وما نزل من الحق" (57:16). Ibn Mas'ud, may God be pleased with him, said: "Since our acceptance of Islam and the revelation of this verse in which God has shown annoyance to us, there was a gap of four years". God also said: "Certainly will the believers have succeeded: They who are during their prayer humbly submissive". " قد أفلح المؤمنون. "الذين هم في صلاتهم خاشعون" (23:1-2).

Humility means submissiveness to God. He, the Almighty, says: "and [all] voices will be stilled before the Most Merciful" "وخشعت الأصوات للرحمن" (20:108). The earth is also described of being humbled as it does not grow except by God Who gives life to it by sending down rain. God says: "And of His signs is that you see the earth stilled, but when We send down upon it rain, it quivers and grows". " ومن آياته أنك ترى الأرض خاشعة. فإذا أنزلنا عليها الماء "اهتزت وربت". (41:39).

Humility necessitates submission to truth. It means coming over lusts, magnifying God and relieving heart by strong faith in God.

It is agreed that heart is the place of humility which has good effects on the rest of body organs. If heart is humble to God, the whole organs of the body will be so. The Prophet (PBUH) said: "Piety is here (and he pointed out to his chest thrice)". Chest implies heart.

Humility combines magnifying and loving God with submissiveness to Him. It includes three degrees:

First degree: is yielding to the religious judgement, i.e.: not to oppose it out of pursuing one's own lusts and thoughts, and yielding to the fatal judgement, i.e.: not to be dissatisfied with it. Humility is to obey commands of God and defer to His decree. Heart and body organs become humble when a slave is certain of that God is acquainted with their inner details. This is one of the two interpretations of God's saying: "But for he who has feared the position of his Lord are two gardens". " وَلِمَنْ خَافَ مَقَامَ رَبِّهِ جَنَّتَانِ". (55:46), and His saying: " But as for he who feared the position of his Lord and prevented the soul from [unlawful] inclination". "وَأَمَّا مَنْ خَافَ مَقَامَ رَبِّهِ وَنَهَى النَّفْسَ عَنِ الْهَوَى" (79:40). When Man fears the position of God (His full Acquaintance with everything,

His Omnipotence and Lordship), inevitably his heart will be humble to God.

Second degree: is to regard defects of the soul; such as arrogance, weak certainty about God, insincerity of doing good deeds ... etc. This consideration makes a slave's heart be humble to God. This degree also includes that a slave should fulfill people's rights, be grateful and disregard the self's grace upon others.

Third degree: is that a slave should conceal his humbleness to God from people as much as possible in order not to become conceited or delightful. Consequently, his worshipping to God will not be sincere. This degree also includes to know that God is the only one who grants grace and reward without any intervention by Man.

A slave must yield to God in his prayer. God shows in the Holy Qur'an that those who pray will not be rewarded for their prayer unless they are humble to God in it.

Humbleness and concentration are the soul of prayer. The Prophet (PBUH) said: "When the Adhan for the prayer is pronounced, then Satan takes to his heels passing wind so that he may not hear the Adhan and when the Mu'adh-dhin finishes, he comes back; and when the Iqama is pronounced he again takes to his heels and when it is finished, he again comes back and continues reminding the praying person of things that he used not to remember when not in prayer till he forgets how much he has prayed. If anyone of you has such a thing (forgetting the number of rak`at he has prayed) he should perform two prostrations of Sahu (i.e. forgetfulness) while sitting".

There is a great reward for being humble to God in performing prayer in the world; e.g. firm faith, peace of mind and delight of worshipping. In addition, a slave humble to God in his prayer will be rewarded with the highest degrees in position on the Doomsday plus accompanying those brought near to God.

The End

The End of Part 1.

* 9 7 8 1 9 9 9 1 7 1 1 5 5 *